Women Patrons and Collectors

Women Patrons and Collectors

Edited by

Susan Bracken, Andrea M. Gáldy, and Adriana Turpin

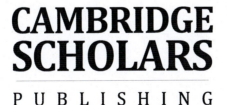

CAMBRIDGE
SCHOLARS
PUBLISHING

Women Patrons and Collectors,
Edited by Susan Bracken, Andrea M. Gáldy, and Adriana Turpin

This book first published 2012

Cambridge Scholars Publishing

12 Back Chapman Street, Newcastle upon Tyne, NE6 2XX, UK

British Library Cataloguing in Publication Data
A catalogue record for this book is available from the British Library

ISBN (10): 1-4438-3464-5, ISBN (13): 978-1-4438-3464-3

TABLE OF CONTENTS

LIST OF ILLUSTRATIONS

ABBREVIATIONS

Alnwick Archive	Archives of the Duke of Northumberland, Alnwick Castle
ASF	Archivio dello Stato di Firenze
British Library, Add. MSS	British Library Additional Manuscripts
BPA	Buckminster Park Archives
DG	*Depositaria Generale*, Parte Antica
FM	*Fabbriche Medicee*
GM	*Guardaroba Medicea*
HMC	Historic Manuscripts Commission
MNM	Budapest, Magyar Nemzeti Múzeum
NPG	National Portrait Gallery
NRA	National Register of Archives
ÖNB, *Hss.*	Wien, Österreichische Nationalbibliothek, *Handschriftensammlung*
ÖStA, HHStA, *FAE*	Wien, Österreichisches Staatsarchiv, Haus-Hof- und Staatsarchiv, *Familienarchiv Erdődy*
RCHM	Royal Commission on Historic Monuments
SNA, *ÚAE*	Bratislava, Slovenský národný archív, *Ústredný Archív rodu Erdődy*

ACKNOWLEDGEMENTS

We as the editors of this volume would like to thank first of all the contributors to our third volume of collected essays for their articles and for their collaboration during the editing process. Most of these essays are based on papers given at the *Women Collectors* conference held in London in July 2008. As always they have benefitted from the participation of the audience; thank you for your feedback and for returning to our seminars and conferences. Our particular thanks go to Professor Sheila ffolliott for her *Introduction* to this volume. Her expertise and ability to pull together connections between and beyond the contributors' essays made this an even better book.

The conference was held at the Institute of Historical Research, University of London, whose continued support means much more than giving a home to the regular Collecting & Display seminars in London and for hosting two of the summer conferences and the recent methodologies workshop (July 2011) so far. We owe thanks to IHR administrative staff who have supported our seminars and conferences in the most helpful manner. We are also deeply grateful to the Henry Moore Foundation for generously sponsoring this and the two previous summer conferences.

Our thanks go to Nick Hess and Irene Campolmi for their readiness to lend each an extra pair of eagle eyes and to Sara King who greatly helped with the formatting of the bibliography. John Hoenig's help with the Index of the previous and with supplying Figure 5 to the present volume is also much appreciated. Carolyn Murin kindly helped with creating the Index to the present volume.

Finally, we would like to thank Cambridge Scholars Publishing for their wonderful collaboration and continued support at a time when multi-authored art historical studies are very difficult to place.

FOREWORD

Joan heard her out, checking a strong disposition to giggle. Her viewpoint was that of the Average Person, and the Average Person cannot see the importance of the scarab in the scheme of things. The opinion she formed of Mr. Peters was of an eccentric old gentleman making a great to-do about nothing at all. Losses had to have a concrete value before they could impress Joan. It was beyond her to grasp that Mr. Peters would sooner have lost a diamond necklace, if he had happened to possess one, than his Cheops of the Fourth Dynasty.

It was not until Aline, having concluded her tale, added one more strand to it that she found herself treating the matter seriously.

"Father says he would give a thousand pounds to anyone who would get it back for him."

"What!"

[...]

"It isn't really very much for father, you know. He gave away a hundred thousand dollars a year to a University."

"But for a grubby little scarab!"

"You don't understand how father loves his scarabs. Since he retired from business, he has been simply wrapped up in them. You know collectors are like that. You read in the papers about men giving all sorts of money for funny things."

—P.G. Wodehouse, *Something Fresh* (1915), republished by Mayflower: London, 1961, 49-50

Today's readership may think it rather unfair of Mr. Wodehouse to ascribe these purely mercenary attitudes to the heroine of his novel. Her lack of appreciation for (in her eyes) the rather eccentric collecting preferences of Mr. Peters is, however, not only shared by her friend Aline, the collector's own daughter, but also the result of a long period of considerable poverty which has taught her the necessity of sufficient income. Hence, she, even less than Aline, can understand the squandering of large sums on "funny things" like scarabs. Expenditure on diamond necklaces and fashion items such as suits and hats made in Paris constitutes a very different matter.

Only men are inclined to give "all sorts of money for funny things" —that is a well-known fact in the world of Joan and Aline. Collecting is, therefore, a pastime for men, such as Mr. Peters, the former owner of the Cheops scarab of the Fourth Dynasty. Women, to the contrary, are practical, down-to-earth, and have neither the time nor the money to spare for building collections; certainly not for collections of "grubby" little things such as scarabs.

Although we may not share this view, collecting has traditionally been regarded as a hobby not all that attractive to women. There were, of course exceptions among the great collectors of the past, for example Isabella d'Este, who was a dedicated and successful collector. Her treasures and the settings in which they were displayed have long been the object of careful study. While she was hardly the only one, she seems to be among those best remembered, while a considerable number of other female collectors has been largely forgotten, despite the interest, substance, high quality and peculiar display of treasures.

Why should the collection of a female owner be less worthy of regard and study than that of a male equivalent? Has it to do with past role models for women, in particular for dynastic brides whose main task in life was to produce an "heir and a spare" and who were not supposed to be distracted from this important goal by intellectual pursuits? Or could it be the case that the close philosophical connection made since Classical Antiquity between princely rule and princely collecting had perhaps more to do with the ideological exclusion of women from the realms of high-end collecting?

As the present volume shows, women—particularly aristocratic women—have not only resisted this discrimination through the ages, they also built important collections and used them to their own advantage: whether to make a statement of lineage, power, cultural heritage or of their religious preferences. Not to forget that an increasing number of middle-class women became draughtswomen, painters and natural scientists and developed a professional interest in collecting. Through the ages, female collectors, whatever their rank in society, chose to collect and what to collect; they chose how and where to present the collection; they also decided if to preserve and when to dispose of objects, thereby taking on a curatorial role.

Women have nonetheless been seen as gatherers of furnishings, jewellery, dress and objects of domestic life. This volume challenges these perceptions by the detailed analysis of different types of collections amassed by women and thus seeks to give a voice to a group of important female collectors from the sixteenth to the early nineteenth century whose importance for the history of collecting has not yet, or not sufficiently, been acknowledged. Not only are the authors of each essay trying to establish the composition of the respective collection but also to present the relevant forms of display and the raison d'être and significance of the objects and their context.

Collecting & Display are the keywords in the name of the working group founded by three scholars in 2004 (www.collectinganddisplay.com). The group has been running a research seminar at the Institute of Historical Research at the University of London since 2005 and in Florence since 2008. Collecting & Display has organised summer conferences in London, Ottobeuren and Florence since 2006. We would like to present, with this book, the third volume of proceedings of these conferences and hope that it will be followed by many more tomes dedicated to different aspects of collecting and display. At the time of writing, the papers of our fourth conference, held in June 2009 and entitled *Collecting East & West*, are being prepared for publication.

London and Florence, July 2011

INTRODUCTION

SHEILA FFOLLIOTT

Francis Haskell's authoritative *Patrons and Painters* (1963, 1980), the first compendium of work on the topic of early modern patrons, set the standard for this line of inquiry.[1] Haskell surveyed the Italian élite—the affluent and the powerful—and what he saw as their proper quarry. In his related *Rediscoveries* (1976), he complicated the issue, investigating changes in taste together with the constant desire to establish universal aesthetic values.[2] Considerable research on women patrons and, to a lesser extent, collectors, has emerged since the appearance of Haskell's books and we now know that many sixteenth- to eighteenth-century women commissioned and collected artworks.[3] Exhibitions have featured the collections of Empress Josephine; Archduchess Isabella Clara Eugenia; governors of the Netherlands Margaret of Austria and Mary of Hungary; Catherine of Austria, queen of Portugal; Isabella d'Este; Christina of Sweden; Caroline Louise of Hesse Darmstadt, margravine of Baden-Durlach; Juliette Récamier; and the duchesse de Berri, among others: a very small number compared to the great quantity on male collectors.[4] It is still worth remembering, therefore, that few women appeared in Haskell's narratives and some of his assumptions about patronage and collecting persist. Perhaps two assessments of a sixteenth-century woman patron and collector, Catherine de' Medici, will indicate why.

Catherine's patronage was by no means outstanding. (Knecht 1998).[5]

and

---

[1] Haskell 1963, 1980.
[2] Haskell 1976.
[3] Collections of essays include: Anderson 1996; Lawrence 1997; Johnson and Matthews-Grieco 1997; King 1998; Matthews-Grieco and Zarri 2000; Reiss and Wilkins 2001; Hills 2003; Wilson-Chevalier 2007 and Strunck 2011.
[4] Di Gioia 2003; Duerloo 1998; Eichberger 2002; Ferino Pagden 1996; Vergara and Cabrera 1999; Jordan Gschwend and Beltz 2010; Lauts 1983; Pougetoux 2005; Biblioteca Apostolica Vaticana 1989; Réthelyi and Basics 2005; Zvereva 2002; Paccoud and Ramond 2009; Kiefer 2005.
[5] Knecht 1998, 244.

> Catherine de' Médicis (1519-1589) fut sans doute le plus important
> mécène français de la seconde moitié du XVIe siècle. (Turbide, 2007).[6]

Such opposing views are typical of historians writing about this
controversial queen of France during the period of the religious wars, but
they also demonstrate differences in attitude about patronage. Knecht drew
from Haskell's model in which choice of artist and genre determines a
patron's merit. Rose Marie San Juan's work on Isabella d'Este made an
important contribution in helping to define an appropriate context for
Renaissance women collectors.[7] Turbide's assessment, similarly, more
fully considers the larger milieu in which Catherine operated. She notes,
moreover, that we no longer realise the extent of Catherine's vast
collecting and patronage: her sumptuous and sophisticated court fêtes were
ephemeral, her buildings have been altered or destroyed, and her varied
collection dispersed. To notice the range of women's involvement, as
contributors to this anthology have done, one must question some
traditional assumptions about where and what to look for in patronage and
collecting, seek alternative explanations, and consider legal, societal, and
circumstantial constraints on women's behaviour.

The essays in this volume treat women patrons and collectors from the
sixteenth through the nineteenth centuries. Some chapters introduce
figures like the Hungarian noblewoman, Erzsébet Rákóczi, to English-
speaking audiences, while others bring up unfamiliar aspects of better
known patrons like Eleonora of Toledo. In this introduction, I shall try to
identify some collecting patterns among women and provide context for
understanding their actions, referring to the individuals under discussion
here, as well as to other collectors. I shall also try to point out some issues
bearing on how collecting is interpreted that have helped to marginalise
women's contributions. But it is important to acknowledge that, in most
respects, patrons and collectors exhibit shared behaviours regardless of
gender. Salvation was everyone's concern and in Catholic Europe
patronage of religious institutions and art and architecture was one way to
help both men and women achieve it. Piety was a virtue seen as
appropriately female; thus women with means could openly practice
charity in the form of religious patronage. Although not the focus of these
essays, many of the women discussed here, e.g. Duchess Eleonora and
Countess Erzsébet, operating within a Catholic sphere, engaged in visible
charitable patronage, as did Marie Caroline, duchesse de Berri, on her
tours around France in the 1820s. In addition, Rákóczi, like other royal

---

[6] Turbide 2007, 511.
[7] San Juan 1991, 67-78.

and aristocratic women across Europe, supervised the construction of her husband's tomb. But religion is never entirely absent, for Protestant women commissioned religious paintings for display in private—possibly indicating Catholic leanings, as Christopher Rowell suggests here for Elizabeth Murray, countess of Dysart and duchess of Lauderdale, in England and Scotland. Heike Zech recounts the history of a jewelled cross that Otto von Wittelsbach gave his Protestant mother, Queen Marie of Bavaria (1825-89), at the time of his Catholic confirmation, which she, in turn, gave a lady in waiting at the time of the latter's and her own conversion to Catholicism.

With the exception of holy relics, which some women collectors avidly sought, collecting *per se* is neither a charitable nor a pious act. So what is (or was) collecting, precisely, and what other terms made collecting possible and acceptable, but also left it relatively unheralded, for women? Charlotte Gere and Marina Vaizey proposed the following definition: "collecting (as opposed to accumulating) must significantly alter the repute of the objects collected, not only by adding to knowledge and expanding appreciation, but perhaps even more by conferring status"[8] For the Renaissance and Baroque eras, however, accumulation in itself was not necessarily a bad idea. Witness the extensive inventories of Henry VIII, Charles V, or the Medici documents to get a sense of the sheer quantities deemed necessary for prestige.[9] Drawing from Aristotle's theory of Magnificence, patronage and collecting, practised properly, was, in fact, a virtue; necessitating spending to create splendour, tempered with sufficient judgment so the results appeared neither vulgarly ostentatious nor overly mean.

Such a view moderated in the Enlightenment, "forceful reasoning" replacing simple dazzling as Paula Rea Radisch noted.[10] But other forces were also at work that complicated the perception of collecting. A nineteenth-century observer, Anna Jameson, characterised various well-known collectors of the seventeenth and eighteenth centuries as follows: "What had been *taste* in Arundel, *magnificence* in Buckingham, *science* in Lely, became in the next century a *fashion*, subject to the freaks of vanity, the errors and absurdities of ignorance, the impositions of pretension and coxcombery."[11] Contemporaries like John Ruskin did not respect her

---

[8] Gere and Vaizey 1999, 10.
[9] Starkey 1998; Hayward 2004; Checa 2010; The Medici Archive Project (www.medici.org).
[10] Radisch 2003, 48.
[11] Jameson 1844, 69.

judgment, declaring that she "knows as much about art as the cat."[12] Nevertheless, she hit the nail on the head with this remark, for by the eighteenth century, because more people, including women, had access to the market, collecting had become fashionable. Writing at the end of that century, Lady Mary Berry made the connection clear, dismissing one of London's art display venues as unlikely to be a major player, being inconvenient to female and male viewers alike as it was near neither the "great haberdashers" nor "Bond Street or St. James's" for the men.[13]

Any would-be collector needs money, position, and access in order to pursue the various goals of collecting: building and decorating spaces, gaining prestige—through the acquisition and display of what the individual collector or peer group desired, or pursuing scientific interests. Are women's motivations essentially different from men's or, rather, is it commentators who have cast those activities in different lights? There is certainly nothing conventionally feminine in Queen Christina's urging Swedish troops in 1648 to raid Prague Castle for its art, as did some of her male counterparts, notably Napoleon. Although most well-known collectors are male, there is nothing essentially masculine about collecting. In fact, Sir Thomas Roe, English ambassador to the Ottoman Empire, wrote to Henry Howard, Lord Arundel in 1621: he waxed lyrical about the interesting things he was finding in Constantinople, but at the same time expressed fears that collecting might be thought effeminate.[14] Such qualms persisted into the early eighteenth century, in the context of women's increasing participation in purchasing art. Women had, in fact, been buying at estate sales in sixteenth-century Spain and they regularly attended auctions in seventeenth and eighteenth-century London.[15] Purveyors there, such as Edward Millington, advertised "galleries set apart for ladies and gentlewomen."[16] Such public auctions served also as sites for art education for middle class women who lacked access to private collections but were desirous, nevertheless, of observing what was being bought in order to acquire sophistication.[17]

As a result, Lord Shaftesbury proposed, in effect, an important distinction: that connoisseurship, entailing judgement and knowledge

---

[12] Haskell 1976, 106. Haskell himself disparaged Mrs. Jameson, introducing her as a "one-time governess and jilted wife … no connoisseur;" but does acknowledge her contributions to iconographical studies.
[13] Ibid., 25.
[14] Peck 2005, 183.
[15] Álvarez 2008, 35.
[16] Cowan 1998, 160.
[17] Ibid.

(Mrs. Jameson's "*taste*" and "*science*"), required "real men" as opposed to simply acquiring paintings for domestic interiors, which involved feminine taste and reflected the luxury market generally.[18] Here we see something typical of gendered discourse: brain activity is aptly male while the more vulgar pursuits pertain to women. In addition to de-emphasising market forces, stressing individual choice and connoisseurship seeks also to remove collecting from the full spectrum of patronage practices informing early modern society. Many objects, moreover, circulated as part of gift exchange. As such, they are not a collector's choice (unless a specific gift was solicited), but nevertheless, many presents remain treasured components of collections, adding to the complexity of analysis.

Research on consumption by historians like Richard Goldthwaite and John Brewer, among others, has made a significant impact on collecting studies.[19] Many scholars of patronage and collecting now orient their work to the inevitability of the market.[20] Welch reminds us, however, that, "court expenditure is still presented as élite and individual, rather than as market-led or market-driven. But the division of purchase and patronage was often a matter of degree."[21] An uneasy tension remains, nevertheless, between views of élite art collecting and consumerism: in Marcia Pointon's words, it remains a "contradiction, and competition—between displayed artefacts and known but repeatedly disavowed discourses of money."[22] The additional role of artworks as fungible assets, often included in dowries, will be discussed below.

"But is it Art?"[23] Distinctions like Shaftesbury's further disparaged women collectors by relegating their activity to the domestic sphere: what Gere and Vaizey called "a by-product of homemaking in the form of furnishing and decorating."[24] Collections of paintings now have the greatest cachet and women like Christina of Sweden and Catherine the Great, but also less famous ones like Barbara Sanseverino Sanvitale (1550-1612), Cristiana Duglioli Angelelli (1614-1669), and the countess of Verrue (1670-1736) formed impressive paintings collections on a par with their male counterparts.[25] Paintings, however, were not always the

---

[18] Peck 2005, 185.

[19] Goldthwaite 1993; Brewer and Porter 1993; Brewer and Trentmann 2006.

[20] North and Ormrod 1998; Welch 2002, 2005; Fantoni,, Matthews-Grieco, and Matthews 2003; Cavazzini 2008; Spear and Sohm 2010.

[21] Welch 2002, 306.

[22] Pointon 1998, 202.

[23] See Kipling's poem "The Conundrum of the Workshops" (1890).

[24] Gere and Vaizey 1999, 11.

[25] For Angelelli, see Curti 2007; for Verrue see Oresko 1996, XXXII, 368; she

most prized objects for collectors of either sex who may have preferred the prestige and monetary value of sculpture, whether ancient or contemporary and of luxury fabrics or tapestries. In fact, in the early modern era, notably Elizabeth Percy, duchess of Northumberland, and Catherine Questiers in this volume, plus many collectors (e.g. Pope Paul II, Lorenzo de' Medici, Isabella d'Este, and Peter Paul Rubens *inter alia*) valued small objects made of precious materials, like cameos, engraved gems, and medals. These small objects were often stored in cabinets, which could be viewed by a select company in a small, therefore exclusive, space.

Women's supposedly natural affinity for the domestic sphere was sufficient to "explain" why, when presented with the opportunity to collect, they chose porcelain, metalwork, furniture, embroidery, dress, jewellery, fans: what are now lumped into the category "decorative arts," often placed lower than painting in hierarchies of aesthetic value. Joy Kearney relates how Mary Stuart, wife of William III of Holland, collected blue and white Delftware and, with the aid of the Dutch East India Company, imported a variety of Asian ceramics. When she and her husband William ascended the English throne in the late seventeenth century, she brought this taste to England, seen most notably in Kensington Palace and Hampton Court. In the nineteenth century Lady Charlotte Schreiber gained real expertise in ceramics and formed an important china collection.[26] Many women collectors focused on gems, which combined the intrinsic worth of materials, an early modern priority, and craftsmanship. Electress Anna Maria Luisa de' Medici's main collecting focus was jewellery: she formed one of the richest collections in the eighteenth century (now Florence, Pitti). But to limit such interests to women is fallacious, as men such as August the Strong also eagerly collected decorative arts.

Collectors can confer status on their objects if they are deemed to be trend setting, to return to what Gere and Vaizey state are criteria for differentiating a collection from simple accumulation. In this volume, Christopher Rowell characterises Elizabeth Murray's employment of the painter Verrio as avant-garde and Philip Mansel uses the same term to describe the duchesse de Berri's patronage. But there were many other innovative collectors including two sixteenth-century Habsburg women, Margaret of Austria, governor of the Netherlands, and her niece Catherine, queen of Portugal, among the first to amass exotica newly coming into

---

owned van Dyck's *Le Roi à la Chasse* (*c.* 1635; Paris, Louvre) and Claude Lorrain's *Landscape with Aeneas at Delos* (1672; London, National Gallery).
[26] Herrmann 1972, 330. She referred to it as her "china mania".

Europe.[27] The former eagerly sought objects from Habsburg possessions in America and the latter was the greatest collector of Asian objects in her century. As Anne Marie Jordan has amply demonstrated, her collection included ivory caskets made in Sri Lanka, prized by many collectors, and she was an innovator in importing Asian fans, the envy at courts in the Iberian Peninsula and beyond.[28] In this volume, we learn about Agnes Block in Holland who used her connections with the Dutch East India Company to procure botanical specimens and then hired artists to depict them. Other women also maintained an avid interest in botany and plant collecting.[29] Elizabeth Percy set up her own museum incorporating objects of all sorts and wrote a catalogue divided into volumes by classification. As Adriano Aymonino informs us, her *artificialia* consisted of pictures, prints, medals and coins; ethnographic materials, primarily utensils; then "everything carved or sculpted"; then a hodgepodge of items not easily subsumed into other categories; then her *naturalia*, fossils and stones, and finally books. Coincidentally, it was James Smithson, her husband's illegitimate son, who left money to found the great American research institution that bears his name. In the nineteenth century, the duchesse de Berri maintained a menagerie and garden with exotic plants at her château of Rosny.

Notwithstanding the concept of Magnificence, unlike their male counterparts, it seems as though women collectors are more often accused of greed: claims of extravagance were levelled at Madame du Pompadour and Empress Josephine, among many others.[30] In this volume, for example, Elizabeth Murray, duchess of Lauderdale, was said to have "a ravenous cormorant appetite in her to devour all," upon receipt of her husband's movables at his death. Such views persist when modern commentators find ways to insert jabs even while praising. Oliver Millar, as Rowell points out, describes Murray as "one of the most acute, politically minded and rapacious ladies of her day." Do modern scholars seem more willing to excuse males who spend and spend? Jonathan Brown said of the king of Spain: "Despite the parlous state of the royal treasury, depleted by almost four decades of war, Philip [IV] continued to buy whenever a good opportunity arose. The dedication of scarce funds for this purpose is quite remarkable when, as one observer noted, there was not enough ready money for food."[31] Words like passionate, flair, or

[27] Eichberger 2002, 2003 and Jordan, "Mujeres," 1999 and 2010.

[28] Jordan, "Exotic," 1999 and Jordan Gschwend, 2010.

[29] Gere and Vaizey 1999, 77.

[30] Ibid., 61.

[31] Brown 1995, 141.

magnificent, are ascribed to George IV's collecting, despite the effects of his extravagance on the national balance sheet. Those discussing collecting by and large excuse such behaviour and, in fact, just regard these kings as among the greatest collectors.

An interesting solution was proposed (and justified) for one male collector whose spending habits merited remark: "[Ramiro Núñez de Guzmán, Duke of] Medina [de las Torres] was a profligate spender ... and supplied his needs by marrying a succession of rich women."[32] Marrying heiresses is, of course, a practice of long-standing for families needing infusions of cash, but more than one collector found it useful. Archduke Ferdinand of the Tyrol's marriage in 1557 to the wealthy commoner Philippine Welser added sufficiently to his coffers to enable him to assemble his extensive collections at Schloss Ambras, near Innsbruck. Thomas Howard, earl of Arundel, only started collecting after his marriage in 1606 to Aletheia Talbot, daughter of the wealthy earl of Shrewsbury.[33] But it worked both ways, for Aletheia's grandmother, Bess of Hardwick, had amplified Shrewsbury's fortune through a series of marriages (and widowhoods), which permitted her to build, commission, and collect.[34] And, like her fellow noblewomen, Elizabeth Murray and Elizabeth Percy, Aletheia was herself a collector, in tandem with and independently of her husband.

Another means of denigrating women's collecting is to assert that it is motivated by sentiment; the objects acquired for personal meaning and not for some abstract and intellectually based higher purpose (whatever that might be). In this volume, Zech investigates princely mothers in seventeenth to nineteenth-century Bavaria. Acknowledging that mothers do collect items relating to their children, she seeks to find what artworks and precious objects might fit into such a category without belittling its implications. Catherine de' Medici's collecting of portraits of her offspring has been dismissed as comparable to what a more modern mother or grandmother might do in assembling a photo album.[35] While I do not wish to deny her motivation in wanting depictions of her family, who, like most royal children, lived in a separate household at some distance, at the same time, it must be noted that in collecting these materials, she was a trend-setter, cultivating a new appreciation for the type of pencil drawing produced by François Clouet and others, generally held in reserve by the artist to use in making painted portraits which were

---

[32] Ibid., 134.
[33] Ibid., 17.
[34] Howarth 1998.
[35] Knecht 1998, 244.

often ordered in multiples. Catherine herself kept and treasured portfolios of these drawings, not just those of her children, but of relatives and courtiers, dead and alive, and she pored over them, sharing them with her ladies.[36] She was not alone: we learn here that Elizabeth Murray also collected pencil portraits of family members. Portraits typically decorate public spaces in palaces, but looking at them in a smaller domestic environment provides more intimate memory experiences, perhaps more genuinely a concern for élite women than men.

Married women moved to their husband's house, sometimes as early as their mid to late teens, and some royal women never saw birth family members again. Portraits reminded them of those left behind. Fifteenth-century Ippolita Sforza, the bride of Alfonso II of Naples, wrote to her mother in Milan about what she wanted for her *studiolo*:

> I pray your Illustrious Highness . . . to have made for me portraits from life of His Excellency my father and of Yourself, and of all my Illustrious brothers and sisters, for beyond the adornment of my studio, looking on them would give me continual consolation and pleasure.[37]

Most of the women treated in this anthology collected and displayed portraits, e.g. Elizabeth Murray in her Private Closet at Ham. Susan James has demonstrated how several other aristocratic Englishwomen collected paintings, primarily portraits: Lettice Knollys's rooms were well furnished with portraits, some of herself, as were those of Anne Parr, younger sister of Queen Catherine and second wife of the earl of Pembroke.[38] As Dagmar Eichberger and others have demonstrated, such women collected portraits—not just of their immediate families, but their enlarged kin network—and hung them in spaces under their control, such as their apartments, to enhance their status.[39] Margaret of Austria and Catherine de' Medici, for example, filled their living spaces with portraits of powerful relatives: ammunition in case a visiting ambassador had doubts about their authority. In this collection, Zech discusses a print depicting the Electress Kunigunde Therese (1676-1730) in which family portraits hang on walls around her in an imagined *studiolo*, creating a family unit that did not reflect the reality of a mother living on her own in exile. Zech also describes nineteenth-century Queen Caroline of Bavaria's disseminating portraits of her children on factory-produced porcelain. So

---

[36] Zvereva 2002, 2007, 2011.
[37] Thornton 1997, 90.
[38] James 2009, 55.
[39] Eichberger 1996, 259-79; Eichberger and Beaven 1995, 225-48.

many manifestations demonstrate how the larger family is stronger than the individual.

Portraits are the common denominator of aristocratic and royal collecting. In public spaces, they define family lines and kinship ties. The dynasty may bear his name, but it is also hers. Several women patrons, in fact, saw the benefits of demonstrating the expansion of dynastic connections through the female line. The decoration of Catherine de' Medici's Parisian hôtel, and her small book of hours, contained portraits of her children of both sexes and the families into which they married, and the decoration of the Innsbruck Hofburg, supervised by Empress Maria Theresa, similarly included the dynasties into which her daughters married. Dynastic continuity makes the state stable, whence the anxiety to produce an heir. Mansel sees "an obsession with family life" in the collection of another princely mother, the duchesse de Berri in the nineteenth century. Her paintings collection featured many domestic subjects, including depictions of mothers with children, not only portraits of herself with her own children. Inventories indicate that some were by women painters, including Marguerite Gérard and Jeanne Marie Catherine Desmarquest, known as Madame Auzou. The latter's work (untraced?) depicts a woman surrounded by her healthy family watching Louis XVIII return to Paris. Mansel points out how this domestic theme has much greater implications: what it takes to keep a family healthy is a healthy nation, and vice versa. In this case, as the duchesse's son was in line for the restored throne and she, like other mothers of heirs presumptive before her, e.g. Louise de Savoie, mother of the future François I, wanted to present him (and herself) in the best possible light.

Another problem in determining women's roles in collecting is that narratives tend to present males as the sole protagonists, even when they act with the dynasty in mind. If their female relatives played a part, their activity is often submerged.[40] Women with a paper trail might more openly acknowledge their familial role. Returning to the domestic sphere, early modern behavioural treatises advocated a custodial responsibility for élite women regarding family property.[41] This normally meant the property of the patriline, for the patrician residence and its contents embodied family identity. Significantly, most women neither selected nor owned the majority of objects in their care and with which they spent most of their time. We know from inventories that in the early fifteenth century,

---

[40] Southron 1988, passim. This book, like similar compendia, contains information on women collectors, but one must hunt for it as the sections are organised by the men in the family.

[41] Alberti 1969, 202.

for example, when she married Gianfrancesco Gonzaga, marquis of Mantua, Paola Malatesta received "217 pieces from the ... storerooms for her own use: metalwork, jewellery, books of hours, but [these] remained inalienable Gonzaga possessions."[42] While the collectors treated in this volume are exceptional in their ability to collect, when compared to women in general, documents also suggest that a range of women possessed some property, including pictures, which they could bequeath.[43]

Occasionally women used their custodial role assertively to preserve family honour and memory through attention to material vestiges even when they may not have assembled the collection themselves.[44] This impetus is the main thrust of Orsolya Bubryák's essay on Erzsébet Rákóczi. Zech demonstrates how in the nineteenth century, Queen Marie of Bavaria acted as a sort of family curator, labelling objects to preserve their context for future generations. Even in the early twentieth century the idea persisted, the countess of Radnor having stated in the preface to a catalogue that "it has been the privilege of ... (the present writer) to arrange and classify the family Collection of Pictures," meaning those of the family into which she had married.[45] Significantly, one of the greatest acts of female guardianship was the feat of Electress Palatine Anna Maria Luisa de' Medici, last of her line. With the Family Pact of 1737, she ensured that her birth family patrimony remained in her native Florence and did not transfer to her husband's family or her nearest male kin, either of which eventuality would have removed many treasures far away from Florence.[46]

Although the women themselves may not have been active collectors, it must be noted that many artworks entered their husband's family collections via dowries or when their brides were their parents' sole heir. Part of Claudia de' Medici's dowry, when she wed Habsburg archduke, Leopold V in 1626, was an Antonio Rossellino *Madonna* (Vienna: Kunsthistorisches Museum).[47] Among the better known works that Olimpia Aldobrandini brought, upon her marriage to Camillo Pamphili in 1647, were some of the contents of Alfonso d'Este's Alabaster Chamber [e.g. Bellini's *Feast of the Gods* (Washington: National Gallery of Art) and Titian's *Bacchus and Ariadne* (London: National Gallery)]; also Raphael's *Aldobrandini Madonna* (London: National Gallery), and Annibale Carracci's, *Coronation of the*

---

[42] Welch 2002, 308.
[43] Weatherill 1986, 150.
[44] ffolliott 2007, 32.
[45] Herrmann 1972, 122; Chaplin 1910.
[46] Ciletti 1984, 23-7.
[47] Holst 1967, 161.

Virgin (New York: Metropolitan Museum).[48] Similarly Vittoria della
Rovere's inheritance included paintings from her family's collection that
transferred to the Medici with her wedding to Ferdinando II: works like
Piero della Francesca's *Portraits of the Duke and Duchess of Urbino* and
Titian's *Venus of Urbino* now appear at the Uffizi rather than in Urbino.
Once in Florence, Vittoria pursued her own patronage and collecting
interests.[49] In France, similarly, Louis XIV's brother, Philippe, duc
d'Orléans received paintings collected by his first wife, Henriette Anne,
daughter of Charles I.[50] Further paintings formed part of the inheritance of
his second wife, Elisabeth-Charlotte von der Pfalz at the death of her
brother, the elector palatine, in 1685. A mortified Lieselotte had to watch
her brother-in-law's troops invade the Palatinate so that her husband could
pursue her inheritance in her name. Catalina Méndez de Haro y Guzmán's
marriage to the tenth duke of Alba in 1688 brought paintings that now bear
his name, including the National Gallery in Washington's prime Raphael,
the *Alba Madonna*.[51]

It is not always clear what, if any, affinity these women had for the
objects that transferred with them, but it is evident that many carried on
with their fathers' collecting priorities. In this book, we learn that Eleonora
of Toledo's love of luxury textiles came from her father's similar
penchant, that Elizabeth Murray's father had been a collector in the circle
of King Charles I, that Erzsébet Rákóczi dedicated herself to carrying on
her father's metalwork collection, while Elizabeth Percy built on her
father's numismatic collection and that, in Holland, Maria de Wilde
(1682-1729) both recorded the appearance of her father's *Kunstkammer* in
drawings and added items to his collection. At the same time in Rome,
Maria Camilla Pallavicini, princess of Gallicano and wife of Giovanni
Battista Rospigliosi, was an active collector of contemporary works, e.g.
Lanfranco and Luca Giordano, adding to the Rubens works left her by her
father and resulting eventually in the extensive group of works in the
Galleria Pallavicini in Rome.[52] Other paintings entered this collection
through additional marriages: Maria Camilla's son married Giustina
Borromeo, whose family had given her paintings and at the end of the
eighteenth century a Colonna bride's dowry further enriched the collection.

Some women worked closely with male relatives to form collections.
Aletheia Talbot, informed her husband about available works while she

---

[48] Rossi 1996, I, 594 [and in Grove Art Online] on Olimpia Aldobrandini.
[49] Straussman-Pflanzer, 2010.
[50] Brown, 1995, 225.
[51] Pita Andrade 1965, 274.
[52] Zeri 1959, 11-9.

was travelling independently of him. One of the more interesting bits of evidence of such a partnership occurred in Mantua. In 1604 not only did Duke Vincenzo Gonzaga write to his mistress, Agnese Argotta, the marchesa di Grana, seeking an Andrea del Sarto *Madonna* in her possession, but his duchess, Eleonora, also wrote to her.[53]

In the cases in which women had discretion over the spaces they occupied, there is ample evidence that they paid very close attention to the objects displayed within. And it is naïve to assume that these are simply women consigned to an isolated domestic sphere for such interiors played important roles as ceremonial spaces. First, some women discussed in this anthology actually were owners, or co-owners, of great houses. Elizabeth Murray had her own standing as countess of Dysart and thus exercised control over her family seat, Ham House, which her mother, Catherine Bruce, had fiercely protected from seizure by Parliament. And Elizabeth Percy, as Adriano Aymonino demonstrates, put her stamp on two houses she inherited in her own right: Alnwick Castle and Northumberland House. Generally speaking, women of higher rank than their husbands had the most leverage and the stature to assert their birth identity within spaces belonging to their spouses. Andrea Gáldy and Robert La France demonstrate the connection between the apartments known as the Golden Chambers that Eleonora of Toledo used on the third floor of the Palazzo Vecchio (a floor above her better known suite), with projects by her father, Don Pedro, the Spanish viceroy in Naples. This volume contains further explorations of women's influence over the imagery in their spaces: as Zech points out, the rooms refurbished in 1665 by Henriette Adelaide, consort of Ferdinand Maria of Bavaria, emphasise hearts and love knots alluding both to her marriage and to her natal House of Savoy. Similarly, in the décor of Eleonora of Toledo's Golden Chambers, falcons refer both to her birth and marital families. A few examples of other women whose decoration of interior spaces indicates their particular efforts include the countess of Arundel at Tart Hall in London; Margaret of Austria at Mechelen in the southern Netherlands; and Caroline Louise of Hesse Darmstadt (1723-83).[54] In Karlsruhe, she formed a collection of works by Rembrandt, Chardin and other seventeenth and eighteenth century Dutch, French and German artists, displayed in her apartments for the exclusive perusal of her guests.[55]

Collecting creates both competition and community. Women collectors often received compatible women at home for salon-style gatherings.

---

[53] Rebecchini 2002, 48.

[54] Chew 2003, 285-314; Eichberger 2003, 25-46.

[55] Laurie 1996, XXXIII, 593-4 on the House of Zähringen.

Because of the political situation during the English civil war, the earl and countess of Arundel fled, he to Italy, she to the Netherlands. After her husband's death, in Padua, the countess remained in Amsterdam with their, now her, extensive art collection and was known to interact with artists and people of letters at her house. Agnes Block and other women collectors in seventeenth-century Holland similarly gathered like-minded people around them. In eighteenth-century London, Elizabeth Percy was part of a circle of collectors including Queen Charlotte, the artist Mary Delany, the duchess of Portland (Margaret Cavendish Bentinck), and others. While we have images of men engaged in the close examination of artwork, we seem to lack similar depictions of women connoisseurs. Somewhat ironically, perhaps, Johan Zoffany's *Tribuna of the Uffizi* (London: Royal Collection), famously depicting a group of male connoisseurs in Florence, was a gift from Queen Charlotte to George III. Lucy Harington, countess of Bedford and in the circle of Queen Anne of Denmark, wrote to her friend Jane Cornwallis, wife of Nathaniel Bacon, about some Holbeins in her father-in-law's collection, urging her to purchase them for her lest they go to Arundel, explaining that she was "a very diligent gatherer of all I can get of Holbein's or any other excellent master's hand."[56] For the duchesse de Berri, collecting provided the opportunity for dynastic competition; she promoted a "Bourbon style" for her son Henri, count de Chambord, versus an Orléanist style favoured by the rival dynasty.

Although I do not want to suggest that quality (however defined) be the sole criterion for examining women collectors, it is clear that women did have connoisseurial interests, abilities, and the means for expressing their views. We have evidence, primarily from letters, that women cared deeply about the quality of paintings. Margaret of Austria described Jan van Eyck's *Arnolfini Wedding*, given to her, as "*ung tableau fort exquis.*"[57] Similar terms were applied to other works in her collection while phrases like "badly done" or "of little value" also appear. Many women demonstrated their ability to evaluate objects. In 1591 Eleonora de' Medici, duchess of Mantua, had correspondence with a Medici agent in Florence about a painting by Andrea del Sarto she wished him to obtain for her from its owner. In a later letter, she noted with great pleasure that the painting is actually by Raphael, not Sarto, plus she requested more information as to the attribution of additional works in his possession.[58] Lucy Harrington

---

[56] Hearn 2003, 225.
[57] Eichberger 1996, 268.
[58] ASF, *MP*, 2941; Medici Archive Project Documentary Sources database, entries 4859, 4866, and 4878.

asserted her expertise, writing to a friend that she had "found in obscure places, and gentleman's houses, that, because they are old, made no reckoning of them; and that makes me thinke itt likely that there may yet be in diverse places many excellent unknown peeses."[59] In a letter to her half-sister back in Heidelberg, Elisabeth-Charlotte von der Pfalz stated that:

> There are few antique medals I do not have already, for I have nearly nine hundred of them. I started out with only 260, which I bought from Madame Verrue, who had stolen them from the then Duke of Savoy ... They did not cost me much since I bought them by weight, and yet the lot contained a few very rare items. I like Merian's copper engravings very much, but I think that landscapes are what he does best.[60]

Christina of Sweden wrote, c.1650, that she possessed:

> an infinite number of items, but apart from 30 or 40 original Italians I care nothing for any of the others. There are some by Albrecht Dürer and other German masters whose names I do not know ... I swear that I would give away the lot for a couple of Raphaels.[61]

Despite such evidence, commentators still find ways to denigrate women collectors with specific goals. According to Niels von Holst, Caroline Louise of Hesse Darmstadt was "an active art lover who championed Parisian taste with an anxious narrow-mindedness." (Would not "a razor-sharp focus" have conveyed the same intent?) He also mentioned that "A list of her requirements in 1761 began with Dou and Netscher, with Rembrandt's name only in tenth place."[62] She was hardly alone at that time in her relative lack of enthusiasm for Rembrandt. Significantly, however, her collection formed the basis of the Staatliche Kunsthalle Karlsruhe. Women did form collections that satisfied contemporary male connoisseurs: publisher Robert Dodsley reported that Elizabeth Percy's "fine collection of pictures ... afford[s] a most pleasing and almost endless entertainment to a connoisseur." The duchesse de Berri received similar praise for the taste demonstrated in her collection.

This anthology features studies of individual collectors, with the exception of Agnes Block, all royal or aristocratic. They collected paintings,

---

[59] Hearn 2003, 225.
[60] Förster 1984, 251.
[61] Holst 1967, 115.
[62] Ibid., 187.

sculptures, the range of decorative arts, coins and medals, and botanical and other scientific specimens. They displayed portraits and, as time went on, paintings with secular subjects in the domestic environments that some built or refurbished. Women in general had to confront, or more often work within, legal and social norms that made difficult their spending money or owning property. Nevertheless, a few modern scholars seek to maintain a de-contextualised notion of "taste" that devalues some of women's past motivations and results. A number of women with access to education very much concerned themselves with what we now call connoisseurship, but they and others saw their collecting as pursuing additional aims, which also gave their objects status. Through collecting, they promoted their families—birth and marital—and themselves thereby; they pursued a passion to share with others; they advanced scientific knowledge; and they maintained a sense of identity as a widow or in a foreign land.

Thus after centuries of neglect and denigration, the important role of female collectors in contributing to new scientific disciplines, to the beginnings of public museums and to the cultural exchange between European courts and states can no longer be ignored. The present volume tries to pay them some of their dues.

CHAPTER ABSTRACTS

Chapter One
Andrea Gáldy and Robert La France

From 1549 to 1555 Duchess Eleonora of Toledo expanded her apartments in Florence's Palazzo Vecchio to its third floor. A tower-like block attached to the south-east corner of the mediaeval palace contained the duchess's new Golden Chambers with a study, chapel, toilet, and open loggia or terrace that not only connected with her earlier Green Chamber suite below, but also to her Spanish female attendants' rooms and her children's bedchambers on the third floor. This configuration evokes Eleonora's previous residence with her father, Don Pedro de Toledo, in apartments adjacent to the Golden Tower of the Castel Nuovo in Naples, c. 1534-9. After examining a 1553 inventory of the contents of the palace's third floor, this essay proposes that the duchess's Golden Chambers were also fitted with a precious series of tapestries entitled the *Months*, which display the duchess's benign stewardship of Tuscany's agricultural resources and the eclectic style popular at the Spanish courts.

Chapter Two
Christopher Rowell

Elizabeth Murray (1626-98), 2nd countess of Dysart (1655) in her own right and duchess of Lauderdale by marriage (1672), was one of the most formidable females of the seventeenth century. Her father, William Murray, 1st earl of Dysart (c.1600-55), was a childhood friend of Charles I, travelled with him to Spain when he was prince of Wales, and was equally imbued with the ideals of the High Renaissance. Ham House (NT), completed 1610, first leased to him by the king in 1626 and then purchased outright in 1637, remains a rare monument of Caroline Franco-Italian taste in interior decoration, where much of the early- and late-seventeenth-century collection remains in situ. Ham was doubled in size, redecorated and re-furnished in the 1670s by Elizabeth Dysart, and her second husband, John Maitland, 1st duke of Lauderdale. Famous already in the eighteenth century for its untouched state, its furniture, its portraits, and its décor, Ham retains its reputation for antiquity, thanks to the conservative approach of Elizabeth's successors in title. Ham is romantically evocative of the reign of Charles I, the Civil War and the

Restoration, and owes much to the heroine of this chapter, which aims to sift the available evidence about her personal tastes, purchases and commissions. The family archives hold a rich vein of information about her life and times, and about the history of her paternal seat by the Thames near Richmond.

Chapter Three
Joy Kearney

In the seventeenth century, when the Netherlands were enjoying unprecedented prosperity, there were a remarkable number of women who devoted themselves to collecting, and in many cases to illustrating, the wonders and curiosities of the natural world. At a time when most women were not educated and did not have the opportunity to travel, these women were at the forefront of scientific and academic discoveries, breaking down gender-related barriers. Two, whose interests brought them in contact with each other, were Agnes Block and Maria Sibylla Merian. Both had a major impact on the distribution of cutting-edge knowledge regarding flora and fauna in the Early Modern period and were pioneers in the field of both natural history research and botanical and zoological illustration. Many other women of means had important collections and libraries and were thus instrumental in advancing the practice of collecting and stimulating the study of science and natural history in the Dutch "Golden Age".

Chapter Four
Orsolya Bubryák

Art collecting of the seventeenth-century Hungarian aristocracy was confined almost exclusively to silverware. Owing to the constant threat caused by the Turkish invasion, which hit a large part of the country from the mid-sixteenth century onwards, the noble families made efforts to amass golden and silver works of art which were easily movable and preserved their value. The huge *Schaukredenz*, consisting of gilded silver dishes, bowls and other tableware presented at feasts, was the most important part of aristocratic representation. Nonetheless, we can hardly speak of continuously existing treasures, since a noble family's existence was based mainly on landholding. Female family members' dowry or inheritance was therefore usually paid in cash or precious objects. It follows that the content of a families' collection frequently changed, according to the demographic situation of the family. This study aims to reconstruct one such case, the history of the collection of Countess Erzsébet Rákóczi (1654-1707). She was the last descendant of one of the most important noble families in the kingdom of Hungary. Her treasure consisted of pieces inherited from her parents and acquired by herself. After her death her collection was merged with the possessions of her first and second husbands' family, the Erdődys. Many pieces that once belonged to the countess, mainly silver dishes, can be identified with the help of written and visual sources. Furthermore, contemporary documents have shed new light on the collecting aims and attitude of Erzsébet Rákóczi.

Chapter Five
Adriano Aymonino
The private collection of Elizabeth Seymour Percy, 2nd countess and later 1st duchess of Northumberland (1716-1776), was one of the largest—but today mostly unknown—private cabinets of curiosities of eighteenth-century Britain. As one of the very few collections independently assembled by a woman in the Georgian period, the duchess's *Musaeum*, as she called it, encompassed almost the whole spectrum of the *naturalia* and *artificialia* collectibles. Its contents were originally displayed in the apartments of the duchess at Northumberland House and, after the demolition of the large palace on the Strand in 1874, relocated to other family residences. During the course of the twentieth century the memory of this fascinating collection was further compromised by a series of sales which dispersed it to the four corners of the world. This article offers an introduction to the contents of the *Musaeum* and to its original principles of organisation and display at Northumberland House.

Chapter Six
Heike Zech
Two objects from the collection of Queen Marie of Bavaria are the starting point for exploring if and how the role as mother informed the acquisition and use of objects and pictures by members of the House of Wittelsbach from the seventeenth century onwards. Taking into account the methodological limitations and the problem of survival of such intimate, informal and hence very dynamic collections, Zech identifies dynastic representation and self-identification as well as maternal love as motivations for collecting. From the early nineteenth century onwards a shift towards the later can be observed which coincides with a revolution in the culture of childcare and motherhood.

Chapter Seven
Philip Mansel

As part of dynasties' attempts to establish their political and patriotic credentials, in their efforts to win or stay on the throne of France, in the nineteenth century the Bonaparte, Bourbon and Orléans dynasties each produced dynamic individual collectors, as well as sovereigns intent on encouraging and expanding the national collections in the Louvre. The Bonapartes had the Empress Josephine, Cardinal Fesch and Lucien Bonaparte; the Orléans Ferdinand-Philippe, duc d' Orléans and eldest son of Louis-Philippe; and the Bourbons the younger son of Charles X, Charles-Ferdinand, duc de Berri, and his wife Marie Caroline of the Two Sicilies. After her husband's murder in 1820 the duchesse de Berri was a leader of taste and entertainment in Paris until the revolution of 1830, after which she lived in exile in Venice and Graz. She had a large income and in all owned over 1000 pictures. Many of them reflect the aesthetics of Royalism—a preference for domestic subjects emphasising family ties, charitable practices and Catholic piety, as well as landscapes and pictures glorifying Bourbon heroes like Henri IV. The dispersion of her collection began in her life-time and is continuing today: a recent sale at Sotheby's on 14 April 2011 contained drawings by Isabey from Schloss Brunnsee, her home outside Graz.

CHAPTER ONE*

GOLDEN CHAMBERS FOR ELEONORA OF TOLEDO: DUCHESS AND COLLECTOR IN PALAZZO VECCHIO

ANDREA M. GÁLDY AND ROBERT G. LA FRANCE

Leonor Álvarez de Toledo (alias Duchess Eleonora di Toledo, 1519?-1562) grew up in Spain and Spanish Naples before her marriage to Duke Cosimo I de' Medici brought her to Florence in 1539. Well connected with the royal house of Trastámara, the dukes of Alba, and the families of Osorio and Pimentel, she took great pride in her lineage and Spanish heritage. Emperor Charles V appointed Eleonora's father, Don Pedro di Toledo, viceroy of Naples in 1532, while her mother Maria Osorio Pimentel had once been a ward of the court of Queen Isabel I "the Catholic" and inherited the title of marchioness of Villafranca.[1] Eleonora turned out to be a beautiful, fertile and pious dynastic bride. She also showed considerable intelligence, business acumen, and boundless ambition for herself, her family and her new husband. Spanish to the core,

---

* This Chapter is dedicated to Robert Gaston, with thanks for his inspiration and support.
[1] For a summary of Don Pedro's appointment and reign, see Galasso 2005, II, 406-538. Maria Osorio Pimentel's life and collecting interests are discussed in Gaston 2004, 159, and the complex story of the matrilineal inheritance of the marquisate of Villafranca del Bierzo (León) is recounted in Hernando Sánchez 1994, 67-8 and 78-9. Although Eleonora's exact date of birth is unknown (Baia 1907, 89, note 1; Cox-Rearick 1984, 290, note 151; and Rousseau 1990, 436, note 82), she was the youngest of Don Pedro's four daughters. Hernando Sánchez 1994, 98-9.

she imported many Spanish customs to her new residence in Palazzo
Vecchio. Her apartment on the palace's second floor is well preserved and
several scholars have explored its design and decoration. Yet the rooms on
the third floor have been mostly overlooked, including a suite of Golden
Chambers dedicated to the duchess and created during the apogee of her
power.

The Ducal Palace and Eleonora's Apartments after 1540

Eleonora's residence in Palazzo Vecchio can be divided into three distinct
phases: an initial campaign to decorate the duchess's second floor
apartment from 1540; the third floor expansion and decoration of the
Golden Chambers from 1549; and finally, Giorgio Vasari's redecoration
of the second floor with a cohesive programme that celebrated Eleonora's
virtues in the early 1560s. Meanwhile, in 1549 the duchess had also
acquired the Palazzo Pitti which, together with the Boboli Gardens,
remained a work in progress that only became the Medici family's
permanent residence after her death.

Following their marriage in 1539, Eleonora and Cosimo resided in the
Medici palace on Via Larga. Then, on 1 May 1540, nearly a year after the
duchess's arrival in Florence and shortly after the birth of their first child
Maria (1540-1557), the ducal couple moved into the former republican
Palazzo dei Priori (Palazzo Vecchio).[2] Thus, in 1540 this palace effectively
became the ducal palace of Florence, although the building was not yet a
luxurious, noble residence. Many rooms were unfinished (such as the
Great Council Hall), and others were decorated for the needs of the
Republic, such as the Hall of the Lilies (Sala dei Gigli), and the Priors'
Chapel. The first floor contained the rooms fitted out for Piero Soderini,
the last standard-bearer or *gonfaloniere* of the Republic, and the duke
claimed both physical and symbolic possession of these for his private
apartments.[3] The duchess took the former dormitories for the priors on the
second floor, which at times she seems to have shared with her husband.[4]
The duke's mother, Maria Salviati, occupied the mezzanine until her death
in 1543.[5]

---

[2] Allegri-Cecchi 1980, 5; on economic reasons for the move, Parigino 1999, 44;
and Gáldy 2006, 298-9.
[3] Rubinstein 1995, 43-6; Gáldy 2002, 490-1 and 496.
[4] Trachtenberg 1989, 598-601; Rubinstein 1995, appendix I, 97-100 and fig. IV;
Edelstein 2003, 52-3 and note 4. On the duke and duchess sharing accommodation
Edelstein 1995, 167 and document 17 on 629; Gáldy 2002, 496.
[5] Hoppe 2004, 99.

Only Eleonora's second-floor apartment survives in its sixteenth-century form as far as the ceiling decorations are concerned; a number of wall hangings are also still extant.[6] While archival documents and several publications over the past thirty years have afforded a better understanding of how the second floor was organised, functioned, and connected to Cosimo's living quarters below, questions remain concerning how much of the decoration and furnishings were Eleonora's choice. Most of the knowledge gained over the past decades, however, concerns either the creation of the Green Chamber (Camera Verde) suite at the beginning of Eleonora's reign in the early 1540s, or the work projected and executed by Giorgio Vasari and assistants at the end of her life in the early 1560s. Hence, in order to understand the palace and the duchess's apartments more fully, we first need to go back to a time before the installation of Vasari's highly propagandistic decorative programme. The second step will be to look at the expansion of Eleonora's early quarters on the second floor to a new suite of apartments on the third floor, its models and precedents. The final sections concern the organisation, contents, and function of the upper floor rooms.

As customary for princely apartments in the sixteenth century, and for reasons of safety and etiquette, Eleonora's apartment was situated on one of the higher floors of the palace and its layout followed that of her husband's quarters below. The duke and duchess's individual apartments were not only initially the same size; they also had the same suite of halls, state rooms, and semi-private chambers, thereby displaying an ideal of equality and joint rule. In addition, a system of spiral staircases situated at a nodal point, just before the most private of rooms, physically connected the two apartments.[7]

Eleonora: a Lady of Lineage, Means, and Authority

Eleonora not only added aristocratic tone to the Medici family, she also increased her husband's wealth by her dowry, business sense, and income from the administration of papal estates in Tuscany.[8] We also know a fair

---

[6] Allegri-Cecchi 1980, 195-212; for a choice of recent publications see among others Hoppe 2004, 98-118; Edelstein 2003, 51-87 and 2004, 71-97; Gáldy 2006, 293-319 and 2008, II, 615-26. Gáldy's 2002 reading of the apartment's sequence seems to have been accepted in subsequent Italian publications, e.g. by Cinelli 2006, 240-5 and Marcolin and Paccetti 2010, 20-31.
[7] On the lay-out of the ducal apartments see Gáldy 2002, 496-7 and 2006, 300-1; Hoppe 2004, 99-102.
[8] Parigino 1999 on Eleonora's enterprising business sense and the origins of her

amount about how she spent her money, for example on clothes and jewels, and that her choice to do so frequently met with the disapproval of Cosimo, who was often under financial constraints.[9] Occasionally, she even lent money to the duke.[10] An inveterate gambler despite her piety, Eleonora frittered away considerable amounts of her wealth.[11] She also gave generously to charitable causes, saved the survivors of the Sienese War from famine by importing grain, and established the Jesuit Order in Florence by bequeathing them a *palazzo* in Piazza S Lorenzo.[12] Moreover, Eleonora commissioned works of art and also received antiquities as gifts from various sources; like her daughters, she may have wished to acquire some herself.[13]

Nonetheless, the duchess's single largest expenditure out of her dowry must have been the purchase of Palazzo Pitti in 1549. Since this building required decades to be completed and transformed into a quasi-royal residence, she only saw the first phase of the building campaign and of the planning and planting of the Boboli gardens behind it. The available documentation has not made it easy to establish how much Eleonora was involved in guiding and funding these changes before her death in 1562.[14] In the case of her apartments in Palazzo Vecchio we have a similar problem, even though we know that she took a keen interest in the decorative scheme for her suite of rooms, which also served state functions.[15]

Eleonora received important visitors and took over the running of the Florentine duchy, whenever her husband was unable to do so.[16] Hence, her apartments needed to create an appropriate stage and backdrop for such

---

fortune, 96-106; Edelstein 2000, 301-7; 2003, 75-7; 2004, 72-3.

[9] Cellini 1983, e.g. 168, 169, 192; Westerman Bulgarella 2004, 207-24; Franceschini 2004, 184-5; Orsi Landini 2005, 23-38 on Eleonora's style and her love of ear-rings, then a new feature in Florentine fashion.

[10] Edelstein 2003, 75-6 and note 62.

[11] Franceschini 2004, 187.

[12] On the duchess's charity towards projects suggested and run by the Jesuits, for example a school in Pisa, see Franceschini 2004, 189-90.

[13] Gáldy 2006, 306 and note 92 on Eleonora's commission of a different set of wings for the altarpiece in her chapel; Cellini 1983, *passim* remarks various times on her interest in and influence on commissions and artistic judgement and intelligence; Gáldy 2010, 157-8 on her son Giovanni's gift of an ancient *putto* to his mother and his activities as an antiquities scout for his sisters, 159-60.

[14] Gáldy 2006, 306 and note 93 and Gáldy 2009 b, 28-9 and 30-1.

[15] For Eleonora's interest in the decorative programme see Edelstein 2001, 234; Gáldy 2008, 618-9 and note 18.

[16] Edelstein 2000, 295-329.

audiences. On the second floor, the rooms stretched out *enfilade*, forming clear boundaries of access.[17] Contrary to the modern museum visitors' route, in the 1540s a guest visiting Eleonora's quarters would have arrived on the second floor from the main stair, passed through the Sala dei Gigli, the Sala delle Udienze, and then the Priors' Chapel in order to gain access to the first of the duchess's four state rooms (Fig. 1).[18] The second floor suite terminated at the other end with the Camera Verde, once decorated with landscapes by Ridolfo Ghirlandaio. This *camera* functioned as the hub of Eleonora's life, where she kept valuables, performed family duties, gambled, and attended to business matters.[19] The woodworker and ducal architect Battista del Tasso (1500-1555) built two rooms, as well as toilets and closets, into the Camera Verde: a study or *scrittoio*, which housed the ledgers that Eleonora needed for financial and administrative work near the strong boxes in the Green Chamber,[20] and the famous chapel painted by Bronzino for the duchess's private devotional practices which she performed according to the Spanish model.[21]

Twenty years later, in 1560-62, Vasari initiated a campaign to redecorate this apartment according to a programme depicting virtuous women, which provided these chambers with their current names (Fig. 1).[22] Yet Vasari left the earlier Camera Verde cluster essentially untouched and preserved the apartment's processional order. The first on a privileged visitor's path, after passing through the Priors' Chapel, became the Sala di Gualdrada, the room with the most Florentine theme in Eleonora's suite. It probably functioned as an antechamber, and the central ceiling painting depicts the story of the mediaeval Florentine girl Gualdrada, who successfully

---

[17] On the etiquette observed by hosts and visitors and the changed views on what was then regarded as private or public see Thornton 1991, 284-300 and Waddy 1990, 3-13.

[18] Gáldy 2002, 496-7 and fig. 3.

[19] The precise function of the Camera Verde has been disputed for some time. Once considered a bedchamber, Edelstein proposed a different use as audience room (see Edelstein 1995, 189 and 2003, 75). Gáldy 2002, 497 (and in subsequent publications) saw it as a *camera* located at the innermost end of Eleonora's apartment in which the duchess also slept. Multi-purpose rooms were the norm in princely apartments of the sixteenth century, while money chests were often stored in bedrooms.

[20] Edelstein 1995, 189 and 2004, 72-4.

[21] For the Spanish sources for the decoration of Eleonora's chapel see Gaston 2004, 157-180, while Cox-Rearick 1993 had seen it as mostly influenced by ideas developed within the Accademia Fiorentina for the benefit of Duke Cosimo.

[22] See the fundamental chronology for Vasari's second floor decoration in Allegri-Cecchi 1980, 195-212.

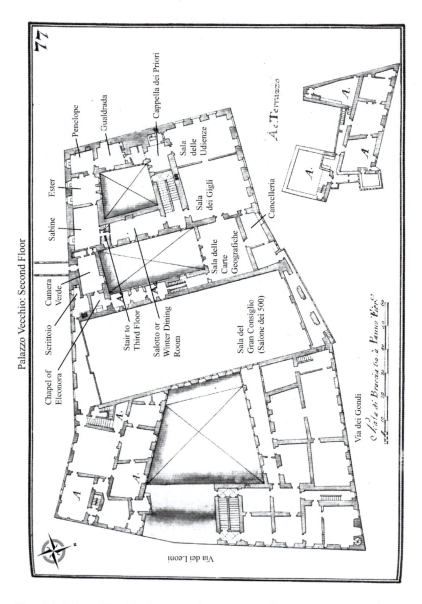

Figure 1: Palazzo Vecchio, Florence, the apartment of Eleonora of Toledo on the second-floor (c.1553).

demonstrated her independence and virtue by refusing Emperor Otto IV's request to kiss her. The second was dedicated to the memory of Penelope, queen of Ithaca, who ruled for twenty years while her husband Ulysses laid siege to Troy and struggled to return.[23] The third room, or Sala di Esther, represents a foreign, virtuous woman crowned queen of Persia by her husband, King Ahasuerus. Eleonora's new title, duchess of Florence and Siena, is inscribed in the frieze below. The fourth room is dedicated to the Sabine women. Despite their abduction, they made peace with the Romans, created a new people out of this union, and ensured the survival of the newly-founded city. These allegories implied parallels with Eleonora's transfer from Naples to Florence, her role in keeping peace between the Empire and Florence, and her elevated rank and family connection to one of the most powerful queens of her age. Eventually, woven tapestries substituted the leather wall hangings that previously adorned these rooms after the Spanish custom.

The Third Floor Apartment

As the second floor became overcrowded during the late 1540s, and before Vasari remodelled it in the early 1560s, the duchess decided to expand her apartment upward. Scholars consider the third floor mainly as accommodation and the nursery for the growing Medici brood, and have dubbed it the "Quartiere dei Signorini."[24] Yet contemporary accounts and inventories specify that the extended chambers belonged to the duchess. Eleonora ruled the palace's third floor, which also housed her children, their nursemaids, and her mainly Spanish servants and ladies in waiting (*damigelle*), including distinct rooms for her favourite attendants Isabel Reynoso and Maria Pimentel. Both of these women came from Spain, had served the duchess's mother in Spain and Naples, and were sent by Don Pedro to assist at the time of Eleonora's first pregnancy.[25] Thus,

---

[23] Even though the original mythological figure was Greek, Penelope was also an important symbol of queenship in Spain and had often been compared to Isabel I and to her mother before her; Gáldy 2006, 311-2 and 2008, II, 621-6.

[24] See Conti 1893, 71-7; Allegri-Cecchi 1980, 10 ("stanze dei Signorini"), and the general discussion of the third floor in the context of the lives of the Medici children in Murphy 2008, chapter 2.

[25] Hernando Sánchez 1994, 139-40. Maria Pimentel had not only served Eleonora's mother, Maria Osorio Pimentel (d. 1539), but was related to her, and probably also kin to Eleonora's sister in law, Inés Pimentel, who married Don Pedro's eldest son Fadrique before 1535. As a noble relation, Maria Pimentel is listed as the head of the *damigelle* in the 1556 salary rolls, assigned a special room

Eleonora's entourage of Spanish women governed the Medici children on the third floor, and formed an aulic environment recalling courts in Spain and Spanish Naples.

Documents indicate that from about September 1549 through at least 1554 Tasso renovated the third floor as part of a larger campaign to expand and embellish the palace.[26] In addition to his role as architect, designing and supervising the construction of roofs, walls, doors, windows, stairs, and chimneys, Tasso also created carved wood ceilings and other ornaments, the payments for which stretched until 1557 and were collected by heirs after his death on 8 May 1555. New construction focused on two chambers and a terrace for the duchess, "dua camere et terrazzo della Signora Duchessa," which crown the block of a tower-like structure attached to the southeast corner of the mediaeval palace along the Via della Ninna (Fig. 2).[27] This block communicates, albeit through a passageway or servant's room, with the second floor rooms adjacent to the Camera Verde via a stairway wedged between the Sala delle Sabine and the Salotto or Winter Dining Room (Fig. 1). This stairwell, with its multiple

---

in the palace, and earned a place in Don Pedro's will of 1553. In addition, the Neapolitan court poet Tansillo praised her virtues and the writer Nicola Terminio dedicated his *Trofeo Toletano* "in servigio de la Eccellente Signora D. Maria Pimontella..."; Hernando Sánchez 1994, 93 and 470.

[26] A letter describing a water leak into the Camera Verde in September 1549 establishes a *terminus ante quem* for the third floor campaign. Cox-Rearick 1993, 80 and 338, doc. 15. See also Allegri-Cecchi 1980, 10, no. 2. At least three problems frustrate efforts to determine a more precise chronology for the third floor. First, the ledgers for the building's fabric (*Scrittoio delle Fortezze e Fabbriche Medicee*) only survive from 1549 forward, starting with the book marked with the letter B. Accounts consistently refer to a lost book marked with the letter A, called the book with the gilt leather ties (*correggie dorè* or "chorreggie doree"), which recorded the initial palace renovation expenses. Furthermore, the detailed payment lists kept by paymaster Francesco Tasselli are also incomplete (see the late example ASF, *FM* 19 "Palazzo Ducale Ricordanze del 1555"). Second, financial difficulties and sloppy record keeping resulted in late payments and accounts fractured across non-consecutive pages. Third, payments for several simultaneous projects intermingle in the same books. These include the construction of the Quartieri degli Elementi and Leone X, the villas at Castello and Petraia, and the completion of the Laurentian Library, making it difficult to isolate the third floor campaign (see the general chronology of some of these projects in Allegri-Cecchi 1980, 14-8, nos. 6-9; Pagnini 2006, 122-5, and Wright 1976). Finally, Giorgio Vasari succeeded Tasso, and disparaged his predecessor's works in the 1568 edition of the *Lives* (La France 2008, 19 for a summary of Vasari's rancour against Tasso).

[27] The quoted phrase appears in several payment records. Appendix 1.

Figure 2: Palazzo Vecchio, south façade onto Via della Ninna with fenestration of the second and third floors.

round-headed doorways, closets, and flights of stairs still functions today as the principal entry to the third floor museum offices.

The construction of the new chambers directly above the Camera Verde nucleus extended the duchess's most intimate, private zone vertically to the next floor. The remains of a spiral staircase in the southeast corner of the third floor's rearmost chamber, rediscovered during the preparations for the Medici exhibitions in 1980, further connected the two new chambers to the terrace.[28] By the time the third floor renovations were completed in the mid 1550s, Eleonora could comfortably rise from the world of *negotium* in the Camera Verde on the second floor, to that of her family obligations and new chambers on the third floor, and then up

---

[28] Allegri-Cecchi 1980, 10.

the spiral stair to the fresh air and *otium* of the terrace.

Florentine record takers repeatedly used the terms *camera* or *camerino* to refer to the duchess's two chambers above the Camera Verde, thereby underlining their significance.[29] These rooms also received special architectural attention in the form of a fireplace with a carved mantle, secured windows, and elaborately decorated ceilings, which are mentioned in tardy payment records. For example, on 1 July of 1554 the suppliers Jacopo Pinadori and Francesco di ser Guglielmi were paid for Volterran gesso, goat hide glue, and Armenian bole, which had been consigned to a painter named Tommaso di Giovanni on 24 April 1553, so that he could paint and gild ceilings in Eleonora's rooms.[30] Two weeks later, on 14 July 1554, another payment covers the turning of 200 bosses (at the price of one *soldo* each) for the duchess's Golden Chambers ("chamere messe d'oro della Duchessa").[31]

The ceilings are more fully described in the final payment to Tasso's sons and heirs (Domenico, Marco, Simone and Filippo) on 27 February 1557, several months after they had been appraised in August 1556 by the woodcarvers "Filippo di Bartolomeo d'Agniolo" (the woodcarver Baccio d'Agnolo's son) and Antonio called Particino.[32] The description specifies "two carved ceilings in the duchess's two rooms above the Camera Verde," which consisted of a total of 70 coffers. Falcons adorned the coffers in one ceiling, and diamonds in the other. Festoons encircled the frieze, while spirals, bosses and other motifs ornamented the framework. The woodwork alone was valued at 160 ducats, as the gold and other materials had already been paid. The entry is one of several in an account that amounts to a post-mortem, partial résumé of Tasso's projects from 1551 through 1555.[33]

The falcons and diamonds recall Piero "the Gouty" de' Medici's (1416-69) heraldic symbols of a falcon holding the Medici diamond ring

---

[29] These terms appear in several payments, e.g., "camere della Duchessa sotto il sopradetto Terrazzo" ASF, *FM* 1, 18 des. and cross reference on 93 des. (payment record of 1 July 1554), or "chamera della D.ssa" ASF, *FM* 1, 59 sin. The more specific term "camerino della Duchessa." appears in ASF, *FM* 2, 63 des. and the variant spelling "chamerino dela Duchessa" in the cross reference on 71 sin. (payment record of 31 October 1553).

[30] Appendix 2.

[31] Appendix 3.

[32] Appendix 4.

[33] Other projects included: a wood model for a palace in Pisa; various windows, doors, and a ceiling in the new wing towards the Via de' Leoni; and two of the carved and inlaid benches for the Laurentian Library reading room. The document is discussed partly in Pagnini 2006, 122-5.

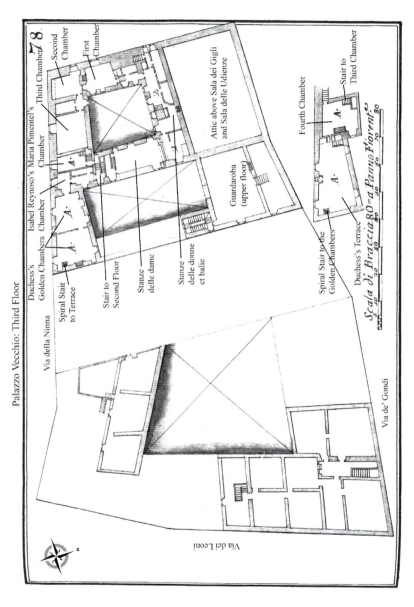

Figure 3: Palazzo Vecchio, the apartment of Eleonora of Toledo on the third floor (c.1553).

and, as Allegri and Cecchi briefly noted, may well represent a minor facet
of Cosimo's vast programme to celebrate and display traditional Medici
imprese to bolster his legitimacy and family's antiquity.[34] Yet, if the
falcon recalled an old Medici device, it also resonated with Eleonora's
Spanish heritage and her father's office as viceroy of Naples. The generic
symbols of diamonds and falcons, and the sport of falconry, constituted a
standard vocabulary of nobility in Eleonora's time. Don Pedro kept a
falcon's eyrie in his palace at the Castel Nuovo in Naples, as had his
illustrious predecessors to the Neapolitan throne, such as King Alfonso V
of Aragon (1394-1458) and his successor Ferdinand I (Ferrante, 1423-94),
who was an avid falconer.[35] Cosimo and Eleonora continued the noble
sport at the time of the construction of Eleonora's chambers, and even
hired a professional falconer named Jacopo di Antonio Zanni in January of
1552, when Tasso began carving the ceilings.[36]

The Golden Chambers and their fittings only survive in modified form.
A thin dividing wall, pierced by a single doorway framed by grey stone
(*pietra serena*), separates the smaller rear chamber from the larger
antechamber. This curtain wall still rests in its sixteenth-century position,
although the door may have been shifted to the wall's centre in relation to
its placement as recorded in an eighteenth-century plan of the palace
preserved in the Habsburg family archives at Prague (Fig. 3).[37] These
rooms still reverberate with echoes of past authority, as the rear chamber
now serves as the office for the chief architect and curator of the city-
administered Palazzo Vecchio, while modern wood and glass partitions
divide the antechamber into offices. The present ceilings in both rooms are
nineteenth-century replacements, yet they reflect their predecessors'
design, albeit without the falcons or diamonds.[38] The gilding is peeling

---

[34] See Allegri-Cecchi 1980, 10 and the discussion of the *impresa* in Cox-Rearick
1984, 16 and 240.

[35] For Don Pedro's eyrie, lion's den, and other captive animals, see Coniglio 1967,
43-4 citing Filangieri 1934, 294, and documents in Filangieri 1940, 32. On
Ferrante's obsession for birds and his multiple aviaries with falcons and rare
species, see Filangieri 1934, 251.

[36] ASF, *DG*, Parte Antica 391, 147 sin.-des.: "Iacopo d'Antoni Zanni nuovo
falconiere da Coreggio con provisione di fiorini nove di moneta al mese
cominiciando addì primo di gennaio 1551 [1552]." Jacopo da Correggio was paid
18 florins for two months work (January to February 1552, modern style). His 9
florin monthly stipend breaks down to 3 florins salary, 2 florins for a 'garzone' or
helper, 2 florins for a horse, and 2 florins for expenses.

[37] For the history of these tax plans (*cabrei*) and related documents, see Manno
Tolù 2007, 5-8.

[38] Allegri-Cecchi 1980, 10.

from the rear chamber's ceiling, which has small rosettes in its shallow coffers. The antechamber's ceiling displays pleasant gilt scrollwork and foliate elements between unadorned, blue-painted coffers. The four window openings in both rooms preserve their original locations (compare with the Prague plan, Fig. 3), and they offer another clue to the chambers' importance and the valuables they once stored. Their sixteenth-century stone frames are preserved on both the inner courtyard and Via della Ninna palace façades, and three display telltale scars from iron grates on their exteriors, while a fourth window still has a flat iron grate set within the frame (Figs. 2 and 4). The frame of the window in the Camera Verde, on the inner side of the palace, is similarly scarred around its face (Fig. 4). Payments in June and July of 1553 recompense the stonecutter Giovanni di Piero for fabricating the courtyard windows, including the one for the Camera Verde, while the blacksmiths Romolo and Filippo di Mariotto were paid for "una ferrata inginocchiata" or "gabbia" (iron cage) to secure the Camera Verde's window.[39] The payments for these security bars on the windows for the duchess's Golden Chambers have yet to come to light, but the physical evidence proves that they once existed in the same cage format as those on the Camera Verde's window.

The large fireplace at the back of the duchess's rear chamber or *camerino* is likely from the sixteenth-century (and is also recorded in the eighteenth-century Prague plan). The fussy carving of the *pietra serena* mantelpiece, however, is suspiciously clean and undamaged, and resembles fireplaces on the palace's mezzanine floor (refurbished in the mid 1540s after Maria Salviati's death). To the left of the fireplace lies a small, shuttered alcove with a convex wall, which is frescoed with a late sixteenth-century image of the Transfiguration above a blank band where an altar once resided.[40] To the right of the fireplace, a doorway leads to the previously mentioned spiral stair and terrace above. Finally, the herringbone-patterned brick floor appears original. Two square, grey stone postholes are inserted into the floor just to the right of the current doorway upon entering the room. The same type of stone frames a trap door in the chamber's southwest corner near the dividing wall. The trap door is now blocked by a radiator, but it certainly opened into a

---

[39] Giovanni di Piero di Giovanni scharpellino" was paid for work on the façades of the palace including five stone window frames for the duchess's rooms plus one for the Camera Verde. Appendix 5.

[40] This space is too shallow to have functioned as a closet or storage space, and most likely served as a small altar/chapel from its inception. The style of the fresco indicates that it was painted in the 1580s, and may date from the time that Grand Duchess Bianca Cappello inhabited these rooms. To our knowledge, this space and fresco are not discussed in the secondary literature.

Figure 4: Palazzo Vecchio, Dogana courtyard with north-facing façade of second and third floors.

safe hiding place for valuables in the subfloor between the second and third levels and above Eleonora's *scrittoio* attached to the Camera Verde.

These stone postholes once fixed a wooden structure to the floor. Although no comparable examples survive in the palace today, documents describe a few contemporary examples, e.g. unpublished payments in 1557 to the woodworkers Marco di Battista del Tasso and Bastiano di Simone Confetti for building a large armoire and a wooden closet divider (which was undoubtedly attached to the floor) in a chamber for the duchess's Spanish servant Antonio Robles Montalvo.[41] A laconic payment record may provide a clue as to the type of structure set into the postholes in the duchess's chamber. On 20 February 1552 the ducal treasury paid a goldbeater twenty *lire* and five *soldi* to provide the painter Bachiacca with 450 gold squares to gild a study for the Lady Duchess in the new rooms ("per metter d'oro uno scrittoio della Signora Duchessa nelle stanze nuove").[42] The most common translation of the word *scrittoio* is study, and in the Florentine context it is often used to describe a *studiolo*, that is a Renaissance study used to keep books and collections of precious objects. While the term may refer to a dedicated room, it and its diminutive form *scrittoino* was also used to describe a movable desk, a stationary piece of furniture, or even an alcove created with wooden partitions, shelving, and cupboards within a larger chamber.[43] The latter type would correspond well with the location of the postholes in the duchess's rear chamber, and a wooden structure in that corner of the room would also have concealed the trap door.

The duchess's *camerino* communicated directly with the larger front chamber and the terrace above. The front chamber has a toilet set into its south wall on the Via della Ninna side of the palace, and two more windows, one on each side of the room (as also visible in the Prague plan). This arrangement of a chamber connected to a chapel and study with a toilet nearby mimics that of the chapel, *scrittoio*, and toilet in the Camera

---

[41] Montalvo's chamber was in the new wing of the palace behind the Guardaroba, that is the northeast corner of the expanded palace along the Via dei Gondi. The payment describes an armoire built for "Montalvo camariere" that was 5 ¾ *braccia* high (3.37m) and the same width, while the "tramezzo… a uso de armario con 4 isportegli" (room divider, used as an armoire with four doors) was 6 *braccia* high and 4 ¾ wide (3.5 x 2.8m). They were completed by 29 April 1557; ASF, *FM 20*, 79r.

[42] Appendix 6. See La France 2008, 305, cat. 164 and 358, doc. 101.

[43] For the general use of the terms "scrittoio" and "studiolo" in Italian Renaissance inventories and the various study types and furnishings, see Thornton 1997, 18, 53-75 and Preyer 2006, 47-8. La France 2008, 88 and 305, cat. 164, discusses the ambiguity of these terms in the 1553 inventory.

Verde suite below. However, on the third floor these rooms were protected from courtiers passing through towards other parts of the palace, a problem best remembered by Cellini's awkward encounter with the duchess at toilet while traversing the second floor Camera Verde in the 1540s.[44] Although modern privacy was neither an option nor a clear concept in sixteenth-century court life, the third floor's location and layout restricted access to only the duchess's most intimate *famiglia*.

As for the terrace, its presence is a vast improvement upon the arrangement in the Camera Verde suite. From the third floor *camerino*, the duchess could ascend via the spiral stair to the large terrace, fresh air, and sweeping southern views towards the recently-acquired Pitti palace and gardens. The terrace was restored in the 1960s, its roof beams (painted by Bachiacca and his workshop) were conserved and attached to a new, reinforced concrete structure, and a modern terracotta tile floor installed. Also at this time, the terrace's south and east faces, which had been bricked closed (as recorded in the Prague plan, Fig. 3), were reopened to reveal the sixteenth-century columns of an open loggia. Payments clearly illustrate that Tasso built the terrace, including the original north wall, which faces towards the palace courtyard and preserves two windows with their reading benches. A third, small, square opening between Tasso's windows pierces an inner alcove (Fig. 4). This window lacks a stone frame, and is likely a later addition. A blocked doorway in the terrace's northeast corner probably led to walkways on the roof of the Great Council Hall in Eleonora's lifetime. This door was sealed when Vasari raised the ceiling for the Salone del Cinquecento in the mid 1560s, thereby changing the relationship between the two spaces.[45] In the sixteenth century, Eleonora could also reach the elevated walkway or *ballatoio* crowning the top of the old block of the palace from the terrace's west end. The Prague plan shows a stair in the northwest corner of the terrace, which certainly ascended to the stone-framed doorway still visible today on the palace's *ballatoio* level (Fig. 3). Eleonora kept a dovecote on this elevated walkway, which afforded a view of the entire city.[46] At present, one enters the terrace from the floor below through a low doorway sliced into the old building and partly cut into the terrace's pavement. This cramped, inelegant solution also appears in the Prague plan, but it may postdate Eleonora's time, when the spiral stair was the terrace's principal entry.

---

[44] Edelstein 2003, 85-87 and Lombardi 2008, 144.
[45] Allegri-Cecchi 1980, 11 and 235-67, cats. 54-55.
[46] Appendix 7.

The Golden Tower of the Castel Nuovo, Naples

At least two main sources of inspiration lie behind the concept of building a tower-like, third-floor addition for the duchess, her children and attendants. Firstly, the authors suggest that traditions of royal complexes in Spain, and Spanish court etiquette, guided Eleonora in the customs and spatial arrangement of her personal court. Eleonora's mother Maria Osorio Pimentel would have passed down her experiences as marchioness of Villafranca and her recollections of the court of Isabel I. Her mother's former servants, Maria Pimentel and Isabel Reynoso, were a daily reminder of Spanish customs. Eleonora followed her father's practice of reserving the most important court positions for trusted Spanish relations, while assigning local Italians to lesser roles.[47] Furthermore, Eleonora's education included the Spanish-language histories of the Castilian and Aragonese rulers, their feats, and their courts in Don Pedro's library.[48]

Secondly, Spanish Neapolitan architectural precedents dominated Eleonora's visual memory. These were of two types: the residences of historical Aragonese rulers and her father's Neapolitan projects. Among Don Pedro's extensive architectural and urban programmes, the renovation of his vice-regal residence at the Castel Nuovo (begun in earnest in 1534) and the rebuilding of the earthquake-damaged villa at Pozzuoli (from 1538) stand out. The choice of grotesque decoration in Eleonora's Camera Verde in conjunction with the duchess's interest in gardens has been linked to the remains of ancient material culture at the villa at Pozzuoli.[49] Yet, the third floor chambers eschew obvious references to Classical Antiquity, and thus any clearly lingering influence of Pozzuoli. In our view, Don Pedro's transformation of the former Aragonese residence in the Castel Nuovo at Naples into his vice-regal palace ultimately had the greatest impact on Eleonora's taste and on the decorative concept for her new rooms in the ducal palace in Florence.[50]

---

[47] Don Pedro selected his top administrators and attendants from among relatives and Spanish families aligned with his house, such as the Valcarcel, Pimentel, Benavente, and Alcocer, leaving the lower level court positions to Neapolitans. Hernando Sánchez 1994, 469-70.

[48] For Don Pedro's interest in recent Spanish history as reflected in his library, see Hernando Sánchez 1988, 21.

[49] Edelstein 2003, 76. The villa was destroyed, along with the rest of Pozzuoli, by a volcanic eruption on 29 September 1538. Don Pedro tenaciously rebuilt the town, and reconstructed an expanded, fortified villa by 1540. See Venditti 2006 (2007), 251-87.

[50] Interestingly, both Don Pedro and Cosimo adopted the main architectural symbols of power and traditional seats of government of their capitals as royal

Admittedly, Eleonora's direct experience of Naples only lasted from the time of her arrival with her elder sister and mother in 1534 until her departure for Florence in 1539.[51] These five years included, however, her formative adolescence and young adulthood, and correspond precisely with Don Pedro's renovation of the Castel Nuovo as the family residence. The castle would have served as an unforgettable example of monumentality and nobility, since it was far larger and grander than any castles Eleonora could have seen in Villafranca or Alba de Tormes her mother and father's hometowns and her presumed childhood homes. Imposing now, the Castel Nuovo was even more so in 1530s, when a second ring of enormous bastions surrounded it.[52]

Don Pedro began building soon after he arrived in Naples, eventually constructing several palaces in addition to the villa at Pozzuoli and transforming the city's entire urban fabric.[53] But in the 1530s, while Eleonora lived in Naples, he strengthened the Castel Nuovo's fortifications and renovated the chambers that once served the Aragonese kings. Don Pedro focused his efforts on the rooms attached to the castle's Golden Tower (Fig. 5; Torre dell'Oro or Torreón de Oro). The last king of Naples of the House of Trastámara, Frederick IV of Aragon (1452-1504), and his second wife Isabella del Balzo had once inhabited these rooms. The Golden Tower acquired its name as the home of the Aragonese treasury, and Don Pedro re-utilised it for the same purpose, placing his own chambers there and making it the storehouse for his "guardaropa" or wardrobe.[54] In addition, blocks of exposed yellow tufa on the tower's exterior have a golden hue different from the rest of the castle's towers and walls, which are re-vetted with a grey volcanic stone called *piperno* (these contrasting colours are clearly recorded in the image of the Castel Nuovo painted in the fifteenth-century Strozzi panel in the Museo di San Martino, Naples).

---

residences and subjected these buildings to extensive renovation campaigns. Indeed, Eleonora's father and husband shared several political, cultural, and architectural parallels, as examined in Hernando Sánchez 1994, 124-5.

[51] Maria Osorio Pimentel (and her children) initially stayed in Spain to administer her marquisate after Don Pedro left for Naples in 1532; Hernando Sánchez 1994, 91.

[52] The outer ring of walls and bastions ("cinta bastionata") were taken down by the end of the nineteenth century, but thoroughly reconstructed in Filangieri 1934, 179-91. For historic views of the Castel Nuovo (including the famous drawing by Francisco de Hollanda of 1540), see Leone de Castris 1990, 15-33 (esp. 24, fig. 9).

[53] See Pane 1975, 81-95.

[54] For the Golden Tower, including the Viceroy's two chambers ("Torréon del Oro, y las dos Recámeras del Virrey") and Don Pedro's first *guardaropa* in the Castel Nuovo, see Hernando Sánchez 1994, 528-9 and Coniglio 1967, 43-4.

Figure 5: Castel Nuovo, Naples with Golden Tower (left) and adjacent Loggia.

A lack of contemporary descriptions and a disastrous fire that struck the Torre d'Oro in 1540 render Don Pedro's renovations impossible to reconstruct with precision. In broad outline they largely followed the footprint and aesthetic established by the Aragonese rulers. Don Pedro selected king Frederick's apartments (in the east wing of the castle, facing the sea, between the Golden Tower and the Palatine Chapel) for his personal residence; while Maria Osorio Pimentel and her courtiers inhabited Queen Isabella's rooms (in the south wing), which had included rooms for Frederick and Isabella's son Ferdinand, duke of Calabria (1488-1550). Don Pedro's renovated quarters retained, either in fact or in memory, Frederick and Isabella's gilt, coffered ceilings, spiral stairs, carved fireplaces, and perhaps even some of the elaborate *paramenti* or wall coverings (e.g. a "ristretto di carmosino" or "del cremesi" was named for its red walls).[55] Don Pedro's quarters also abutted the magnificent pre-existing mediaeval Angevin Palatine Chapel (which he would later renovate) and the fifteenth-century Aragonese additions by the Spanish architect Guillem Sagrera (?-1454), such as the Sala dei Baroni, and an unforgettable monumental spiral stair between the Chapel and the Sala, which connected these colossal spaces to rooftop terraces.[56] Don Pedro

---

[55] Filangieri 1934, 249.
[56] Not to mention the castle's magnificent Renaissance (1453-67) triumphal arch portal. See the overviews of the Castel Nuovo's architecture in Leone de Castris

added two floors with open loggias along the castle's south wing and, for
his personal rooms in the east wing he built a monumental staircase, a
grand hall (the Salone di Carlo V), and an attached loggia facing the sea
(now called the Loggia di Pedro de Toledo, Fig. 5). The hall acquired its
current dedication to the emperor after Charles V lodged in these quarters
subsequent to his conquest of Tunis and triumphal entry into Naples in
November of 1535.[57]

This moment of splendour likely shaped the duchess's taste and
patronage. Yet the apartments and their ornaments would end in ashes. As
told in a letter by Duke Cosimo's informant in Naples, Pirro Musefilo, fire
escaped from a fireplace in a dining room a few hours after dark on a
Thursday in early March of 1540 and set the apartments next to the
Golden Tower ablaze. He added that these had many carved and gilt
ceilings, as well as a hall decorated with images of kings and emperors,
which all burned, along with the contents of the vice-regal wardrobe.
Fortunately, favourable winds prevented the loss of the entire castle and
fire failed to reach the munitions, yet the damage was tremendous.
Musefilo exclaimed that the viceroy did not have a set of sheets, a
handkerchief, or a rug left. He estimated the damage at 12,000 *scudi*, since
the jewels were kept in another place and, although the craftsmanship of
the precious works of art had been lost, the silver and gold had survived,
albeit fused together by the heat.[58] Don Pedro's seventeenth-century
biographer, Scipione Miccio, wrote that the emperor sent 30,000 *scudi* in
compensation, which may be a better estimate of losses.[59]

The form and concept of Eleonora's Golden Chambers in the Palazzo
Vecchio in the 1550s bear a remarkable resemblance to the eclectic
Angevin and Aragonese, yet predominantly Iberian, architectural and
decorative language of Don Pedro's residence attached to the Golden
Tower of the Castel Nuovo before the fire. Eleonora's Florentine quarters
on the second and third floors developed as much vertically as
horizontally, like the multiple levels of rooms in the south and east wings
of the Castel Nuovo. Her Golden Chambers and Terrace use the same
fundamental vocabulary of spiral staircase, carved and gilt ceiling, and
open loggia as in Naples. The block of the Golden Chambers and Terrace
also abuts a mediaeval tower in much the same way as Don Pedro's

---

1990, 35-63 and Pane 1975-7, I, 153-201.
[57] Leon de Castris 1990, 24 and 54-5. For Charles V's triumphal entry, see
Hernando Sánchez 2001, 447-521.
[58] ASF, *MP* 4068, n. p. (letters organised by date) and the discussion in Hernando
Sánchez 1993, 51.
[59] Miccio 1846, 45.

apartments and loggia in the south wing of the Castel Nuovo adjoin the Golden Tower (Figs. 2 and 5). Even the colour of materials in Florence echoes the Spanish-Neapolitan model. The grey *pietra serena* columns of the loggia on the duchess's terrace contrast with the golden *pietra forte* of the Palazzo Vecchio, just as Don Pedro's grey *piperno* loggia stands out against the yellow tufa of the Golden Tower. Indeed, Eleonora's expanded living quarters, including the rooms for her children and Spanish ladies in waiting, evoked those her former residence in Naples, although on a smaller scale and inflected with a marked Tuscan accent.

The Third Floor in the 1553 Inventory

While the architecture and splendid décor of the duchess's Golden Chambers and Terrace generally recall the viceregal residence in the Castel Nuovo, a famous inventory helps us to determine the specific contents, organisation, and functions of all the rooms on the third floor of the ducal palace in Florence.[60] On 27 October 1553, Giuliano del Tovaglia, Giovanni Ricci, and Mariotto Cecchi began taking inventory at the head of the third floor suite in the duchess's Golden Chambers, "Nelle camere nuove di sopra della Illma Sig.^ra Duchessa, sotto il terrazzo."[61] They proceeded to catalogue only the goods belonging to the ducal wardrobe or *guardaroba* that they had easy access to, skipping items owned by others and locked rooms, as well as leaving out many fixed decorations. Also, it is important to remember that the new rooms were not quite finished at the time; for example, the paint was hardly dry on Bachiacca's terrace decoration, and payments suggest that Tasso's ceilings may not have been complete. Consequently, some items listed in the duchess's chambers are disassembled, movable, or put away. This situation fits our understanding of the multiple functions that many rooms served in the palace.

---

[60] In his 1893 publication of the inventory, Cosimo Conti claims that too many obstacles thwarted him from reconstructing the locations of the rooms on the third floor. Conti 1893, 71.

[61] Ibid., 72; ASF, *GM* 28, f. 10v-11r; Gáldy 2009a, 217-8; Gáldy 2009b, 29-30. The inventory became necessary after the duke's former tutor, secretary, and *maggiordomo* Pierfrancesco Riccio suffered a breakdown (see La France 2008, p. 7, n. 27). The contents of the ducal household needed to be re-evaluated before his replacement could take office. Thus, the inventory takers included the new secretary Giuliano del Tovaglia (a banker with substantial interests in the Kingdom of Naples), Giovanni Ricci (a relative of the retired secretary Pierfrancesco Ricci), and Mariotto Cecchi (Pierfrancesco Ricci's former assistant, often charged with the movement of goods from the ducal wardrobe).

Thus, the third floor inventory starts in the most distinguished rooms on that level, and intriguingly combines the contents of both chambers with the plural *camere*. Here we find a painted portrait of the recently deceased Don Pedro de Toledo (now lost) presiding over a white leather chair for the duchess, a stone table, a camp table on its foldable stand, and a disassembled tabletop and stand. These items paint a picture of rooms in which the duchess celebrated her family through the image of her beloved, departed father, and that functioned at that moment as a meeting room. But this furniture could easily be moved to change the rear chamber into a bedroom, and indeed the makings of a ducal bed were housed, as we will soon argue, in a nearby closet. The list of items in the duchess's chambers ends with its blinds ("finestre impannate"), while a separate, indented line states that the duchess's "scrittoino" was not inventoried because it was locked.[62] As mentioned earlier, while the diminutive suffix "-ino" suggests a desk, the term may also refer to a small wooden alcove, fixed to the floor and covering the trap door in the corner of the *camerino*.

The itemisation continues as the inventory takers presumably climbed the spiral stair onto the duchess's Terrace, which featured an old, long table (5 *braccia* or about 3 meters), another white leather chair, a camp chair, and three stool-like *sgabelli*, suggesting that meals could be taken outdoors. Intriguingly, the terrace displayed two large maps of Pisa (2 ½ *braccia* or 1.45m) and Genoa (4 *braccia* or 2.32m).[63]

When the inventory takers finished their work on the terrace, they likely descended the spiral stair and retraced their steps through the Golden Chambers. Subsequently, the inventory continues at the point where the duchess's *camere* meet the fabric of the mediaeval palace, above the second floor Sala delle Sabine. This space, carved into the SE corner of the old palace wall, has two windows and is shown divided into two rooms and a closet in the eighteenth-century plan, although it may have been a single room or partitioned differently in the sixteenth century. In any case, it is most likely the next space in the inventory and the chamber of Isabel Reynoso (Fig. 3). A location just outside of the duchess's Golden Rooms seems appropriate for Eleonora's oldest and most trusted lady in waiting. According to the inventory, Isabel slept and attended the duchess there, as there is a bed on benches with its mattresses and cover, as well as two red leather chairs, one large and one small.[64]

---

[62] "Lo scrittioino della Sig.ʳᵃ Duchessa in dette camere non s'è inventariato per esser serrato"; Conti 1893, 73; ASF, *GM* 28, f. 11r; Gáldy 2009a, 218.

[63] "Nel terrazzo della Sig.ʳᵃ Duchessa"; Conti 1893, 73; ASF, *GM* 28, f. 11r; Gáldy 2009a, 218.

[64] "Nella camera della S.ʳᵃ Isabella de' Renosa"; Conti 1893, 73; ASF, *GM* 28, f.

In our opinion, Del Tovaglia, Ricci, and Cecchi proceeded from the Golden Chambers, walked across the landing of the staircase leading down to Eleonora's second floor suite, and continued their inventory in the space that is currently a large, unified hall directly above the second floor Salotto or Winter Dining Room. Several scholars believe that this entire space was a kitchen, and perhaps part of it was in the fourteenth and fifteenth centuries. Yet the monumental cooking fireplace centred on the hall's north wall may not have been used for that purpose in the sixteenth century or was closed into a smaller room.[65] The Prague plan shows a full wall partition underneath one of the two surviving diaphragm arches in the hall, suggesting that the space was divided into two rooms or more in previous centuries, rather than an oversized kitchen (Fig. 3). In addition, the frieze of small round windows or oculi on the east side of the mediaeval palace's courtyard that still lights this space provides a clue as to the rooms' function at the time of the inventory. On 4 August 1553, a certain Battista di Francesco *tiraferro* was paid for fabricating iron muntins that separate the panes of glass in the oculi for the "stanze delle damigelle," indicating that these rooms once housed the ladies in waiting.[66] In fact, a few months later, Del Tovaglia, Ricci and Cecchi called this area, likely the next rooms on their list, the "stanze delle dame."[67] The items recorded here belong in a multi-purpose workroom and dormitory for female servants: battered pillows, mattresses, and spreads for four beds and three trundles; used painted and unpainted benches; four stools or *sgabelli*; two desks; a leather camp chair; and a pair of table stands. Perhaps part of this area constituted the "disvano" or closet that appears next in the inventory, where extra tables and chairs were stored, as well as three large armoires with much higher quality mattresses, featherbeds, and pillows that may have constituted a portable, provisional bed for the duchess.[68]

The inventory takers continued counter-clockwise through the rooms, in the same general direction that they proceeded while compiling their lists on the floor below. They would have subsequently entered a hall

---

11r; Gáldy 2009a, 218.

[65] The room was altered and the fireplace may have been moved there during extensive late nineteenth and early twentieth-century restorations, as suggested immediately after mentioning the so-called large kitchen or "cucinone" in Allegri and Cecchi 1980, 10. In addition, sixteenth-century palace inventories do not mention a kitchen on this floor.

[66] Appendix 8.

[67] Conti 1893, 73-4; ASF, *GM* 28, f. 11v; Gáldy 2009a, 218.

[68] "Nel disvano..." Conti 1893,. 74; ASF, *GM* 28, f. 11v-12r; Gáldy 2009a, 218.

along the north side of the palace courtyard. The same frieze of small, mediaeval oculi as in the rooms for the *damigelle* continues here, but an upper clerestory of rectangular, sixteenth-century windows gathers additional southern light to illuminate a larger space or spaces. At present this area has been reduced to its mediaeval function as a corridor connecting the fourteenth-century stair (adorned with a lion newel) that ascends from the second floor landing just outside the Sala dei Gigli to the third floor entrance into the old palace's tower. It is further narrowed by partitions inserted to create storage spaces along the north wall that date back to at least the time of the Prague plan (Fig. 3).[69] However, like the rooms for the ladies in waiting, this space may have been divided differently in the sixteenth century, as the inventory labels this the "stanze delle donne et balie" (the rooms for the ladies and wetnurses), and begins by listing a number of green leather wall coverings (208 skins) with gilded frieze and pilasters, as well as a lined door cover or *portiera*, which would have blocked drafts from the medieval stair. And the contents suggest that these rooms functioned as personal storage and a schoolroom for the Medici children. They included a painting of the Virgin and Child; an inlaid *cassone* or chest with the duchess's goods, two strongboxes, and a large armoire; plain, gilt, and carved boxes; a likely teacher's desk; "two desks for the little lords' school"; and a long bench.[70]

In order to continue the inventory Del Tovaglia, Ricci, and Cecchi would have crossed through the narrow, wooden-floored passage behind the palace's tower, and stepped up one half level to just above the frieze of oculi into the next suite of four chambers along the old palace's western and southern flanks. The inventory shows that wall coverings decorated all four, and they functioned as bedrooms where, as the large beds suggest, the Medici children slept in pairs or more. The first or "prima camera" lies directly above the second floor Sala di Gualdrada (Figs. 1 and 3). The inventory states that it had cracked red leather wall coverings with a gilded frieze and pilasters, one wide bed (4 x 3 *braccia*; 2.32 x 1.74m), various mattresses, and a few chairs.[71] The second room, above the second floor Sala di Penelope, had similarly worn red leather wall coverings, an even wider bed (4 x 5 *braccia*; 2.32 x 2.9m), a locked chest, an image of the

---

[69] The hall is also next to the attic above the carved ceilings over the Sala delle Udienze and Sala dei Gigli, a vast, uninhabitable space strictly reserved for maintenance access to the ceilings' armatures.

[70] The teacher's desk is described as "uno desco di noce co' piè d'una cassa a seppultura con balaustri," and the childrens' desks are "2 deschi per la squola de' Signorini." Conti 1893, 74-5; ASF, *GM* 28, f. 12r.

[71] "Nella prima camera"; Conti 1893, 75-6; ASF, *GM* 28, f. 12r-v; Gáldy 2009a, 218.

Virgin with gilded festoons, and a small armoire "a uso di credenza".[72] The third chamber, which straddles the Sala di Ester and Sala delle Sabine below, has twice the amount of torn red leather wall coverings as the second room (80 skins v. 46 skins) and is, in fact, nearly twice the size of the preceding chamber. It held a bed of the same size, but also a trundle or *carriuola*.[73] Entering the fourth chamber required ascending a few stairs, and is nearly on the same level as the duchess's Terrace (the two are clustered together on the Prague plan, Fig. 3). It displayed about 70 skins of old red leather wall coverings, which is an appropriate number given its size compared to the larger third and smaller second chambers. Its bed was like those in the previous two rooms, but it also held a cradle.[74]

The smaller space underneath the fourth chamber, and on the same level as Isabel Reynoso's room, is most likely Maria Pimentel's room, mentioned next in the 1553 inventory. As illustrated in the Prague plan, by turning left (west) after exiting the door, Pimentel could climb low stairs that connected directly to the third and fourth chambers. By proceeding straight out of the door (north), she would have entered the main stair that communicated vertically between the duchess's second and third floor suites, as well as horizontally between the rooms of the *damigelle* and Golden Chambers on the same floor. This central position would have been ideal for Pimentel, the chief of the ladies in waiting. A Spanish noblewoman, Maria Pimentel brought her own furnishings and wardrobe to court, and since these did not belong to the Medici, they were not inventoried.[75]

After passing Maria Pimentel's room and noting it in their inventory, Del Tovaglia, Ricci, and Cecchi logically entered the stairwell and descended to the second floor.[76] They turned north to continue their task

---

[72] "Seconda camera"; Conti 1893, 76; ASF, *GM* 28, f. 12v; Gáldy 2009a, 218.

[73] "Terza camera"; Conti 1893, 76-7; ASF, *GM* 28, f. 13r; Gáldy 2009a, 218.

[74] "Quarta camera"; Conti 1893, 77; ASF, *GM* 28, f. 13r; Gáldy 2009a, 218.

[75] "Nella stanza dove sta la S.^ra Pimentella non s'è inventariato cosa alcuna perchè son sua"; Conti 1893, 77; ASF, *GM* 28, f. 13r; Gáldy 2009a, 218.

[76] Subsequent entries in the inventory confirm that the ducal secretaries were on the second floor. A recent reconstruction suggests that, at the time of the inventory in 1553, Del Tovaglia, Ricci, and Cecchi left the Salotto, traversed the Sala dei Gigli (which they would have called the Sala dell'Oriuolo and omitted to mention, since they had completely inventoried it the previous day) and entered the Chancellery, which was then called the first room of the Guardaroba. From there, the successive listing of rooms in the manuscript indicates that they followed a path of balconies and spaces crossing the attic at the north end of the Salone del Gran Consiglio and into the new ducal apartments along the Via dei Gondi. This path is described in Lombardi 2008, 144 with the floor plan reconstructed and

and breached "the Salotto where the duchess's things are," listing it as the
next space in the inventory after Pimentel's room.[77] This Salotto is certainly
the room consistently called either by that title or less frequently labelled
the Winter Dining Room, located at the foot of this stairwell on the second
floor.[78] At the time it served at least two functions: as a seasonal dining
hall for the ducal "famiglia" and as a reception room for Eleonora's
second floor suite. Del Tovaglia, Ricci, and Cecchi had already taken a
partial inventory of this "Sesta camera et salotto" after cataloguing the
second floor's contents on October 26. But they had limited themselves to
general and dining-related objects, such as the supper table, tablecloths,
and wall coverings.[79] After finishing the third floor and returning to the
Salotto on October 27, the three secretaries twice specified that they were
now exclusively itemising the duchess's goods. These are of the kind
expected from a reception area: a camp table, white and red leather chairs
(like those in the Golden Chambers), and locked furnishings ranging from
painted chests to several coloured leather and suede strongboxes, and an
armoire.

The Months Tapestries

A final point concerns the decoration of the duchess's Golden Chambers.
The 1553 inventory lists wall coverings in all of the Medici children's
chambers on the third floor, while the servants' rooms, closet, and
curiously, the Golden Chambers, are without wall hangings. Blank walls
in the most luxurious chambers on the floor were likely reserved for the
display of tapestries. In general, inventories do not list tapestries hanging
in the rooms for which they were specifically fitted; rather, all of the
Medici tapestries are listed in the ducal wardrobe for safekeeping. This is
the case for rooms on the second floor, such as the Joseph tapestries
(designed mostly by Bronzino) for the Sala dei Duecento and the

---

rooms labeled on 146. Vasari changed this circulation pattern in the 1560s by
raising the Salone's roof and transforming Tasso's Loggia della Guardaroba into
the Sala delle Carte Geografiche. He further altered this area with the terrace over
the Custom House (Dogana) in 1565-66, replacing Tasso's stairway to the
Guardaroba, and Ammanati added the workroom on that terrace in 1581-2. At that
time the wall of Eleonora's chapel was pierced with a doorway to access the
terrace, workroom, and Guardaroba; Allegri-Cecchi 1980, 351-2, no. 62.

[77] "Nel salotto dove stanno le robbe della S.ra Duchessa"; Conti 1893, 77; ASF,
GM 28, f. 13r-v; Gáldy 2009a, 218.

[78] La France 2008, 87, note 73 (with bibliography) and Edelstein 1995, 261-94.

[79] Conti 1893, 68; ASF, *GM* 28, f. 10r; Gáldy 2009a, 217.

Grotesque Spalliere (designed by Bachiacca) for the Sala delle Udienze.[80] The latter audience hall possessed ornate carved and gilt ceilings as well as a fresco cycle by Francesco Salviati (1543-1545) illustrating the deeds of the Roman hero Camillus.[81] The hall has been compared in the past to the Sala di Costantino in the Vatican, a commission by two Medici popes that Cosimo may well have seen during his visit as a six-year-old to pope Clement VII.[82]

The ten *Grotesque Spalliere* were specially fitted to hang along the lower register of Sala delle Udienze and establish an important precedent for the Golden Chambers. Designed by the court artist Bachiacca beginning in 1545 and woven by the Flemish master weavers Jan Rost and Nicholas Karcher mostly before 1549, these tapestries feature a series of *all'antica* style swags and candelabra grotesques teeming with an abundance of birds, flowers, fish, lamps, masks, and fruit. Putti play under baldachins against a buttercup-yellow silk background, recalling the famous *Giochi di Putti* tapestry set commissioned for the Vatican. The medallions and grotesques contain allegorical references to the duke and duchess's heraldry, virtues, and beneficent joint rule, such as the Medici family's gold balls, personifications of Charity and Abundance, and a representation of a peacock (Eleonora's personal emblem).[83] The opulent decorative scheme of the Sala delle Udienze—a courtly audience hall ringed with tapestries and crowned with a carved and gilt ceiling—anticipates the Golden Chambers dedicated entirely to the duchess and her interests on the third floor. Indeed, the court architect Tasso and court painter Bachiacca continued their work on that floor in the next phase of the palace's redecoration.

Yet another set of tapestries, the series of the *Months* also designed by Bachiacca and woven in the Florentine workshops of the Flemish master weavers Nicholas Karcher and Jan Rost, appear in the cabinets of the ducal wardrobe in the 1553 inventory.[84] At least four pieces of evidence corroborate the suggestion that the *Months* were designated for display in the duchess's Golden Chambers. First is their size. At about half the height

---

[80] For the Joseph tapestries, see Meoni 2010, 193-265 with bibliography. For the *Grotesque Spalliere*, see La France 2008, 229-44, cats. 69-78 with bibliography.

[81] Allegri-Cecchi 1980, 40-5, no. 13.

[82] Rohlmann 1994, 153-69.

[83] Many scholars overlook the joint character of this combined Medici-Toledo imagery. See the new interpretation in La France 2008, 83 and cat. 69-78, as well as the illustration of the Sala delle Udienze outfitted with the tapestries in Meoni 1998, 41.

[84] La France 2008, 252-64, cats. 85-9.

of the monumental Joseph tapestries (approx. 5.7m), the *Months* (approx. 2.7m) belong in a more intimate space, such as the Golden Chambers. This intimacy is reinforced by their smaller imagery, which requires close inspection, unlike the large figures of Bronzino's tapestry designs, which remain legible from a greater distance. Second, the date of the commission and completion of the *Months* corresponds precisely with the third floor building campaign. Bachiacca received the commission to create tapestry cartoons for the *Months* about 1549, and weavers completed the entire set before their inventory in September of 1553. Third, the choice of the artist also associates the *Months* with the Golden Chambers. Battista del Tasso had married Bachiacca's cousin, and their family bonds extended into their court careers.[85] The two men worked hand in hand on the duchess's new rooms. As discussed above, Tasso built the duchess's Terrace and Bachiacca (with his workshop) decorated it. Tasso and his shop carved the ceilings for the duchess's Golden Chambers and Bachiacca painted its gilded "scrittoino." Consequently, it is likely that since Tasso erected the Golden Chambers, Bachiacca designed their tapestries.

Finally, the *Months*' subject matter illustrates the duchess's agricultural interests and stewardship of Tuscany, as would be appropriate for display in her personal chambers. The tapestries depict the labours of the year divided into panels for each month that include the harvesting and threshing of grain, making of wine and cheese, slaughtering of pigs, gathering of firewood, shearing of sheep, and dressing of flax. Eleonora invested and traded in all of these agricultural commodities and purchased the farms and land necessary to produce them across Tuscany.[86] Furthermore, the *Months* include an idealised representation of Eleonora, accompanied by two ladies in waiting (likely Maria Pimentel and Isabel Reynoso) holding a picnic in the month of May.[87] A procession of revellers, led by a page and a court dwarf (Pietro Barbino) on a donkey, present her with a platter loaded with the fruit of these labours.[88] The *Months* celebrate Eleonora's authority and the prosperity of her

---

[85] Ibid., 7 and 32.

[86] See Ibid., 256, Parigino 1999, 90-114, and Edelstein 2008 with bibliography.

[87] La France 2008, 259, cat. 85, plate LVIII and fig. 45. Like a saint's attribute, the parrot perched on the basket just below the central female figure in this damaged and restored tapestry confirms the identification of the duchess's portrait. Eleonora was particularly fond of parrots, as testified by several examples painted in the vault of the Camera Verde and her documented request for the construction of a parrot cage in 1539; Lamberini 2002, 138.

[88] The physiognomy is that of the thinner Pietro Barbino, rather than the hefty Morgante. See Gadessi-Fleming 2007, 79 and fig. 26.

investments. Their silver, gilt silver and silk threads would have added to the general splendour of the duchess's Golden Chambers.

Conclusion

In January 1553, the elderly Don Pedro sailed from Naples to Tuscany leading troops for the siege of Siena. As recounted by Miccio, the winter weather aggravated one of Don Pedro's perennial bouts with fever and catarrh, forcing a recuperative stop first in Livorno, then Pisa, before he was well enough to join his daughter and son-in-law in Florence. The viceroy spent the last weeks of his life in the ducal palace, finally succumbing to his illness on 22 February 1553.[89] While no known documents record where Don Pedro lay for his final hours, historical imagination and common sense place him where his portrait appears in the palace inventory eight months later, in his favourite daughter's Golden Chambers. The fact that their decoration was not quite finished would not have troubled a man who endured a constant state of construction in his palaces and capital city. Don Pedro likely felt most at home in the duchess's new suite of rooms in Florence modelled after his former residence at the Castel Nuovo in Naples.

Some or all of Eleonora's recently-woven tapestries likely surrounded her moribund father. Even if the contents of the viceroy's apartment and wardrobe at the Castel Nuovo were lost in the 1540 fire, an inventory of Don Pedro's Neapolitan goods taken after his death in 1553 provides a sample of his taste for the decorative arts, which he handed down to his daughter. His numerous "paños de tapiçeria, camas, paramentos de cama, pavillones y otras ropas" show a preference for luxury textiles that confirms Mantuan ambassador Nicola Maffei's eyewitness report of large tapestries in the residence at Castel Nuovo in 1536.[90] The ubiquitous presence of tapestries of Flemish origin and their fundamental place in Spanish courts and European Renaissance court culture at large is well known; it is not surprising that both Don Pedro and Eleonora decorated their residences with tapestries in both Naples and Florence. What is remarkable is that the series of the *Months*, which probably hung in the Golden Chambers, are as eclectic in style as anything produced for the Neapolitan court. The subject of the labours of the year is Flemish in origin and the iconography of Bachiacca's tapestries derives mostly from German prints. Yet the figures and motifs mix Flemish landscapes and

---

[89] Miccio 1846, 85-6 misprints 12 February.
[90] Hernando Sánchez 1993, 51-2 citing Coniglio 1959, 351-2.

Italian sources into a hybrid whole, matched only by the fact that Flemish weavers (and their Florentine assistants) had woven the tapestries in Florence, in a newly-established tapestry works based on Flemish models. Thus, Eleonora's *Months*, like her Golden Chambers, embody the alluring variety of styles and international influences characteristic of the pan-European courts in general and the Spanish court of Naples in particular.[91]

---

[91] The attraction of cosmopolitan art at the court of Eleonora and Cosimo has been historically underrated, not least by Vasari. This is a central theme of La France 2008, 8, 77, 90, and 116 with bibliography. More recently, Loconte (2010, 24) similarly concludes: "Essentially, Vasari was unable to appreciate the variety of styles and international influences which co-exist in a world city [mid sixteenth-century Naples]."

Appendix

1. ASF, *FM* 1, 164 sin; "Spese di muramenti in acrescimento del palazzo di S. E. Ill.ma. [28 February 1550/1]... E addi detto [28 feb. 1551] lire settecentonovantauna soldi xiii denari iiii piccioli si fanno buoni a maestro Batista di Marcho del Tasso e compagni intagliatori di legniame per la monta d'un conto di piu manifatture et lavori datoci d'addì 16 di giugnio addì 18 dicembre 1550 in usci, finestre, sportelli, per cammini et soppannare di noscie usci e finestre nelle dua camere et terrazzo della S.ra D.ssa e per altre stanze di detto dove erano i magazini di dogana et altri luoghi di detto come appare al Giornale a c. 58 avere in questo a c. 132 ----- ducati 113 lire – soldi 4."

2. ASF, *FM* 2, fol. 18 des., and more detailed in the cross reference on fol. 91 sin.: "E addì detto [1 July 1554] lire tredici soldi 1.o piccioli si fanno buoni a Jacopo Pinadori e Francesco ser Guglielmi e compagni speziali per la monta di libbre 30 di gesso volterrano e libbre 22 di gesso impani e per libbre 90 di linbellucci di capretto e per libbre 11 1/2 di bolio armenio dato tutto a Tomaso di Giovanni dipintore sotto dì 24 d'aprile 1553 per dipigniere et comettere d'oro dua palchi di dua camere per la S.ra D.ssa..."

3. ASF, *FM* 1, 91 des.: "E addì 14 detto .... [payments for workers and building materials, including:] e per torniatura di 200 borchie a soldi 1.o l'uno per le chamere messe d'oro della D.ssa..."

4. "E addì 27 di febbraio 1556 [1557] lire millecentoventi piccioli si fanno buoni a maestro Batista di Marcho del Tasso e compagni per la dreto per loro manifattura di 70 quadri fatti in dua palchi nelle dua camere della S.ra du.ssa sopra la Camera Verde intagliati che in una v'è falchoni e nel'altro punte di diamanti con festoni a' torno e chiociole et borchie e altre chornicie intagliate che chorrano la piana di detto palcho a lire 16 l'uno di detti quadri di fattura rivisti et pregiati per Filippo di Bartolomeo d'Agniolo et per Antonio detto Particino legniauioli soto dì 16 d'agosto 1556 e' lor' datoceli finiti per tutto di 6 aprile 1556 come al Giornale a c. 140 avere in questo a c. 177 ----- ducati 160." ASF, *FM* 2, 176 sin. and cross ref. on 177 des. (discussed but not transcribed in Allegri-Cecchi 1980, p. 10).

5. ASF, *FM* 2, 11 des. "Giovanni di Piero di Giovanni scharpellino" was paid for various work on the facades of the palace including five stone window frames for the duchess's rooms plus one for the Camera Verde, which (still today) has an iron grate: "E addì 9 di giugnio 1553 ducati trentotto di moneta lire dua piccioli si li fanno buoni per la monta di 5 finestre di pietra bigia con chornicie e davanzale per ducati 6 l'una e per du'altre finestre ricinte di braccia x e per un'altra finestra di detta pietra ferrata a gabia dateci in palazzo ducale per la muraglia d'adì 4 di febbraio 1552 a questo di dare spese di detta moneta in questo a c. 56 ----- ducati 38 lire." The 849 pound iron cage enclosure for the Camera Verde window is also mentioned in entries on ASF, *FM* 28, sin-des., 56 des. (as "una finestra di detta pietra ferrata a gabbia murata nela sala dipinta a grotesche sopra la dogana"), and 60 des.

6. ASF, *FM* 1, 43 sin.: "E addì 20 di febbraio [1552] lire venti soldi v piccioli pagati a Antonio di [blank] battiloro portò contanti per 450 pezzi d'oro fine hauto da llui il Bachiacha pittore per metter d'oro uno scrittoio della S. D.ssa nelle stanze nuove a Uscita a carta 134 in questo a carta 212 ---------- ducati 2 lire 6 . 5." Also folio 252 sin.: Spese di muramenti in acrescimento del palazzo di S. E. Ill.ma deono dare per tanti poste debbino avere per resto d'un' lor' conto in questo a c. 251 ----- ducati 13242 ire – 9. 4." After listing various other expenses on the same page: "E addi detto [28 Febbraio 1552/3] ducati millecentottant[cancelled repetition]otto cioe ducati millecentoottantaotto di moneta lire tre soldi xvii denari iiii piccioli sono che tanti n'era debitore spese di pittori e lor' pertinenzie per spese fatte in far' dipigniere sale, camere scrittoj et altro in detto palazzo però se ne fa debitore questo conto eccezionale dette spese di pittori in questo a c. 43 ----- ducati 1188 lire 3 . 17 . 4." See La France 2008, p. 305 cat. 164 and p. 358, doc. 101.

7. ASF, *FM* 1, 29 sin.-des. records payments to the woodcarver Bastiano di Simone Confetti for various projects, including 14 ducats for repairs to the duchess's dovecote on the uppermost *ballatoio* level of the palace: "achoncimi fatti nela cholombaia della Duchessa e per una stanza di legniame fatta sul ballatoio per servitio di S. Ecc.tia." The *ballatoio* also had a ball court (now the Sala delle Bandiere), where Cosimo could indulge in his passion for ball games (Marcolin and Paccetti 2010, 29), or watch a hired ballplayer, e.g., "Alessandro detto Napoli giuocatore di palla," who was paid 2 florins per month for his services in the mid 1550s. ASF, *DG*, Parte Antica 1514 (*Salariati MDLIIII*), f. 102.

8. ASF, *FM* 2, 43 des. "Batista di Francesco tiraferro di contro de' avere addì 4 d'agosto 1553 lira nove soldi x piccioli si li fanno buoni per tre pezzi di rete di filo d'ottone per tre ochi et per du'altre rete simile per sopra un tetto dateci addì 15 di luglio e questo dì per le stanze delle damigelle nel palazzo ducale dare spese dela muraglia di detto in questo a c. 62 ----- ducati 1 lire 2 . 10." Cross reference: ASF, *FM* 2, 62 sin.

CHAPTER TWO

ELIZABETH MURRAY, COUNTESS OF DYSART AND DUCHESS OF LAUDERDALE (1626-1698), AS A COLLECTOR AND PATRON*

CHRISTOPHER ROWELL

Elizabeth Murray (1626-98), 2nd countess of Dysart (1655) in her own right and duchess of Lauderdale by marriage (1672), was one of the most formidable females of the seventeenth century. Attractive, with then unfashionable red hair, intelligent, well-read, independently-minded, able, articulate and energetic, the story of her life is the story of one of the most turbulent periods in British history. She was born into the collecting purple. Her father, William Murray, 1st earl of Dysart (c.1600-55), was a childhood friend of Charles I, travelled with him to Spain when he was prince of Wales, and was equally imbued with the ideals of the High Renaissance. Ham House (NT), completed 1610, first leased to him by the king in 1626 and then purchased outright in 1637, remains a rare monument of Caroline Franco-Italian taste in interior decoration, where much of the early-seventeenth-century collection remains in situ. Elizabeth's mother, Catherine Bruce, Scottish like her father, was portrayed, dressed in the height of fashion, by both Van Dyck and Hoskins (c.1637 and 1638), the approximate date of her life-size bronze bust.[1] Such

---

* For permission to consult the family archive, and for their generous help, I am indebted to Sir Lyonel Tollemache, Bt., Richard Tollemache and Lord Tollemache. I am also most grateful to my colleagues, Victoria Bradley and Alastair Laing, and to Susan Bracken, Andrea Gáldy, and Adriana Turpin for their comments on the text and their advice. A modified version of this chapter will appear in Rowell 2013.
[1] For Van Dyck's portrait of Catherine Murray, see Barnes et al 2004, no. IV. 167, 559-60 (entry by Oliver Millar). The Petworth portrait was in the collection of Van

tangible reminiscences of the doomed court of Charles I would have been significant in themselves, but what makes Ham quite exceptional is that it was doubled in size, redecorated and re-furnished in the 1670s by Elizabeth Dysart, and her second husband, the 1st duke of Lauderdale. Again much survives from this second phase of major alterations, so Ham remains redolent of the reigns of both Charles I and II. Famous in the eighteenth century for its untouched state, its furniture, its portraits, and its décor, Ham retains its reputation for antiquity, thanks to the conservative approach of Elizabeth's successors in title. Even George III was not allowed admittance, the 5th earl of Dysart declaring that "Whenever my house becomes a public spectacle, His Majesty shall certainly have the first view". Horace Walpole's beloved niece was the wife of this somewhat eccentric peer, so Walpole had the entrée, but was strangely disappointed (as he was, also surprisingly, at Knole): "The old furniture is so magnificently ancient, dreary and decayed, that at every step, one's spirits sink, and all my passion for antiquity could not keep them up". To this day, its gloomy grandeur can be off-putting, but most visitors would disagree with Walpole, finding Ham romantically evocative of the reign of Charles I, the Civil War and the Restoration. Subsequent alterations were always undertaken in an antiquarian spirit, thus preserving its seventeenth-century distinction as the collection expanded and further redecoration and re-furnishing was undertaken. Ham owes much to the heroine of this chapter, which aims to sift the available evidence about her personal tastes, purchases and commissions. The family archives hold a rich vein of information about her life and times, and about the history of her paternal seat by the Thames near Richmond.

Sir Peter Lely painted two portraits of the flame-haired Elizabeth Murray as a young woman of twenty to twenty-five.[2] In the first she must be under twenty, still very much a girl. The second, with a black servant, portrays her in the height of fashion, presumably as a young married woman (she married in 1648 aged twenty-two). Lely's double portrait of the duke and duchess of Lauderdale (c.1672) depicts Elizabeth and her second husband, John Maitland, 2nd earl and 1st duke of Lauderdale, KG

Dyck's generous patron, the 10th earl of Northumberland, whose collection of female portraits by Van Dyck is discussed in Rowell 2003. A post-Restoration copy remains at Ham. Catherine Murray's portrait bust will be discussed by Charles Avery in Rowell 2013.

[2] All the works of art cited here are at Ham House, Surrey and belong to the National Trust (NT) unless otherwise stated. For further information about Ham House, its inventories and collections, see especially Dunbar 1976, Thornton and Tomlin 1980, Moore, Rowell and Strachey 1995 and Rowell 2013.

Figure 6: Sir Peter Lely, *The Duke and Duchess of Lauderdale*, oil on canvas, c.1672, Ham House, ©NTPL/John Hammond.

(1616-82), seated together on a carved stone bench in an arbour within the precincts of Whitehall Palace, where—as senior courtiers—they had lodgings.[3] (Fig. 6) What a contrast! The youthful sitter in the earlier portraits has become a faded, but still handsome, woman of the world. The duchess (who succeeded her father as countess of Dysart in her own right in 1655) had eleven children by her first husband, Sir Lionel Tollemache, 3rd Bt, (1624-69) of Helmingham Hall, Suffolk. In 1672, when she married John Maitland, 2nd earl of Lauderdale, he had been recently widowed, and his haste in re-marrying, not to mention their previous notorious liaison, had been the subject of much gossip. Even so, Sir Robert Moray, who had been one of Elizabeth's original suitors and knew her well, declared that "there was nothing in that commerce between them besides a vast fondness". It was clearly a love match, and Lauderdale was created 1st duke of Lauderdale soon after the February marriage ceremony in the little

---

[3] For a full account (by Oliver Millar) of this portrait, see Jackson-Stops 1985, no.100, 170. In 1677, it hung in the Great Dining Room at Ham, and was valued at £80 in c.1683. It still hangs in the same room, now the Hall Gallery (the floor was removed 1698-1728).

church at Petersham near Ham.[4] Lely's telling double portrait (one of his most perceptive) is in its original giltwood frame and has hung at Ham since at least 1677. The duke had also been a former patron of Lely. He wears the Garter ribbon and star, conferred in 1672, while the duchess is enveloped in the loose dress of the court, in fashionable Lely-esque *déshabillé*, holding a diaphanous gold-trimmed handkerchief in her left hand.

Family Life

Elizabeth was fourteen when her father's works at Ham were completed around 1640, when there was little time for her to imbibe the sophistication of the Caroline court, so amply represented in the new state apartment at Ham. This is one of the most complete survivals of Caroline court style, now only equally tangible, in a secular setting, at the Banqueting House, Whitehall, the Queen's House at Greenwich, and at Wilton House, Wiltshire. In 1644, two years after the outbreak of Civil War, when Elizabeth was eighteen, she was described by a friend of the family as 'the jewel, and indeed a pretty one but for her deep coullerd hayer...'tis said that she is like to be a very great fortune...such a pretty witty lass, with such a brave house and state as she is like to have, m'thinks might make a young fellow think her hayer very beautifull'.[5] The Civil War (1642-9) changed Elizabeth Murray's life. Her father, William Murray (c.1600-55), who was one of Charles I's most loyal adherents—a childhood friend, fellow collector and patron—spent the years after the regicide of 1649 as a peripatetic royal agent on the Continent and in Scotland. He was created earl of Dysart by the future Charles II in 1651, but as the patent had not passed the great seal, Elizabeth—as his successor in title—had the peerage confirmed in 1670, ten years after the Restoration, and a year after the death of her first husband, Sir Lionel Tollemache, 3rd Bt. (1669). Elizabeth's three surviving sons and two daughters were born between 1649 and 1661. Her mother, Catherine Bruce, died in the year of the regicide (1649), having indomitably defended Ham from sequestration by Parliament. This defence of the estate was continued by Elizabeth's husband after their marriage in 1648, and the ménage at Ham included her three sisters.

---

[4] Burnet 1823, I, 518: "I [Burnet] was in great doubt whether it was fit for me [as a bishop] to see his [Lauderdale's] mistress. Sir Robert [Moray] put an end to that; for he assured me, there was nothing in that commerce that was between them besides a vast fondness".

[5] Henry Knyvett to his wife, 23 May 1644, in Schofield 1949, 151-2.

Despite her growing family, Elizabeth could not—given her royalist sympathies and her determined character—devote the interregnum solely to motherhood and domesticity. She and her husband were in Paris in 1656, and in 1657 "Sir Lionel Talmash and his lady" were reported to the Protectorate as being "spies" in Flanders.[6] No doubt this was some sort of royalist mission. A member of the secret royalist society, the Sealed Knot, Elizabeth was involved in intrigue.[7] She is reputed to have charmed Oliver Cromwell with the partial aim of mitigating the danger to her lover, Lauderdale, imprisoned in the Tower since his capture at the battle of Worcester in 1651, and not released until 1660. Lauderdale's will (1670) bequeathed £1500 in gold to Elizabeth "as a token of my gratitude…in preserving my life when I was a prisoner in the year 1651".[8] Before the defeat at Worcester, Lauderdale and the future Charles II had cemented the closest of friendships, to which the king remained loyal. From 1660, Lauderdale was Scottish Secretary, with vice-regal dominion over his home country. Both Elizabeth and Lauderdale benefited financially from Charles II's Restoration. She received £800 pa for life and he—as well as being given the chief role in Scotland—had his lands restored and others granted.[9]

Marriage to John Maitland, 2nd Earl and 1st Duke of Lauderdale, KG

The late Sir Oliver Millar described the half-length portrait of Lauderdale (NPG of Scotland, Edinburgh) as "One of Lely's most baroque portraits, painted c.1665, and a powerful presentation of a formidable, well-educated, unprincipled and unattractive man". Sir Oliver described the future duchess as: "One of the most acute, politically minded and rapacious ladies of her day".[10] Bishop Burnet thought she was a "woman of great beauty but of much greater parts. She had a wonderful quickness of apprehension, and an amazing vivacity in conversation. She had studied not only divinity and history, but mathematics and philosophy. She was violent in everything she set about, a violent friend, but still more violent enemy".[11] Lauderdale was in her thrall, but as a strong character himself,

---

[6] Cripps 1975, 49; quoting Macray 1876.

[7] See Cripps 1975 for the duchess's biography, and for the general history of the Tollemache family, Tollemache 1949.

[8] Cripps 1975, 41; quoting MS 578 (100), the National Library, Edinburgh.

[9] Cripps 1975, 67.

[10] Millar 1978, nos. 23 and 37, 47-8, and 56-7.

[11] See Marshall 2004.

they were evenly matched.

The duke and duchess clearly had much in common, including their red hair. His temper was notorious, and she was also prone to anger. Elizabeth's first husband, a rich country baronet, had been far too nice and unambitious for her. It was presumably with his own wife in mind that Sir Lionel advised his son, Lionel, later 3rd earl, on the treatment of his future spouse:

> love her intirely but let her not know it, for all wifes are but too apt to take advantage of the fondness of theire husband, and upon it to grow insolent and imperious, and inclined to pervert the laws of nature by indeavouringe a superiority over the husband, and if she getts the reignes in her own hands, away shee will runn with it, and you scarce ever will stopp her in the whole course of her life.[12]

John Evelyn knew Lauderdale well: from 1671, they both sat on a board for the Royal Plantations in the West Indies, and dined in each other's houses. On 2 March 1664, Evelyn gave a dinner party. Among the guests were "the *E: of Lauderdail* His Majesties greate favourite, & Secretary of Scotland".[13] Other guests belonged to the Royal Society. Lauderdale's learning was considerable: he spoke Latin, Greek and Hebrew. In 1671, such was the weight of the books in his library at Lauderdale House, Highgate, London, that the structure of the house was endangered.[14] The Library at Ham, with its shelving and cedarwood-fitted secretaire, created for him in 1673 by the joiner, Henry Harlow, was connected by a staircase to his bedroom and dressing room. This type of civilised domestic arrangement, which must have been due to Lauderdale himself, became popular among collectors in the eighteenth century, but was pioneering in its day.[15] The sale catalogues of his books, the bulk of which was auctioned 1687-92, reveals an impressive range; he also owned Old Master drawings and designs.[16] Despite his boorish appearance and manners, lampooned by Bishop Burnet, who noted that the king had to have his snuffbox re-designed to stop Lauderdale putting his fingers in it, he clearly had many other strings to his bow. The eminently urbane Evelyn remained a friend, as most importantly did the king. However, Ronald Hutton, Lauderdale's biographer, concluded that: "When every

---

[12] Quoted in Cripps 1975, 36.

[13] De Beer 1959, (4 March, 1664), 459.

[14] Cripps 1975, 101.

[15] An eighteenth-century example is Henry Holland's design for Clive of India at Claremont, Surrey in the early 1770s; see Rowell 2001, 14-22.

[16] For the Lauderdale library, see Purcell 2003.

extenuation is made, his career remains a classic illustration of the corrupting effects of power".[17]

A Glorious Decade, 1672-1682

The high point of the duchess's career as a collector and patron was undoubtedly her participation in the duke of Lauderdale's massively extravagant building and furnishing campaigns, conducted between their marriage in 1672, and Lauderdale's death in 1682. The duchess seems to have had a considerable influence on her husband. According to Burnet, in his last decade he "became quite another sort of man than he had been in all the former parts of his life".[18] His interest in architecture seems to have derived largely from her enthusiasm "for Lauderdale does not seem to have shown any interest in building until about the time (a year or two before their marriage in February 1672) that she began to exercise a deep influence upon his thought and conduct".[19] In 1671, the duke was already writing from Ham to give precise orders about the alterations at one of his Scottish seats, Lethington (now Lennoxlove), declaring to his brother, Halton (future 3rd earl) "When you give occasion, I shall never wearie to send answers, for I am fond of this work."[20]

During the glory years, the Lauderdales conjoined in the extension, redecoration and refurnishing of Ham, while engaged on similar works in London, Edinburgh and elsewhere in Scotland, where Lauderdale's aggrandisement of his family's chief stronghold, Thirlestane, and other Scottish houses, is tangible evidence of his political power as Secretary of State (and virtual ruler) of that kingdom. Stone was transported by water from Scotland to Ham: most notably for the massive piers of the Northern entrance gate facing the river, which was designed and erected in 1671 for the future duchess by her cousin, William Bruce (c.1630-1710), who was also the architect of Thirlestane. Ham must therefore be regarded as part of a joint property empire, spreading from London to Edinburgh, albeit of particular importance to the duchess (both as her paternal home and as the seat of her earldom).

---

[17] Hutton 2004.
[18] Quoted in Dunbar 1976, 221.
[19] Ibid., 202.
[20] Quoted in Dunbar 1996, 206.

The Transformation of Ham, 1672-1676

Taking her cue from her mother perhaps (whose iconography included one of Van Dyck's best English female portraits (Petworth House, NT), as well as a hugely expensive bronze, which she kept in one of her private closets at Ham), Elizabeth Murray was portrayed as a girl by Lely, and retained her loyalty to this most distinguished of Van Dyck's immediate successors. Her three subsequent portraits by Lely, all at Ham, reveal her in fashionable guise with a black page (soon after her first marriage), with the duke in middle age, and as an older woman in a revealing and honest portrayal which shows that she retained much of her beauty.[21]

Both the duke and duchess were well aware that for a very political duke, image was especially important. The duke's iconography includes portraits by Lely, Benedetto Gennari, Paton and Ashfield as well as the silver medal (1672) by Jan Roettiers. It depicts him in profile like a Roman Emperor, wearing *all'antica* armour decorated with a Herculean lion's pelt, while on the reverse is a seated figure of *Minerva*, bearing a shield of the Maitland arms encircled by the Garter, and holding up an elaborate helmet with the ducal crest.

1672, the year the medal was struck, was an *annus mirabilis*, when Lauderdale was raised to a dukedom, awarded the Garter, and married Elizabeth Dysart. The *mise en scène* of all their properties was clearly considered to be fundamental to the ducal projection of power. Elizabeth was now at the peak of Restoration Society, a countess in her own right, as well as the consort of one of the most powerful men in the kingdom, who was also a bosom companion of the king. She was only too aware of the advantages of such an elevated social position, both socially and culturally. One feels that at last she had found the proper sphere for the exercise of her many talents and interests. And yet, although Ham, Helmingham, and the Lauderdale properties were aggrandised, the new duke and duchess achieved a synthesis of grandeur and *grande luxe*, with an eye to comfort and practicality. First and foremost they were leaders of fashion and innovation in building, installing sash-windows and double-glazing at Ham,[22] where the new works of the 1670s incorporated not only a first floor extension of the state apartment, but also libraries and closets, where they could pursue their own particular interests, and be surrounded by their favourite things. The duchess also installed a "Bathing Roome" in the basement, accessible via a staircase from her bedroom. Equipped with a

---

[21] For the portrait with a black servant, see Thornton and Tomlin 1980, fig. 48; and for the last portrait, see MacLeod and Marciari Alexander 2001, no. 89, 192-3.

[22] For these innovatory windows, see Dunbar 1976, 219 and 224-5.

fireplace for warmth and a bed to relax in *après le bain*, this indicates the duchess's concern with personal hygiene, a virtue not often accorded to our ancestors, but which was clearly very much a part of civilised aristocratic life at Ham House.

The Lauderdales' extensive remodelling of Ham was hailed by their contemporaries as both exceptionally splendid and sophisticated. The house had originally been designed as a *maison de plaisance*, within easy reach of London. The main addition from 1672-1676 was the cleverly managed transformation of Ham into a double-pile house, creating new apartments on the South front. These works by the gentleman-architect, William Samwell, were praised by the discriminating Roger North (1651-1734): "for I do not perceive any part of the old fabrick is taken down, but the wings... are joined with a strait rang[e] intirely new. And there are all the rooms of parade, exquisitely plact... so that the visto is compleat from end to end...".[23] At either end of this enfilade overlooking the formal garden on the South side were the duke and duchess's private rooms, with the black and white marble-floored Dining Room in the centre of the house. Upstairs was a State Bedroom apartment constructed for Queen Catherine of Braganza, a personal friend of the duchess, who certainly "Dined there [at Ham]" in 1674, soon after the royal apartment's completion.[24] Indeed, the king and queen were already expected as early as the summer of 1671.[25]

The house was meant to be read as a villa, in the Italian sense. There was a small agricultural estate, and although many things were bought from London, Ham was self-sufficient in dairy products, and there were the usual offices including a large Still Room for the production of distilled waters and liqueurs, as well as stables, a kitchen garden, and an Orangery. The river was used as a prime means of access, due to the poor roads, but both were clearly in regular use. The posthumous inventory of Lauderdale's possessions in 1682 included a "six oar'd barge", a "foure oar'd barge", as well as a "great Coach", a "mourning Coach" and a "Chariot".[26] We have a vignette of Lauderdale being rowed down the

---

[23] Roger North, *Of Building*, after 1684, MS in British Library (BM, Add. MS 32540) quoted (by Strachey) in Moore, Strachey and Rowell 1995, 67. See also Colvin and Newman 1981.

[24] Buckminster Park Archives (henceforth BPA), MS 413: "Account of Receipts and Disbursements of E. Masters for the Duchess of Lauderdale" (1672-81; 1674), "Given to 2 Cookes yt work'd at Ham when ye Queene Dined there".

[25] Quoted in Dunbar 1976, 222.

[26] BPA MS 358: "A true and perfect Inventory of all and singular the Goods Chattels and Creditts of the most Noble John Duke of Lauderdale, lately

Thames to Ham before his marriage to its chatelaine. Soon after her husband's death in Paris, he was on his way from London:

> It is so hard to write heir for the shake of the barge that I can write no more. I am going on a visit of charity to my Lady Dysert who is a most melancholy woman upon her double loss.[27]

The river and road approach—via an avenue leading through an iron grille framed by a great gateway, with Bernini-esque embracing courtyard walls beyond, formal planting, and lead busts set in wall niches framed in Italian style by the clipped evergreen, *phylleria angustifolia*—was devised with Baroque effect. Arcades on either side of the front door are decorated with landscapes in perspective, probably replacements of earlier ones, and still contain what may be the earliest documented pieces of garden furniture in England: the pair of "carved benches" made in durable oak by Henry Harlow in 1674. John Evelyn—who knew Italy at first hand—memorably described his impressions on 25 August 1678:

> After dinner I walked to *Ham*, to see the House & Garden of the *Duke of Laderdaile*, which is indeede inferiour to few of the best Villas in Italy itselfe, The house furnishd like a greate Princes; The Parterrs, flo[wer]: Gardens, Orangeries, Groves, Avenues, Courts, Statues, Perspectives, fountains, Aviaries, and all this at the banks of the sweetest river in the World, must needs be surprizing &c.[28]

---

dec[ease]d, not disposed of by him in his Lifetime…in the year of our Lord One thousand Six hundred and Eightie & Two". I am indebted to the late Chris Nicholson for the following definitions of a "Coach" and a "Chariot": "A coach is a permanently closed four-wheeled carriage with a body that is symmetrical about a door in the middle of each side, so it has a backward-facing seat (normally for two but occasionally for three in early coaches) ahead of the doors, and a forward-facing seat behind the doors. A similar carriage, but without the seat ahead of the doors and therefore seating two, is logically called a *coupé* in Continental Europe because it is effectively a coach with the front part of the body *cut off*. In Britain we call it a "chariot", as in "state", "town" and "travelling" chariots. The earliest surviving chariot in Britain is the "Darnley Chariot" at Cobham Hall, Kent, believed to be c. 1720."

[27] As well as her husband, her daughter Catherine had also recently died. Cripps 1975, quoting Patton 1939, letter LXXVII (30 January 1669).

[28] De Beer 1959, (26 August, 1678), 653.

The Duchess as Patron and Paymaster

The voluminous Ham papers reveal *in extenso* how this great work was achieved between its inception in 1672 and Evelyn's visit in 1678.[29] The payments to craftsmen and suppliers reveal Dutch, French, German and Italian, as well as English names. The alterations were largely complete by 1676. Further evidence is provided by inventories, primarily those taken in 1677, 1679 and 1683, as well as the "Estimate of Pictures", a complete list of valuations (c.1683), which—in tandem with the inventories recording the number of pictures in each room—indicates the crowded picture hangs.

Bills for building, for joinery, and for carving tended to be addressed to the duke, whereas most—though not all—of the bills for furniture and furnishings came to the duchess.

The duchess's personal accounts (1672-81) include payments to fringemakers (Dufresnoy, Hanesworth); embroiderers (Lanoine); upholsterers (Coke, Poictevin); drapers (Mr. Allen); cabinet-makers ("Johnson" and "Mr Jensen"[Gerrit Jensen], "Jorkim Andler", Balthasar Gray, Johannes van Santvoort); frame-makers (Norris, Naylor); gilders (Cousin, Nicholas Dessesas); silversmiths (Josias Ibart); tapestry makers (Mr Poyntz); dealers in china and silk (Mrs Taylor); joiners (Henry Harlow, "Hendrick Mainners the Dutch Joyner", "Johan Christian Ulrich a Dutch Joyner", Thomas Gally); carvers ("ye Dutch carver"); scagliola makers (Baldassare Artima); plasterers (Henry Wells); gardeners ("John Flaigmill, ye French Gardiner"); "Mr. Remp Pottmaker", and so on.[30] Many of the tradesmen's accounts were annotated by the Lauderdales' men of business, including Kirkwood, the family agent. Often the duchess would write "Kirkwood pay in full, E Lauderdale", always adding the date of her instruction. This was presumably the John Kirkwood who was among Lauderdale's attendants on 8 June 1672 during his inaugural arrival at Holyrood as Secretary of State for Scotland.[31] On the whole, it is fair to say that the duchess, rather than the duke, had her finger on the pulse. This is hardly surprising: Ham was her house after all, and the duke had many other fish

---

[29] MSS mainly preserved at Buckminster Park, Lincolnshire, the seat of Sir Lyonel Tollemache, Bt. and Richard Tollemache; at Helmingham Hall, Suffolk, the home of Lord Tollemache; the Surrey History Centre at Woking; and Ham House (NT). See also Dunbar 1976, 202-30; and Dunbar 1970.

[30] BPA MS 413.

[31] Cripps 1975, 115. Kirkwood may have been related to James Kirkwood, the Latin Grammarian and Head Master of Linlithgow School, near Edinburgh, which William Tollemache, the duchess's youngest son, attended (Cripps 1975, 118).

to fry, and it is also not untypical. The duchess's mother, Catherine Bruce, Mrs Murray (d.1649), signed off bills for payment during the 1630s alterations at Ham.[32]

One particular extravagance was the huge cost of ropes and tassels, mainly for the suspension of pier glasses. Many of these were made up from gold and silver bullion. The embroidered damask wall- and bed-hangings, as described in the inventories, were the acme of richness and expense. Some were changed from time to time, and in the Queen's Bedchamber, in summer and winter. Many survive *in situ*, on exhibition in the Ham Textile Museum, or in store. They are trimmed with the richest raised work and *passementerie*, in some cases so elaborate as to resemble spun sugar. This reflects an extremely rare conspectus of Charles II court style in furnishing textiles.

Another rare survival of Restoration luxury at Ham is the preponderance of silver fireplace furniture, of which Mary Evelyn famously wrote in *Mundus Muliebris or The Ladies Dressing Room Unlock'd and her Toilet Spread* (1685): "the chimney furniture of plate for iron's now quite out of date". The fashion had come from France, where silver furniture was the chief ornament of Versailles until it was melted down in 1689 to pay Louis XIV's armies.[33] In England, silver and silver-mounted furniture and fittings were made fashionable by the mistresses of Charles II. At Whitehall Palace on 4 October 1683, Evelyn accompanied the king to the duchess of Portsmouth's *levée* in her dressing room, which was hung with tapestries, some "of His Majesties best paintings" and "huge *Vasas* of Wrought plate, *Tables, Stands, Chimny furniture, Sconces, branches, Braseras* &c they were all of massive silver, & without number".[34] The set of "*Chimny furniture*" in the Queen's Bedchamber at Ham may well have been there since 1679, when the inventory lists: "One Broome and one bellowes garnisht with silver", which were hanging from "two silver hooks". The inventory also lists a firepan, firedogs and a grate all "garnisht with silver". The engraved cipher, beneath a ducal coronet, on the front of the bellows, has been read as the "JEL monogram of the Duke [John] and Duchess [Elizabeth] of Lauderdale",[35] but the cipher actually appears to read "EJL". The silver-mounted firegrate in the Queen's

---

[32] Signing herself "Catherine", and not "Katherine", as her name is usually spelt in the literature on Ham. The 'K' derives from the inscription on her coffin plate, but "C" is followed here.

[33] For seventeenth-century French silver furniture, see Arminjon 2007.

[34] De Beer 1959, 756-757 (4 October 1683).

[35] Jackson-Stops 1985, cat. no.135, 210-11 (entry by Hardy).

Bedchamber has the clearly legible monogram 'EJDL'.[36] The elaborate embossed silver mounts of the bellows indicate awareness of "Roman foliage' patterns"[37] (the kind of acanthus-based arabesque design that was disseminated via Roman, then French, Dutch and English engravings), and the floral marquetry is very much in Franco-Dutch style, the whole presumably made in London. Silver-handled iron fireplace implements (c.1690) also survive in the Danish Royal Collection.[38] The 1677, 1679, and 1683 Ham inventories reveal that the main rooms at Ham all had silver fireplace furniture, and several silver-mounted firepans still survive, including an exquisite small scale example in the Green Closet, c.1637-9, which is complete with a filigree fender and silver detachable "feet". One suspects that this helped to set the trend for such things at Ham in the 1670s, by which time—as Evelyn remarks—silver-mounted furniture had become synonymous with conspicuous expenditure by luxurious female courtiers. The duchess personally ordered at least one set of silver-mounted fireplace equipment from the goldsmith, George Bowers: "pay Mr Bowers in full for one pair of Silver Andirons one Shuffle & one pair of tongs Sixteen pounds".[39] A set of bellows, also mounted in silver and marquetry (Royal Collection, Windsor Castle) was reputedly made for Nell Gwynn, so this certainly tended to be thought of as a female extravagance. The sole silver-mounted fireplace furniture in the Lauderdales' London apartment at Whitehall Palace, was the "One fire Iron with Silver feet & handles" in "Her Graces Closset".[40] At Ham, however, the Duke's Dressing Room, as well as the Green Closet, was also furnished with silver fireplace impedimenta.

Although at Ham there is no silver furniture completely given over to the precious metal, there is one silver-mounted piece that was certainly commissioned by Elizabeth, before her second marriage to Lauderdale. This is the *carved, bronzed and gilded silver-mounted ebony-topped side table, with caryatid legs*, c.1670 (the top? and the ebony stretcher added c.1730), which has stood in the Green Closet since at least 1677 (Fig. 7). On the ebony top, the seven plaques of decorative silver and contrasting

---

[36] Thornton and Tomlin 1980, fig. 132.

[37] Thornton 1998, 108 (the Ham bellows are illustrated at plate 216, 107) and Snodin and Llewellyn 2009, no. 168, 354, and pl. 5.76 (entry by Rowell).

[38] See Bencard 1992, cat. nos. 19-20, 70 (Copenhagen, c.1690, attributed to Henri de Moor).

[39] BPA MS 450 (memorandum dated 11 October, 1673). I am grateful to Tessa Murdoch for this reference. She will describe the metalwork, jewellery and clocks at, or previously at Ham, in Rowell 2013.

[40] BPA MS 183.

silver-gilt, bearing a countess's coronet above "ECD" (for "Elizabeth, Countess [of] Dysart"), date the table between 1655, when she inherited the title, and 1672, when she became a duchess after her second marriage. Stylistically, the table seems to date around 1670, the year that Elizabeth had her Dysart earldom confirmed by a new patent. The table may have been commissioned as a memorial of this re-affirmation of her *suo jure* earldom, and placed symbolically in her father's Green Closet. The carved elements of the support, were probably originally silver and gold, and were bronzed later. The remaining carved furniture in the Green Closet—both seat furniture and stands for a pair of Japanese cabinets—appears to be part of the same set, and the *pair of Japanese lacquer cabinets* (Kyoto, c.1630-50), flanking the chimneypiece, were also listed first in 1677. These were probably purchased by Lady Dysart, given her love of Oriental lacquer and japanned furniture.

Figure 7: Carved, bronzed and gilded silver-mounted ebony-topped side table, with caryatid legs, c.1670 (the ebony stretcher added, and the top possibly renewed, c.1730) in the Green Closet, ©NTPL/John Hammond.

The duchess certainly took an interest in the *minutiae* of the Ham project, but the rooms that she could call her own, rather than the state apartments, reflect her personal tastes most specifically. She had been the chatelaine of Ham since her father's death in 1655, but seems to have begun its embellishment in earnest after the death of her first husband in 1669. A set of japanned furniture bearing the cipher of the chatelaine of Ham— this time "EDL" ("Elizabeth Duchess [of] Lauderdale" or "Elizabeth Dysart Lauderdale") beneath a ducal coronet—was clearly made for her own private sanctum on the ground floor, still known as the Duchess's Private Closet. (Fig. 8) Three of these exotically designed and decorated *cane-bottomed faux lacquer backstools*, c.1675, survive, and were probably from the set of "six Japan'd backstools with cane bottoms" listed in her Private Closet in 1683.[41] The cane seats were provided with cushions matching the wall hangings. The Duchess's Private Closet is situated at the South-East corner of Ham, at ground floor level. Adjacent, at the end of the South front enfilade, is the White Closet, which gave onto the garden, and beyond was the duchess's bedroom (the present Volury Room, remodelled in the 1740s, but still named after its *quondam* birdcages constructed outside the windows in the 1670s). The overdoors are depictions (1673) of birds by Francis Barlow (1626-1702). A "pair of Casements" in "My Lady Chamber"—presumably the Volury Room at this time—were decorated by "Mr Moor the Paynter" with "gilding & blewing", in 1673-4, which is typical of the grand style of Ham.[42] Originally, the duke's bedroom was presumably at the West end of this *enfilade* of rooms, given that the ancillary closets were described in the inventories as his, and also because it is decorated with seascapes (1673) by William van der Velde the younger (1633-1707). However, in the 1677 inventory, this room (with its bed alcove) was described as "Her Graces Bedchamber", so the duchess had clearly taken it over (hers seems to have been originally in the Volury Room, adjacent to her closets). The reason for this change is unknown, but she cannot have been driven out by the noise of her pet birds as there were birdcages outside both bedrooms. However, she and the duke retained their original dressing rooms. Assuming that the duke took over her former bedroom in the Volury, this inconvenient arrangement suggests that they liked the intimacy of having to cross each others' bedrooms to reach their dressing rooms.[43] However,

---

[41] They were probably also listed here in 1677 and 1679, but the descriptions are less precise. For this japanned seat furniture, see Aldrich 2009, 30-41.

[42] BPA MS 443.

[43] For a comprehensive account of this assumed bedroom swapping, see Thornton and Tomlin 1980, 47-8 *et seq.*

as there is no bedroom in the inventories of 1677, 79 and 83 designated specifically for the duke, it is more likely that they both shared her bed in what had been called "My Lady's Alcove Room" in Henry Harlow's 1672 carpentry bill. They certainly shared the same bedroom at Brunstane, where in 1672, the duke instructed William Bruce to take down a wall in "my wife's bedchamber and mine, where there is a corner chimney, because for inlarging of that bedchamber...".[44] A similar indication of their intimacy is the fact that the 1677 inventory of their lodgings at Whitehall Palace lists a bed in "Her Graces Chamber", but he only had a bed in "His Graces Dressing Room". Between them was "The Hole", which contained "One cedar close Stoole box with two velvet seates".[45]

Figure 8: Ham House, the Duchess's Private Closet, ©NTPL/John Hammond.

---

[44] Dunbar 1976, 215 (1672).
[45] BPA MS 183: "A true Inventory of his Grace the Duke of Lauderdales Goods at Whitehall taken the 4th of August 1679".

The Duchess's Private Closet

From the evidence of the 1677, 79 and 83 inventories, and the c.1683 "Estimate of Pictures", it is possible to establish what the Duchess's Private and White Closets contained, and to get a good impression of how the duchess used them. The Duchess's Private Closet was conveniently placed next to a servants' staircase, and could be maintained discreetly without the need for them to approach it via the White Closet or the Volury bedroom beyond. Its contents were fairly consistent between 1677 and 83. As well as the japanned backstools, the furniture consisted mainly of other Oriental or pseudo-Oriental things. Ever since Far Eastern imports had increased in the early-seventeenth century, particularly via the Dutch East India Company (VOC; founded 1602), lacquer or japanned furniture and other artefacts had become particularly popular among female collectors, who had also begun the lasting seventeenth-century craze for Far Eastern porcelains. A classic case was that of Amalia von Solms, the German consort of Prince Frederik Hendrik, stadholder of The Netherlands (m.1625) who may be said to have invented the concept of the Orientalising closet in the 1630s, decorated with lacquer, porcelain and other artefacts. Her son, the future Willem II, married Princess Mary of England in 1641, and this must have hastened the fashion in England, just as her daughters spread the fashion in Germany.[46] The Duchess's Closet in the Lauderdales' lodgings at Whitehall Palace also contained "One lakerd Cane Chayre wth a sky colour Satten Cusheon embroidered" and her bedroom had "Three lakerd Arme Chayres wth Cane bottomes" and "Two great Indian [ie. Chinese or Japanese] Screens", so she definitely had a taste for things Oriental.[47] The following were listed in the Duchess's Private Closet in 1683:

> Two cases of Shelves for bookes, Japanned/ One Table of the Same./ One Scriptore [fall-front secretaire] of walnut tree./ One Cedar table./ One Japan box for sweetmeats & tea./ One Tea table, carv'd and guilt.

The books, the secretaire, and the tea things indicate that the room was used for private study, reading, writing and amusement. The lacquer furniture could not have been more appropriate for tea drinking, and one can easily imagine the duchess and her friends seated on the japanned backstools, clustering around the "Tea table, carv'd and guilt", which is presumably identical with the red, black and gilded low table that was

---

[46] Van den Ploeg and Vermeeren 1998, 76-86 (chapter by C. Willemijn Fock).
[47] BPA MS 183.

provided with an ebonised English stand, c.1675, to bring it up to the height of Western seating. This unusual table—and the very similar example at Dyrham Park, Gloucestershire (NT)—has previously been thought to be "Javanese", but such tables were in fact produced at Arakan in the Bay of Bengal.[48] The Closet also contains what is by Tollemache family tradition known as the "Duchess's teapot". This is a white crackled glaze Chinese porcelain teapot made at the Zhangzhou kilns in Fujian province (c.1650-70). The craquelure is due to underfiring, and such porcelain was not made for export. Its English gilt bronze mounts were presumably added for the duchess. The pink tinge was probably caused by years of hot tea seeping through the glaze.[49]

Figure 9: Antonio Verrio (c.1639-1707), *The Penitent Magdalen, surrounded by Putti holding emblems of Time, Death and Eternity,* c.1675, on the ceiling of the Duchess's Private Closet, ©NTPL/John Hammond.

---

[48] Veenendal 2002, 24. I am grateful to Simon Jervis for pointing this out (Jervis 2009, 370). For the Ham table, erroneously described as "Javanese", see Snodin and Llewellyn 2009, no. 48, 335-6 and pl. 2.79 (entry by Rowell).

[49] The teapot was given to the National Trust by the late Ronald Lee, a prominent London antique dealer, who gave it via the NA-CF [now the Art Fund] in 1994 in memory of his wife. Lee was a neighbour of both Sir Lyonel Tollemache, 4th Bt (1854-1952) and his son, Sir [Cecil] Lyonel Tollemache, 5th Bt. (1886-1969), the joint donors of Ham, and acquired various things from the Ham collection. For details of the teapot, I am grateful to Patricia Ferguson, whose account of Ham ceramics will appear in Rowell 2013.

The walls of the Closet were hung with exotically paned hangings, which were different each year that the inventories were taken, culminating in 1683 with "foure pieces of Dark Mohayre bordered with flowered Silke with purple & gold fringe". Over the door from the White Closet and over the corner chimneypiece, are paintings by Henry Ferguson (b.The Netherlands, before 1655-d.Toulouse, 1730), listed here in 1677.[50] The overdoor, *Capriccio of Classical Reliefs*, and the overmantel, *Medea casting spells among Ruins*, were both *in situ* by 1677. *Medea* is an unusual subject. The theme of love, betrayal, and of avenging wife and sorceress, is not an obviously attractive choice for the duchess to have made. The imagery of the ceiling painting by Verrio, *The Penitent Magdalen, surrounded by Putti holding emblems of Time, Death and Eternity* is exceptional for England at this date, c.1675, and suggests Catholic leanings, especially as it is in the duchess's inner sanctum. (Fig. 9) Her choice of female saint strikes a chord, with its theme of luxurious immorality and subsequent penitence. Given that this was always her room, it is clear that the choice of subject matter for the fixed paintings would have been hers. However, there is no overt religious symbolism, such as a crucifix, for instance. Verrio's employment by the Lauderdales marks them out as *avant-garde*. His style, at this early date in England, is imbued with current Italian and French sophistication, evident in both the figural and architectural elements of his painted décor.[51] The Closet walls were also covered by paintings, which in 1679, amounted to:

> Foure pictures with guilt carved frames whereof two small ones/ One picture of her Graces mother, in an Ebony Case/ Seaventeen other pictures all in Ebony frames of severall sizes.

This hang has recently been recreated, in so far as it is still possible. The 1677 and 79 inventories usually mention the number of pictures in each room, and the type of frame, with occasionally a mention of a particular picture, such as Hoskins's 1638 portrait of the duchess's mother, *Mrs. William (Catherine) Murray*. By contrast, the "Estimate of Pictures" (c.1683) of which two slightly variant versions survive, includes full descriptions of the paintings. This inventory (valuing the bankrupt duchess's pictures in order to raise ready money) begins in the Duchess's

---

[50] See Eidelberg 2000, especially 28-30 and figs. 3 and 4. I am grateful to Alastair Laing for this reference.
[51] For this and Verrio's other work at Ham and the beginning of his English career, see Brett 2009-10.

Private Closet, thus enabling the recent re-hang based upon it.[52] The precedence of the Duchess's Private Closet illustrates the importance of the room at the time the inventory was made, and by this time the duchess had been widowed for the second time, and was once again the sole chatelaine of Ham.

The c.1683 mix of paintings and drawings listed in the Duchess's Private Closet ranges from family portraits and portrait drawings to Venetian Old Masters. This remains the second most important Cabinet Room in the house, after the Green Closet, and the original mix remains, albeit in slightly reduced numbers. In its original ebony case with doors is the large miniature portrait of the duchess's mother, *Catherine, Mrs. Murray, with Ham House in the background* by John Hoskins the Elder (c.1590-1665), signed and dated 1638. A set of family portrait drawings in plumbago by the Scot, David Paton (active c.1660-95), covers both Maitlands and Murrays, including the sole image of the duchess's father, *William Murray, 1st \Earl of Dysart*, her mother, *Mrs. William (Catherine) Murray* and portraits of her sons: her heir in the earldom, *Lionel Tollemache, 3rd Earl of Dysart (1649-1727)*, and her beloved second son, *General Thomas Tollemache (c.1651-94)*, whose heroic death at the disastrous Siege of Brest was widely mourned. Also by Paton, and continuing the theme of her father's Green Closet, are *drawings after Raphael, Titian and Andrea del Sarto*. All these are in their original ebony frames, and only three paintings in gilt frames. A pair of Venetian sixteenth-century round-headed panels depicts *St. Sebastian* and *St. Anthony Abbot*. On the backs is an attribution to "Leonard Davinshaw" [Leonardo da Vinci], and the c.1683 value of £25. They retain their sixteenth-century carved and gilded Venetian frames. Finally, there is a glazed pastel portrait of *John Maitland, 1st Duke of Lauderdale, KG* initialled and dated 1675, by the first English pastellist, Edmund Ashfield (active 1669-76), a pupil of John Michael Wright. This is in its magnificent original carved and gilded auricular frame of c.1675.

In 1677, Sir John Reresby wrote of a visit to Ham:

---

[52] Laing and Strachey 1994, 3-9. This article re-interprets the c.1683 "Estimate" identifying its correct starting place. The previous interpretation of the picture hang, which was used by the V&A as a basis for hanging the surviving pictures, was published in Thornton and Tomlin 1980. Their account is based on the incorrect premise that the "Estimate of Pictures" starts in the Duke's Dressing Room rather than in the Duchess's Private Closet.

The next day [13 May] I went to visit the Duke and Duchess of Lauderdale at their fine house at Ham. After dinner, her Grace entertained me in her chamber with much discourse upon affairs of state. She had been a beautiful woman, the supposed mistress of Oliver Cromwell and at that time a lady of great parts.[53]

Perhaps this interview took place in the Duchess's Private Closet? It was certainly the kind of confidential exchange for which it was intended.

The White Closet

The duchess's adjoining White Closet was more simply furnished and hung, and the pastoral landscape overdoors by Dirck van den Bergen (1640-90) depict the Ovidian *Mercury and Battus*, and a generalised scene of *Herdsmen and Animals*. The room takes its name from the *faux* white marbling and from the 1677-83 inventory descriptions of wall hangings of white "tabby" or ribbed silk, bordered with "sadd coloured" tabby, fringed with silver. The only picture which has hung here since the duchess's time is the head of *St. Paul* by Benedetto Gennari (1633-1715).[54] There were four other heads, and *The Baptism of Christ* by Abraham Bloemaert (1564-c.1651), valued at £15 in 1683, and re-framed in the 1740s by the 4th earl of Dysart [Withdrawing Room]. Above the corner chimneypiece still stands a bronze bust of Catherine Bruce, the duchess's mother, (c.1637-8) previously given to Hubert Le Sueur (c.1590-after 1658), but probably by another sculptor in the Caroline court circle.[55] The bust was listed in the White Closet as a "brasse head of her Graces mother" in 1683 but clearly had a coat of black shellac varnish by the time of the 1728 inventory, when it was ignorantly described as a "blackamoor over the chimney". The black patination, shown in photographs, was removed, though not entirely, in 1976 by the V&A. Examination in 2011 by Rupert Harris indicated that the bust has never been gilded, and was perhaps darkly patinated from the outset.

The painted cove and ceiling, again by Verrio, depicts *Putti with medallions of the Four Cardinal Virtues, and Sphinxes* and *Divine Wisdom presiding over the Liberal Arts*. This is one of his most accomplished

---

[53] Reresby 1743, 49 (entry dated 13 May 1677).
[54] This is no.27 in the "Estimate of Pictures": "St. Paul's head of Jenaro – £10. 00. 00".
[55] For the attribution to Le Sueur, see Avery 1980-82, which was repeated in Jackson-Stops 1985, no. 68, 142-3 (entry by Avery). The authorship of the bust will be reappraised by Charles Avery in Rowell 2013.

performances at Ham, revealing the Italian source of his inspiration. The concept is particularly reminiscent of Pietro da Cortona and the painted and stucco decoration of the Pitti Palace (begun 1642) which is entirely in tune with French fashion and the décor of Versailles as conceived by Charles Le Brun. Verrio had come to England from France, encouraged by the duke of Montagu, Charles II's ambassador to Louis XIV. These early Ham painted ceilings represent some of Verrio's most sophisticated work in England: much of his subsequent English work is coarse and lumpen by comparison.

As for the contents of the White Closet, the *Chinoiserie* theme of the Duchess's Private Closet was continued in the seat furniture. In 1683, the White Closet contained "Six arme Cane Chayres Japaned", as well as "One Childs Chayre gilt", which must have been for the duchess's grandson, Lionel Tollemache, viscount Huntingtower, born in 1682. The only surviving piece of furniture is the superb "Scriptore of Prince wood, garnished with Silver", c.1675. (Fig. 10) "Prince wood" is an early term for rosewood (in this case, *dalbergia nigra*, from South America, which in the late-seventeenth century was distributed in Northern Europe by the Dutch).[56] The internal drawers of the cabinet are of solid rosewood, the veneers on the front and sides are applied to the oak carcase. The standard of workmanship is of the highest order, and the design is individual, with turned Salomonic legs, joined by a sinuous stretcher, and terminating in vases of acanthus, and distinctive pad feet which appear in furniture by Gerrit Jensen (d.1715), to whom large payments were made by the Lauderdales. The silver mounts, escutcheons and circular handles are also of the first water. This secretaire or "scriptore", of royal quality, testifies to the highest standards specified by the duchess. Where was it—and the companion piece made for the Duke's Private Closet—produced? We do not know, but the likelihood is that this type of furniture was produced in London, very probably by foreign craftsmen, familiar with French and Dutch taste: someone, indeed, very like Jensen.

---

[56] See Zinnkann 2003, 60-2.

Figure 10: "Scriptore of Prince wood, garnished with Silver", c.1675, attributed to Gerrit Jensen (d.1715), oak veneered with rosewood (*dalbergia nigra*, from South America), ©NTPL/John Hammond.

French Taste and Commissions

The duchess's private rooms at Ham represented the height of fashionable patronage. The rooms were also comfortable, with the signal advantage of small size for heating, and of ventilation in the summer. Indeed, the White Closet door, whose 36 glass panes were fitted in 1674, allowed the duchess direct access to the garden.[57] As we have seen, she was probably the leading light in the extension and furnishing of Ham between her second marriage in 1672, and the duke's death in 1682. She was up to date with international fashion, and was well travelled. She took chamber and household plate with her into France in 1669-70, and on 27 April 1671, she wrote: "all the discourse is now of ye King of France [Louis XIV] and of his splendid Court, Many doe go from hier to see him".[58] Indeed, the

---

[57] BPA MS 440; Mr Bear, the Glazier, 8 December 1674, "For 36 panes in ye dore going into the Cherry Garden £2.02.00".
[58] Cripps 1975, 97, quoting Tweeddale Papers, Acc. 4862, Box 3, f. 3 (a), letter from Elizabeth Dysart at Ham to countess of Tweeddale, 27 April 1671.

duchess had been in France several times, and her father, partly due to his exile during the Commonweath, had been imbued with Continental taste. Her silver included '2 stands for dishes of the French fasion'.[59] Just as the Stuart royal family continued to look to Paris for the *dernier cri* of luxury and style, so did the sophisticated court. One can assume that Lady Dysart, who clearly had more freedom to indulge her collecting proclivities after her first husband's death in 1669, and immediately embarked on a French tour, was only too familiar with the latest French fashions. In 1672, shortly before her marriage to Lauderdale, rich clothes "made by my Ladye Dysert's measure" were sent over from Paris.[60] In those days especially, there was less distinction between dress and furnishing textiles, so it is hardly surprising—given the rich heritage of seventeenth-century textiles at Ham—that the duchess was ordering clothes from the French capital, then as now the capital of taste in women's clothes.

Although no fully documented French pieces of furniture survive at Ham, there are bills from French *ébénistes*, partly published by James Yorke in 1990.[61] On 20 April 1673, M. Pelletyer of Paris—possibly connected with the Pelletiers who worked at Boughton—billed the duke of Lauderdale and two of his friends, for the supply *inter alia* of four pier glasses, tables and torchère stands, of ebony mounted with gilt bronze.[62] The total cost was £126.19.00. The two Ham sets were listed in 1677, but by 1679 they were marked "Sent to Scotland" in the inventory.[63] Similarly, on 17 June 1673, Philippe Lelarge, the "French joyner", billed the duchess for a state bed and ten chairs, and for cutting down the bed in height. No vestige of this commission is recorded in the Ham inventories.[64] Another important bill in French (1673; unpublished until now) signed in London by the well-known upholsterer, Jean Poictevin, is headed: "Memoire De Ce que Jay Faict et Fourny [pour] Son Altesse Madame la duchesse de Laderdelle".[65] These so-called "Dolphin" six chairs and six armchairs,

---

[59] BPA MS 877. I am grateful to Tessa Murdoch for this reference.

[60] Cripps 1975, 110; quoting Tweeddale Papers, Acc. 4862, Box 101, f. 3, National Library, Edinburgh.

[61] Yorke 1990, 235-38.

[62] For the Pelletiers at Boughton, see Murdoch 1992, 129-30 and figs. 125-6 (chapter by John Hardy); see also Murdoch 1997 and 1998.

[63] Yorke 1990.

[64] Ibid, James Yorke describes the "French Joyner" as anonymous, but the bill was signed at Whitehall on 17 August 1673, by Philippe Lelarge, who is presumably the person in question.

[65] Poictevin's bill (BPA MS 911) was paid at Whitehall on 17 October, 1673, amounted to £81.02.06, and contained three beds, and numerous cushions and ribbons.

retaining seventeenth-century brocatelle top covers, probably the ones provided in 1673 by Poictevin, represent the height of French fashion around 1675. Poictevin charged for: "Plus avoir garny six chesse et six fauteuille deaulphiné d'or detoille rouge a dix chelin l'un piesse [£]6.00.00".[66] The frames are now bronzed and gilded (the result of nineteenth-century intervention) but the original treatment was apparently more colourful so that the dolphins appeared to sport in their own element, the sea. Poictevin's description implies that gilding was predominant.

Dutch and Anglo-Dutch Furniture

The duke and duchess were quite clearly devoted to the unusual and prestigious. The "cabinet entirely inlaid with ivory", first listed at Ham in 1677, is now thought to have been made in The Hague, and to date from c.1650-55.[67] It is an open question as to whether this was acquired at that time, or much later, but it is certainly not listed in the Ham inventory of c.1655. Other passing fashions include a table and pair of torchères in ebonised wood, with the tops of cane, c.1675 [Duke's Dressing Room], originally *en suite* with a "greate looking glasse with an ebony frame caned"; and a similar set veneered with seventeenth-century incised Chinese lacquer [Withdrawing Room].[68] Both these sets have strong Dutch overtones, and furniture and panelling made up from Far Eastern lacquer had been popular in royal circles in The Netherlands since the 1630s. As for the table and stands with caned tops, these can possibly be paralleled by a mention in the 1709 inventory of Montagu House, Bloomsbury, of "a Cained Table" in an Ante Room.[69] There are also superb pieces decorated with Franco-Dutch style marquetry, which must have been made for the Lauderdales in the 1670s, again probably in London by a Continental craftsman. Most splendid [Queen's Ante-Chamber] is the pier table and large pier glass surmounted by a ducal coronet or a royal crown [it is ambiguous in form] above a profile head after the Antique, which are richly inlaid with arabesques of ebony, plain and green-stained ivory, and various woods. Marquetry furniture played a major role in the decoration of Ham, and there are several outstanding pieces still *in situ*, including cabinets and tables. Their style is Franco-Dutch, but these pieces were made in London, and will be discussed by Reinier Baarsen in the

---

[66] Ibid.
[67] Baarsen 2008, 372-80.
[68] For the caned set, see Thornton 1980, 239-40 and fig. 1.
[69] Murdoch 2006, 18. I am grateful to Sarah Medlam for this reference.

forthcoming major study of Ham and its collections.[70] It is this type of supremely fashionable furniture—combined with a rich décor of textiles, decorative painting and a significant art collection—that led Evelyn in 1678 to describe Ham as "furnishd like a greate Princes", and apparently "Ham was sometimes called Ham Palace, a name which it fully deserved".[71]

Enforced Economies and Widowhood

With his stroke in 1680, the duke of Lauderdale's power began to slip away from him. After his death in 1682, a lying-in-state at Ham, and a magnificent funeral in Scotland costing £5,000 (which the duchess tried for years to get her brother-in-law, Lord Halton, 3rd earl of Lauderdale, the duke's heir, to pay for) the bubble burst. Lauderdale's huge debts were described as "the winding-sheet of the earldom", while his widow was accused of "a ravenous cormorant appetite in hir to devour all".[72] She was left all his moveable possessions, so fourteen wagon loads of goods left Thirlestane for England, thus explaining its singular lack of seventeenth-century furnishings. It is said that the fifteenth wagon was stopped by locals incensed at this disastrous depletion. Although the duchess succeeded in avoiding the entire responsibility for the duke's financial liabilities (the majority of which the 3rd earl of Lauderdale had to resolve) she had to lead a much more straitened and economical existence, being reduced to pawning her jewels, her plate and her pictures (thus giving us the invaluable c.1683 "Estimate of Pictures", with the values being inscribed on the backs of the paintings, as first realised by Alastair Laing and Nino Strachey).[73] Among the "mortgaged" jewels were diamonds and pearls, perhaps including "ye necklace of piarl's" for which "Mr Jackson" had been paid the huge sum of £517 on 30 September, 1679. There was also the "great necklace of pearls" which formed part of the Lauderdale jewels, which were left to her by the duke's will.[74] Some £11,000 worth of jewels was pawned, and in 1696, £10,000 was raised from Lord Normanby, by

---

[70] Rowell 2013.

[71] Lady Sudeley, *Gossip Notes* (unpublished; BPA), quoted in Tollemache 1949, 71.

[72] Cripps 1975, 203; quoting *Historical Notices of Scottish Affairs*, selected from the MSS. of Sir John Lauder of Fountainhall, II, 1848, 769.

[73] There are numerous documents in the Buckminster archive attesting to the duchess's debts and money-raising after the duke's death in 1682. See also Laing and Strachey 1994.

[74] Cripps 1975; quoting Tweeddale Papers, Acc. 4862, Box 101, f. 3, National Library, Edinburgh.

mortgaging Ham House itself. These vast sums of money, at a time when a Ham labourer was earning an average of 12s a week, and skilled men about twice as much, give a telling impression of the life of the Caroline aristocracy, whose excesses were noted—disapprovingly but with fascination—by such commentators as John Evelyn.

The Lauderdales' crash was greatly to the chagrin of the duke's own family. A disgruntled epitaph for the duke and duchess's princely extravagance is inscribed on the frame of Lely's full-length portrait of the duke in the dining room at Thirlestane:

> This man enjoy'd all the great offices under the Crown, but ruin'd his family by giving away to an old woman, Lady Dysart, his second wife, an immense Estate handed him through a series of prudent and able ancestors, which estate was the means of raising him to the honours he enjoy'd.[75]

Elizabeth's inheritance was perfectly legal, because she received in accordance with Lauderdale's will, all his movable possessions (hence the cartloads of goods from Thirlestane), while her eldest son, Lord Huntingtower, was granted Lethington. Most significantly for her heirs, she was left Ham House (which on her marriage had become the property of the duke) together with the freehold of the Manors of Petersham and Ham, which had been granted to Lauderdale in 1671.

Although Lauderdale usually gets a bad press, his brother and heir, the 3rd earl of Lauderdale (the dukedom became extinct), wrote to his sister-in-law, the widowed duchess, of the funeral at Haddington, Scotland:

> the companie, lords and others first had dinner in Roums provided for them. And the noblemen's room was hung with Blak and garnished with their Scuchions...My Lords arms and yours...at 5 aclok That noble and Extraordinarie person was placed in his Tumb....Ther was present at the funeral two thousand horse at least; in so much that these filled the highway for full four meils in length, thur was 25 coaches and most of this company came to the Grave....so well was he beloved that the whole Countrie keindly gave ther presence to the assisting in this last dewtie....[76]

She had wanted a dignified but simpler funeral at Lauder and the £5,000 expenditure on this grand occasion became a bone of contention which was eventually settled, together with other legal disagreements over the ducal estate, in 1688.[77] The duchess was required to pay the funeral

---

[75] Quoted in Moore, Rowell and Strachey 1995, 69.
[76] Quoted in Tollemache 1949, 66.
[77] For a detailed account of the terms of Lauderdale's will and the dispute over it,

expenses but had her other inheritances upheld by the Scottish courts. Her own funeral in 1698 was a quiet affair. She is buried in St. Peter's, Petersham, where she was married to the duke, and to which she presented a 1640-1 silver flagon and 1663-4 paten, both of which are engraved with her arms. She requested that she be "carried only by my particular family, in Petersham Church where my honoured mother the Countess of Dysart does lye with three of my sisters and three of my own children".[78]

Bishop Burnet rather confirms that the duke and duchess were made for each other, by being equally vitriolic about both of them. Burnet describes the duke's extravagant "course of luxury and sensuality", in which he "delivered himself up to all her humours and passions".[79] But the duke was no Adam, and the duchess was no Eve. Fortunately, Ham still testifies to their extravagant good taste, and to their devotion, whatever the cost, to fashionable and fine craftsmanship. The Ham summary accounts (not necessarily complete) record architectural expenditure of £9,659 (1672-6), while the posthumous inventory of his goods states that "the Duke bestowed upon buildings and reperationes [ie excluding furniture, pictures etc] at Ham and gardens thereto belonging sixtein thousand pund sterline".[80]

Conclusion

The duchess undoubtedly made a significant contribution to the extension and enrichment of her family's Thames-side seat at Richmond. As the second wife of John Maitland, 1st duke of Lauderdale, she was bequeathed the lordships of Petersham and Ham, granted to him in 1671, a grant which had long been the unsuccessful goal of her father and first husband. Ham, its lands and contents reverted to her in their entirety by the terms of Lauderdale's will, and when the prolonged litigation with her brother-in-law, the 3rd earl of Lauderdale, was settled in 1688, she was able to live out the rest of her life as the chatelaine of Ham. Despite her straitened circumstances, especially her lack of ready money which led her to pawn jewels and paintings, she had the satisfaction of knowing that her heirs would enjoy the benefits of both her first and second marriages, and that they would be secure in the possession of her estates.

How did the duchess measure up to her female contemporaries? She was interested in architecture, works of art, and interior decoration, to such

---

see Pritchard 1995, 20-31.

[78] Moore, Rowell and Strachey 1995, 69.

[79] Ibid., 64 and 68.

[80] Dunbar 1976, 228, quoting the "Estimate of the Duke of Lauderdale's movables at the time of his death, 1682", BPA 24/3/30.

an extent that the duke of Lauderdale caught the building bug only after marrying her, according to Burnet. In this she was exceptional but not unique. Her eldest son's wife, Grace Wilbraham, future countess of Dysart, who was painted, apparently in the garden of Ham House around the time of her marriage in 1680, by John Michael Wright (The Weston Park Foundation),[81] was the daughter of Lady Wilbraham of Weston Park, a building enthusiast, who employed William Taylor (1674) and captain William Winde, a professional gentleman architect like the duchess's cousin, Sir William Bruce.[82] Lady Wilbraham also commissioned the sculptor-architect, Sir William Wilson, to undertake funerary monuments in Weston Church in 1671, a transaction recorded in her annotated copy of Palladio's *First Book of Architecture* (English translation, 1663) in the library at Weston Park.[83] Grace's elder sister, Elizabeth, and her husband Sir Thomas Myddelton, 2nd Bt, employed Taylor at Chirk Castle (NT), in the 1670s, where her mother gave directions on the new additions, including the Long Gallery. [84]

Having inherited her father's property and earldom, the duchess had greater independence than most heiresses. At a time when women's property, possessions, and even their wishes were usually subsumed in those of their husbands, the duchess was fortunate in both her spouses, who treated her liberally both in their lifetimes and in their wills. On Sir Lionel Tollemache's death in 1669, Helmingham and the other Tollemache estates were vested in her as countess of Dysart, on the basis that her son, who had succeeded to his father's baronetcy, would become the 3rd earl of Dysart. He indeed inherited both the Tollemache and the Murray estates and titles on her death in 1698, a unification that continued until the 6th earl died childless in 1821.

The duchess was exceptional for her learning, being better educated than most women and most men. Her wit was also much remarked upon. Her prodigious acumen, energy, and loyalty to the Stuart cause, were also exceptional. These qualities were shared by Lauderdale, and both the duchess and Charles II clearly appreciated such traits, while turning a blind eye to his boorishness, bad manners, bad temper, and moral turpitude. Both the duke and duchess had suffered in the Civil War and it must have been partly to celebrate the Restoration of the Stuart dynasty that they so richly amplified and embellished Ham after their marriage in

---

[81] MacLeod and Marciari Alexander, 2001, no. 80, 180-1.

[82] Colvin 1978 (second edition), under 'Winde, William (-1722)', 902-5.

[83] Ibid., under 'Wilson, Sir William (1641-1710)', 900.

[84] Dean 1983, 24-5 and 51. For the reference to Lady Wilbraham's copy of Palladio, see Colvin 1978, 900.

1672, a process she had begun independently in 1670, having been re-affirmed—as a widow—in her earldom. Queen Catherine of Braganza was her friend, and it was to her that the new State Bedchamber apartment was dedicated. Fashion at Ham was the fashion of the Court, so both the king and queen would have appreciated the novelty and expense of the newly restored house, while realising—as they ascended the Great Staircase to the newly refurbished or constructed State Rooms on the *piano nobile*—that the Lauderdales had built upon the style of the first Caroline reign, when the king's and the duchess's fathers had been close companions. This is borne out in several ways, notably in the Lauderdales' purchase in 1673 for the new Marble Dining Room of a set of overdoor copies after Polidoro da Caravaggio, whose fanciful designs of playing *putti* had inspired Francis Clein's decoration of the Green Closet in the late 1630s.[85]

Reflecting her father's sophisticated tastes during the first great phase of British collecting was her accumulation of small paintings and drawings within her new Duchess's Private Closet along the lines of the paternal Green Closet. Like her father, she favoured Old Masters, or copies of Old Masters, as well as small portraits. The c.1683 "Estimate of Pictures" indicates that she pawned her paintings for ready money, but—unlike the jewels—she also made sure that they were redeemed for her posterity, thus underlining her appreciation of them. More typical of her female contemporaries was her pronounced taste for lacquer and *faux* lacquer furniture (including backstools emblazoned with her initials under a ducal coronet) which was partly for the purpose of drinking new-fangled tea. Her Chinese teapot remains, but the duchess was a-typical in eschewing the massed displays of blue and white porcelain loved by her contemporaries. By 1844, the Duchess's Private Closet was known as the "China Closet" reflecting the porcelain collecting of the 4th earl in the mid-eighteenth century, but in the duchess's day the lacquer shelves were for books, and the 1677, 79 and 83 inventories prove that she was largely immune to the mania for Chinese porcelain first manifested by Dutch and German princesses in the 1630s. Like Charles II's mistresses, however, she loved the display of wealth in interior design, but even the silver-mounted fire furniture and the richest of textiles had already been evident at Ham in the c.1655 inventory taken soon after her father's death. Paris was the source of most new fashions in the duchess's day, and it is hardly surprising that one of her first commissions, between her two marriages, was that of the ebony and silver-mounted table in the Green Closet (Fig.

---

[85] BPA MS 413; 18-24 April 1673: "Paid Mr Norris in full for 6 Peeces after Polidore £30.00.00."

7). Its caryatid-legged design is pure Le Brun and Le Pautre, breathing the sophisticated and extravagant spirit of Louis XIV's court at Versailles. That Elizabeth Dysart fixed her countess's coronet and cipher no less than seven times in silver and silver-gilt upon this new table in her father's Green Closet—as well as installing other similar furniture there, including the two magnificent Kyoto lacquer cabinets—illustrates both her good taste, her addiction to current fashion, and her respect for her patrimony.

The Dysart earldom is now held by John Grant of Rothiemurcus, 13th earl of Dysart (b.1946), having been separated from Ham House since 1835, but the duchess of Lauderdale's other direct descendants, Sir Lyonel Tollemache and his son, Major (Cecil) Lyonel Tollemache, the 4th and 5th baronets (second creation), gave Ham House to the National Trust in 1948. Ham House has thus remained intact, ensuring that the British nation has reaped the benefit of the duke of Lauderdale's bequest to his beloved second duchess. The duke and duchess of Lauderdale are indivisible from the spirit of the place, and Elizabeth Murray, successively Lady Tollemache, countess of Dysart and duchess of Lauderdale, remains to this day the most famous of Ham's many chatelaines, and the most significant in terms of collecting and patronage.

CHAPTER THREE

AGNES BLOCK, A COLLECTOR OF PLANTS AND CURIOSITIES IN THE DUTCH GOLDEN AGE, AND HER FRIENDSHIP WITH MARIA SIBYLLA MERIAN, NATURAL HISTORY ILLUSTRATOR

JOY KEARNEY

Ladies of Leisure

During the seventeenth century, in spite of a succession of European wars, great wealth was to be found in the Northern provinces, with the result that numerous collections of curiosities and art cabinets were created by the landed gentry and the bourgeoisie.[1] Many society ladies at this time were drawn to such hobbies and established important trend-setting collections for themselves. These were, of course, women whose social position and financial circumstances meant that they could indulge themselves in the luxury of collecting at will. They also had the advantage of easy contact with influential individuals and institutions, such as royal and aristocratic circles and the officials of the United Dutch East India Company. Many were either born into, or married into, these social circles, and some inherited the collecting tradition from their fathers or husbands.[2] Collecting art, antiquities or the keeping of a "rariteitenkabinet" or cabinet of curiosities was primarily a male-dominated pastime, which women were encouraged to support and take an interest in but were not expected to initiate themselves. Therefore, few independent women collectors, even though

---

[1] Engel 1986, ii-iv.
[2] Fallon 2003, 1.

some were pioneers in their fields, made major contributions to the history of collecting. Nonetheless, both archival evidence and scholarly traditions obscure the roles women played in Dutch collecting, often giving the credit to their husbands, fathers, or other male members of their families.[3] The arts and the study of the antique was, in fact, a field typically reserved for men.[4]

While most of the women discussed in this essay are not directly connected in any way, they represent chronological development in the history of collecting in the Netherlands, as well as different objects and modes of collecting. While these constitute just a sample of the women who were involved in collecting on a major scale, they were all well-known, prominent members of Dutch society of their time, and contributed to the practice of collecting in the fields of both art and natural history.

A Royal Collector

Even though this essay is concerned with the collecting habits and interests of a number of Dutch ladies of the upper middle classes, their endeavours were nevertheless encouraged by Royal patronage. Queen Mary, a lady of great taste and refinement, was the daughter of James II and his first wife Anne Hyde. Married to her first cousin, the "stadholder" William III, she spent several years in the Netherlands before the Glorious Revolution in Britain forced her father to leave the country and led to her and her husband's joint coronation in 1689. Through her husband and through her time in Holland, Mary had experienced examples of Dutch gardening, of interior decoration and collecting that were going to influence many of her own choices in these fields after her return to Britain.[5] She was instrumental in the development of what came to be known as the "Anglo Dutch garden", a fusion of two distinct cultures.[6]

Mary thus not only became very knowledgable about gardening and botany, she also used her connection with the East India Company to import plants and artefacts from Asia for her own collections, such as the "crystal rose", the "music tree", the "apple of love", the "perfuming cherry of Arabia" and the "silver lotus".[7] While still in Holland, she also started a collection of blue and white Delftware that was eventually going to form the nucleus of the rich holdings of such objects, much of which is housed

---

[3] Ibid., 1.
[4] Ibid.
[5] Dixon Hunt 1988, 8-10.
[6] Ibid, 10.
[7] Ibid.

at Het Loo in Apeldoorn. Her husband shared her interest in gardening and at their two principal houses, Hampton Court and Kensington Palace, they created elaborate new gardens in the Dutch style, comparmentalised into what were known as "parterres", containing neatly trimmed shrubs fashioned into shapes, divided by gravel paths. Many water features were included, as well as statues of Roman gods, as can be seen in many seventeenth century paintings.[8]

The Contribution of the Dutch East India Company

The new awareness of the diversity and complexity of the natural world in the seventeenth century provided artists with the opportunity to paint many new creatures hitherto unknown. The journeys of the Dutch East India Company particularly in the period 1597 to the mid-seventeenth century, meanwhile, resulted in many exotic creatures and tropical plants being imported to the Netherlands.

The Dutch East India Company was founded as an organisation of merchant venturers in order to explore new territories and exploit new products for importation and operated from 1602 to around 1795. While mainly concerned with exploiting the resources of south-east Asia, the company actually brought about considerable wealth for the Dutch middle classes and at the same time contributed to the exploration, cartography and a notable improvement of the knowledge about fauna and flora of the countries under Dutch influence. The success of the Dutch East India Company has been well-documented and the stories of voyages in search of spices, tea and coffee have been told repeatedly, underlining the innovative nature of this extraordinary firm which was in fact the first multinational company, introducing exotica onto the European market.[9]

This period heralded the beginning of a new world view, a new consideration of our fellow creatures and a new approach to painting them. Some painters specialised in the painting of exotic flowers and fruit while others were entirely concerned with painting birds, such as Melchior de Hondecoeter, who painted exotic birds at the menageries of William III at Het Loo and Honselaarsdijk.[10] The taste of the time tended towards the keeping of menageries and botanical collections as a decorative element on the country estate; collectors became increasingly eager to acquire rare

---

[8] See for example the work of Melchior de Hondecoeter, Jan Weenix, Isaac de Moucheron and others.

[9] Wagenaar, 1996, 11-23.

[10] The original Oude Loo was the location of one of the oldest menageries in possession of the Dutch Royal family. See Kearney 2010, 44.

curiosities and unusual, often exotic items with which to impress their visitors.[11] There was competition from abroad as well, since Louis XIV was occupied with the decoration of the gardens and menageries at Versailles, thus the French aristocracy was also interested in having country estates embellished with rare flowers, fruit and exotic creatures. William III even provided animals acquired by the Dutch East India Company for the king's menagerie at the palace of Versailles.

The Fruits of Success: Interest in Botany

Botanical collections and the science of botany seem to have appealed to many of the ladies who formed collections in the Northern Netherlands in the Early Modern period. Magdalena Poulle (1632-99), for example, was the widow of an Amsterdam merchant and a well-known botanical collector who bought Kasteel Gunterstein in 1680 and restored it from a mere ruin to its former glory. Her cousin, the botanist Jan Commelin, commissioner of the Hortus Medicus in Amsterdam, was responsible for the introduction of the tropical hothouse in 1684, which made it possible to grow tropical plants.[12] He had valuable connections in the botanical world both in England and at Leiden. The hothouse became a popular feature in the gardens of the more affluent members of society, and Poulle also possessed one. The hothouse first became known around 1684-5 and was the only manner of propagating tropical species. Poulle's name is firmly associated with the development of Dutch garden history and her contribution included the fact that she had also formed one of the most remarkable collections of plants in the Dutch Republic. After her death her brother sold part of her orangery collection, and the advertisement published in 1699 mentions individual species such as lemons, limes, jasmines, arbutus and oleander, as well as other bulbs, strange fruits and foreign tree roots.[13]

Among the items that were principally collected in the seventeenth century were plants of all varieties, many of them collected abroad by members of the Dutch East India crews, and fruit was a very desirable commodity, the more exotic the better. Inspired by the variety and profusion of fruit being grown in the Netherlands, collectors sought to produce new varieties and introduce new products on the market. During the Dutch Golden Age there was substantial fruit production in Holland

---

[11] Ibid., 47-9.
[12] Sikkens-de Zwaan 2002, .206-10. The pineapple was a particular favourite.
[13] Ibid., 216.

with apples, pears and plums being both popular and easily available. As can be seen from still life paintings of the period, common species of cherries and various berries were plentiful, and if grapes were present then this was a symbol of luxury and wealth. Grapes presented a challenge to the painters of the day, as to reproduce a ripe, shiny grape took a great deal of skill and an understanding of the effects of light on the skin of the grape. Fruit such as lemons and limes were expensive in the seventeenth century, and the Chinese bitter orange, also included in some still life paintings, was a symbol of royalty.

The Dutch East India Company returned to the Netherlands from the colonies with seeds, bulbs and roots from exotic destinations, and this changed the production and consumption of fruit in the Netherlands for good.[14] It also had a major impact on the depiction of fruit in still life paintings, which helped to document lifestyles and indeed diet and health in the seventeenth century. Fruit such as the pomegranate is regularly to be seen in such still life paintings, as indeed are grapes and other imported fruit.[15] This indicated a tendency to want to taste the "fruits of success", perhaps referring to the successful foreign conquests of the East India Company abroad, and was indeed also a sign that globalisation had begun. Fruit was frequently used in a symbolic manner in still life pictures, sometimes having sexual or religious implications. A pomegranate, for example, used in combination with a religious accoutrement such as a crucifix or chalice, could be seen as a reference to the blood of Christ and to his Resurrection from the dead. Such sumptuous exotic fruits were thus instrumental in enriching the art of still life and as such were a great added value in Dutch cultural life.

The above-mentioned example of Magdalena Poulle attests to the fact that botanical collecting was greatly advanced in the seventeenth century thanks to certain notable women whose interest in plants and flowers went far beyond the decorative and was much more scientifically oriented. Their focus was on building up private collections of hitherto unknown tropical plants and on the attempt to propagate them from imported seeds. Paintings and drawings of many different species frequently had both a decorative as well as an illustrative and documentary function. The shared interest gave rise to friendships between some of the collectors and artists of the day, most notably between Agnes Block, a wealthy landowner and collector of exotic plants, and Maria Sybilla Merian, a brilliant artist and

---

[14] Coppens 2005, no pagination.
[15] Grapes are not native to the Netherlands, but grapes and grapevines have appeared in Dutch paintings and prints since the seventeenth century.

draughtswoman who painted both plants and animals.[16] Such connections helped to form banks of knowledge on particular subject areas, to stimulate the study of plant biology and to kick off research into the conditions necessary for propagation.

Agnes Block and Magdalena Poulle gained a reputation as experts in the field of collecting and propagating various species of plants and had access to exotic species via their contacts with the East India Company. This was very advantageous as they were able to order seeds and bulbs from every expedition and thus built up extraordinary collections of such rare and wonderful plants as pineapple and banana, exotic flowers and tropical plants of all descriptions.[17]

Agnes Block—Flora Batava

As a nineteen-year old orphan Agnes Block married the wealthy silk merchant Hans de Wolf, a nephew of the renowned Dutch poet and dramatist Joost van den Vondel, in Amsterdam in 1649. She was very close to van den Vondel, after whom Vondelpark is named. When Agnes became a widow at the age of forty, she used the money she inherited from her husband to realise her dream: she bought a country estate at auction in Loenen aan de Vecht, a small Dutch town, with a piece of land on the river Vecht and established gardens and ponds, hence the name "De Vijverhof".[18] It soon became a popular attraction for Amsterdam and Utrecht patricians, who marvelled at its flower beds, groves of trees and manicured hedges, as well as the greenhouses of exotic plants with mysterious flowers and scents. Eventually, her collection became the nucleus of the Botanical Gardens in Leiden, the famous Hortus Botanicus.

In fact, Agnes Block had become a keen amateur botanist whose passion for plants led her to commission the Dutch East India Company to bring back specimens to adorn her botanical garden. In due course she was going to make a substantial contribution to the science of botany. She became fascinated by stories of an exotic fruit with an Indian name: *nana meant* which means "kostelijke vrucht" or "expensive fruit". During the second voyage of Columbus (1493-1496) one of his crew described the pineapple as follows:

> There were plants that looked like artichokes, but then four times the size and with fruits growing out of them, like pine cones but twice as big. These

---

[16] Reitsma, 2008, 19-37.
[17] Sikkens-de Zwaan, 2002, 206-20.
[18] "vijver" is the Dutch word for pond.

fruits taste very nice and are easily cut with a knife, like a beet.[19]

Having acquired seeds of this unusual fruit, Agnes was not satisfied until she became the first in the country to grow a pineapple. The propagation of the pineapple, however, proved time-consuming and great patience and dedication was required.The British botanist John Rose had produced a ripe pineapple for King Charles II in England in 1675. Eventually, and perhaps even inspired by his example, Agnes succeeded as well in producing a pineapple fruit, which seemed to originate from a myriad of small flowers which then together made up one fruit—a true marvel of nature! It was such a major event that a silver medal was created by the silversmith Jan Boskam on which she is depicted as the goddess Flora, standing in front of a potted pineapple plant with in the background the garden at De Vijverhof. On the other side she is seen as *Flora Batava.*

Agnes is depicted in a group portrait by Jan Weenix together with her second husband Sybrand de Flines and their children in her botanical garden (Fig. 11).[20] Agnes Block remarried after the death of her first husband, this time to a widower with two daughters. The family are depicted in an elegant and yet very personal family portrait that includes De Vijverhof with its greenhouses, aviaries and exotic plant species in the background. In this portrait the artist has also included a pineapple plant very prominently in the lower left foreground.

Figure 11: Jan Weenix, portrait of Agnes Block and Sybrand de Flines and their children in front of De Vijverhof, c.1694, Amsterdam Museum.

---

[19] Coppens, 1997, 19.
[20] Amsterdam Museum inv.no.SA20359.

Figure 12: Georg Gsell, portrait of Maria Sibylla Merian, hand-coloured counterproof, 1717, Artis Library, Amsterdam.

Agnes Block approached botany in a scientific manner, having read a great deal of specialist literature in several different languages on the subject. She ensured her collection was carefully documented.[21] She employed about twenty painters, specialising in botanical and zoological items, to paint plants and flowers propagated by her, as well as birds, in hundreds of watercolours. These included Herman Saftleven, Pieter and Alida Withoos, Maria Sibylla Merian (Fig. 12) and her daughter Johanna Herolts-Graff, Pieter Holsteijn, Maria Moninckx and Johannes Bronkhorst. It appears from dated drawings by Saftleven, among others, that the artists

---

[21] Old herbal almanacs, the *Florilegium* of Emmanuel Sweerts (Frankfurt 1612), Adriaan van Berkel's notes on his voyages (Amsterdam 1695) and the botanical writings of Caspar Commelin are just a few examples of what she would have had access to as sources of botanical knowledge.

spent longer periods of time at Vijverhof. These scientifically accurate drawings, which were divided into a number of volumes, were purchased after the death of Agnes Block by Valerius Röver from Delft and were later dispersed. Due entirely to the catalogue that Röver made of his collection in 1730, it is known exactly which plants and flowers Agnes Block commissioned drawings of, as well as from whom. From her own detailed notes it is known what was contained in her collection before Röver had access to it. This is rare and valuable information which provides an insight into her collecting habits and her network as a collector. On some of these drawings she even wrote these details on the reverse. This was in the form of explanatory notes to further specify what should be illustrated and add interest and information and thus amplify the enjoyment of owning such drawings. In the Rijksmuseum's print room in Amsterdam there are two sheets of paper in one of these "flower books" in which she wrote precise instructions to the artist regarding exactly what she wanted depicted.[22]

On the occasion of her death in 1704 Vijverhof was sold. The gardens gradually disappeared during the eighteenth century and, sadly, the house was demolished in 1813. Most of her valuables were sold and therefore dispersed. Valerius Röver purchased not only the flower books and the bird book but also the majority of paintings from Blocks collection.[23] Nothing remains, however, of her own cuttings and drawings.[24]

Metamorphosis and the Meeting of Science and Art

Maria Sybilla Merian (1647-1717; Fig. 12) was one of the foremost scientific painters of her day and one of the few to have left such a rich legacy of natural history drawings and paintings of this early period. Her extraordinary rendering of the life cycle of insects and other small animals ensured her popularity and her exquisite attention to detail in painting the metamorphosis of tiny creatures places her well before her time. She and her daughter were commissioned by Agnes Block in 1695, 1696 and 1697 to paint, on vellum, all manner of plants, insects and birds in Block's garden.[25] Interestingly, Maria Sybilla Merian produced a magnificent illustration of a pineapple as the first illustration in her book *The Surinam*

---

[22] Coppens 1997, 19-23.

[23] Röver was a citizen of high standing who owned an unrivalled *kunstkabinet* and lived in Delft, near the Prinsenhof. He evidently made these purchases to further expand his *kunstkabinet*.

[24] Missel in http://library.wur.nl/alida/Alida_Frameset/alidaframeset_h3_1.htm.

[25] Reitsma 2008, 125.

Insect Book (1705; Fig. 13), where it is shown surrounded by cockroaches.

At the time Merian's *Metamorphosis* was published in 1705, her masterpiece paved the way for a new approach to natural history and natural history collections. This folio with its magnificent detailed insights and extremely high quality of artwork, was the first book published by a female European artist-naturalist who had travelled as far as the New World specifically to study certain elements of the natural world. All or most of the organisms portrayed in it were painted from living specimens she had collected, and many were kept by Merian for study. In a communication to James Petiver, she related how she was not interested in merely cataloguing exotic specimens, but in the "formation, propagation, and metamorphosis of creatures, how one emerges from the other, the nature of their diet."[26] This was quite an extraordinary focus for a woman of her time, and the emphasis on the life cycles, behaviour and interactions of the species depicted make *Metamorphosis* one of the first ecological studies (though this term had not yet even been invented). Soon after it was published, copies of this book as well as many of the original watercolour illustrations found their way into the eminent collections of such well-known names as Sir Hans Sloane and Richard Mead. There was, moreover, considerable distribution in the form of copies of the images such as those of James Petiver in his 1767 natural history volume. Maria Sybilla Merian's influence was very extensive and may be seen in several important natural history studies that followed. Her work had a huge impact on both art and scientific illustration and influenced the ways in which the organisms were viewed on a larger scale, and she is extremely popular right up to the present, with several exhibitions and publications having been devoted to her work. She continues to fascinate the general public with her minutely-detailed and decorative glimpses into the lives of the tiny creatures she collected and painted.

---

[26] Ibid., 125.

Figure 13: Maria Sybilla Merian, *Pineapple and Cockroaches*, hand-coloured etching, 1705, Artis Library, Amsterdam.

The popularity enjoyed by Maria Sybilla Merian still remains unrivalled to this day, and this is indeed no surprise given the intricacy and fine detail in her depictions of insect and spider life cycles, flowers in various stages of opening from bud to full-blown bloom, and small animals in very naturalistic poses such as lizards, snakes and other reptiles and amphibians. Merian combined science and art to produce some of the first detailed drawings of insect life cycles (Fig. 14). Exotic birds also featured in her work, and were painted accurately according to their species (Fig. 15), providing valuable natural history information about the species she observed. With the still life painter Jacob Marrel as her stepfather, it is not surprising that she turned to natural history and devoted herself to painting detail, and in 1665 she married his apprentice, Johann Andreas Graaf.

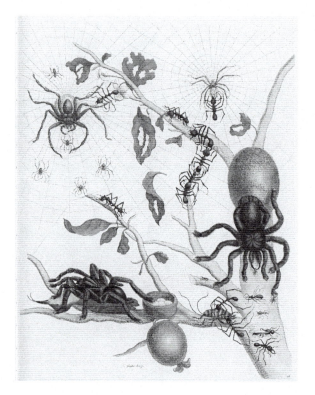

Figure 14: Maria Sybilla Merian, *Guava Tree with Tarantulas and Leaf-cutter Ants*, hand-coloured etching, 1719.

Together with Graff, she produced a book of flowers, the first part appearing in 1675; a second edition, enlarged by volumes 2 and 3, was produced in 1680, entitled *Florum fasciculi tres*. It included 36 engravings intended to serve as patterns for embroidery. Only five copies of this book have survived. The illustrations are remarkably detailed and refined, showing not only artistic merit but also scientific rigour and an in-depth understanding of the natural world.

Figure 15: Maria Sybilla Merian, *Cardinal's Guard, Idomeneus Giant Owl*, plate 60 from *Metamorphosis Insectorum Surinamensium* (1705), watercolour on vellum, 1701-1705, Artis Library Amsterdam.

Dutch Women Collectors of the Golden Age

While Agnes Block and Maria Sybilla Merian constitute two particularly important and well-known examples of female collectors and illustrators interested in botany during the Dutch Golden Age, they were by no means alone in their endeavours. Even though it is not always easy to find out the amount of work ladies with a mind for botany contributed to the emerging science, we are gradually able to gain a clearer picture. In what follows, a few examples of lady collectors operating contemporaneously with Agnes Block will be listed. That does not necessarily mean that they knew, were friends with, or were inspired by Agnes Block directly, but it is nonetheless indicative of the fascination collecting exercised on ladies of the upper middle classes and of the funds they were prepared to spend on their hobbies.

Petronella de la Court (1624-1707) was a woman of independent means, indulging in pastimes befitting her social standing. One of the most famous pieces in her collection was the dolls' house or "poppenhuis" from 1670-1690 now on display in the Centraal Museum in Utrecht.[27] The dolls'house was commissioned in 1670 and took almost twenty years to complete. Eleven rooms are reproduced and many objects are in fact tiny replicas of actual pieces owned by de la Court. In total there are 1600 objects represented in this marvellously crafted dolls' house. Obviously, rather than being a toy for children, this dolls' house was created for the amusement of its grown-up owner. Shortly after her death in 1707 de la Court's collection was auctioned; on this occasion it transpired that she was the owner of no less than 150 paintings.[28] The auction catalogue mentioned that she had amassed her collection over a period of 50 years "with great cost and effort", comprising porcelain, paintings, drawings and curiosities.[29] Her collection was very well documented, even considered to have been on a level with that of the famous collector and Rembrandt patron Jan Six.[30] Her painting collection consisted of old master paintings as well as of paintings from her own time; principally portraits, genre and mythological subjects.

Sarah Hinlopen (1660-1749), daughter of the linen merchant Jan Hinlopen, was another important collector whose beautiful Amsterdam canal house is now the Geelvinck-Hinlopen House Museum. It was built in 1687 by Albert Geelvinck in celebration of his marriage to the much younger Sarah. Her originally Flemish family were cloth merchants and her grandfather Jacob Hinlopen had been a merchant in spices with connections to the Enkhuizen chamber of the Dutch East India Company. Sarah turned out to be the longest living member of her family, and died at almost 89 years old. One of her in-laws mentioned in his diary that she had been blind for a few years but had enjoyed good general health nonetheless.

---

[27] The Centraal Museum, Utrecht.

[28] Fallon 2003, 1.

[29] Ibid., 1. The quotation in Dutch reads as follows: : "Met grote kosten en moeite in meer dan 50 jaren bij een vergaard en nagelaten door Petronella de la Court, weduwe wijlen Adam Oortmans, in zijn leven brouwer in de Zwaan." (English: with great cost and effort in more than 50 years amassed and bequeathed by Petronella de la Court, widow of the late Adam Oortmans, in life a brewer in 'The Swan'; translation by author).

[30] Ibid., 1.

We know that Sarah was portrayed by Gabriel Metsu together with her parents and siblings in the Amsterdam canal house she inhabited. This was a measure of the family's prominence and wealth since Metsu was fashionable and most probably an expensive portrait painter, and Sarah continued this trend, her income having been estimated in 1742 at 8,000 guilders per annum. When she died in 1749 she had amassed a fortune of 350,000 guilders, which was a very considerable estate at that time. The house, situated on the Keizersgracht in a very fashionable area of Amsterdam, was beautifully furnished and decorated in a taste befitting the finest houses in the seventeenth century.

Not having had children, on the occasion of her death in 1729 most of her possessions, including the house, her stocks and shares, her paintings and her books, and cash were divided into lots and passed to her sister-in-law, nephew and his three sisters. The last will and testament unfortunately does not mention any paintings individually, and this may have been due to the fear of incurring inheritance tax.

Maria de Wilde (1682-1729) was a very accomplished Amsterdam draftswoman, poet and collector who made drawings of her father's "kunstkabinet" and added to his collection with items she chose herself, notably antiquities. Her father was chief commissioner of the Amsterdam Admiralty. Collections of antiquities were greatly appreciated at the time due to the recognition of the importance of ancient Roman sculpture and architecture. She married Gijsbert de Lange, a commander in the Amsterdam Admiralty. This undoubtedly ensured a secure future and allowed her to indulge in her creative hobbies. She made detailed drawings of individual pieces from her father's collection, leaving us a valuable record of collecting and taste in the late seventeenth and beginning of the eighteenth century.

The number of women in possession of extraordinary collections in the late seventeenth and early eighteenth century in the Netherlands was nothing short of extraordinary, and yet little has been written about this subject to date. While much literature exists regarding the work of Maria Sibylla Merian, many of the other collectors mentioned here have hardly been mentioned in publications devoted to collecting, and can only be given cursory treatment here. They are, however, worthy of note, and their contributions were considerable. Together they constitute a movement of pioneers for the preservation and promotion of art, science, history and natural history at a time when women were not associated with such pursuits.

Conclusion

While the names mentioned here may not be known, or certainly not well known, outside of the Netherlands, these women were nevertheless nationally important and even acquired fame during their lifetime. These women, and many more besides, played a major role in the history of collecting of *naturalia*, art and other objects, paving the way for future museum collections and curiosity cabinets, many of which survive to this day. The importance of their collecting work was enriched by their writings, indexing or ordering of thei possessions: in some cases they made a very serious contribution to the history of collecting and took up a pioneering role in the distribution of knowledge during the second half of the seventeenth century.

Dutch women collectors, like their peers all over the world, have been largely neglected until very recently, as being collectors of the superficial and the frivolous. Their work has been obscured by time and as well as frequently by lack of documentary evidence. Their stories are now starting to be explored in order to set the record straight. They were not simply helpmates of their husbands and fathers, as was frequently insinuated, but were learned women in their own right who helped to form a very specific taste in the seventeenth century and beyond. It is due to some of these pioneering collectors that we have such developed fields of collecting in botany, antiquities, as well as an in-depth knowledge of plant, animal and insect biology, and this was no mean achievement in the era in which they lived.

Chapter Four

The Treasures of Countess Erzsébet Rákóczi (1654-1707)

Orsolya Bubryák

This article identifies and describes works of art that were once in the possession of a seventeenth-century Hungarian noblewoman, Countess Erzsébet Rákóczi (1654-1707). She is primarily known for her literary activity and considerable correspondence—she was one of the first aristocratic poetesses in Hungary;[1] her letters to her husband were published in 2001.[2] This paper seeks to contribute to the research of her "art collection" and to introduce the long-forgotten art patronage of this lady to an international forum.[3]

Family Tragedies

Erzsébet Rákóczi (Fig. 16) was born into a very wealthy aristocratic family in Hungary. Her great-grandfather was Zsigmond Rákóczi (1544/54-1608), ruling prince of Transylvania and the descendants of his oldest son were elected princes of Transylvania as well. The last elected prince was Erzsébet's nephew Ferenc II Rákóczi (1676-1735). He is today revered as a Hungarian national hero who led the war for Hungarys independence (1703-1711) against the Habsburgs. Erzsébet's grandfather Pál Rákóczi (1596-1636) was the youngest son of Prince Zsigmond who held the office of *judex curiae* (Lord Chief Justice of the Court of Hungary), the second-highest dignity of the country. His son, László

---

[1] Thaly 1900, 481-94; Angyal 1901, 359-60; Uhl 1995, 82-8; Kovács 1996, 121-7.
[2] Benda and Várkonyi 2001.
[3] I wish to thank Éva Bicskei and Andrea Gáldy for their help in translating my text into English.

Rákóczi (1633-1664), father of Erzsébet Rákóczi, was Lord Lieutenant in
the county Sáros. He had a promising military career ahead of him, but
was killed in a battle against the Turks at Nagyvárad (Oradea, today
Romania) in 1664.[4] Erzsébet had lost her mother one year earlier, so she
became an orphan when only ten years old.

Figure 16: Portrait of Erzsébet Rákóczi; nineteenth-century copy after a lost
seventeenth-century painting, oil on canvas, private collection.

Being the only living descendant of her parents, and the last
representative of the younger branch of the Rákóczi family, Erzsébet
became the sole heir to a vast fortune. Her estates were located in the
North, in Upper Hungary (today: Slovakia) and in the South, in Croatia.

---

[4] Horn 1990b, 61-90.

An influential family, the Erdődys, at that time deeply in debt, managed to win the hand of the fourteen-year old girl in 1668. Although the marriage had been decided by Erzsébet's guardians, it seemed to be promising. The chosen fiancé, Ádám Erdődy, the colonel of Petrinavár (Petrograd, today Croatia) (Fig. 17) was a young and educated officer who spoke several languages and soon earned the love of the young girl. His portrait, dated to 1668, was painted probably not much before their wedding by a Flemish master active in Vienna, Frans Luyckx.[5] Three weeks after their marriage the young husband was also killed in a battle against the Turks.

Figure 17: Frans Luyckx(?): Portrait of Ádám Erdődy, 1668 (inscribed with the incorrect date of 1680), oil on canvas, private collection.

This tragedy resulted in what might be called as the first flowering of her art patronage: she organised a splendid funerary ceremony for her beloved spouse, and erected a monument in the cathedral of Szepeshely

---

[5] The later inscription on the painting contains incorrect data.

(now Spišska Kapitula, Slovakia) that still exists today.[6] The iconographic programme of the monument surrounded by military trophies is much influenced by the campaign against the Turks. In the upper part one can see *The Woman Clothed with the Sun with the Moon* (i.e. the Turkish crescent moon) *under her Feet*. On either side stand two important Hungarian saints and kings: St. Stephen and St. Ladislaus. In the lower part of the shield, St. George on horseback commemorates the dead officer. Through the symbolism of the epitaph, Erzsébet assigned the heroic death of her husband to the main protectors of Hungary and Europe. The programme was not her own invention: its exact model can be found in the Jesuit church in Nagyszombat (now: Trnava, Slovakia), where a similar epitaph was created for Count László Esterházy, killed likewise in a battle against the Turks. This epitaph was raised by his younger brother, Pál Esterházy, who became later the palatine of Hungary.[7] But the Erdődy family did not want to lose the huge Rákóczi property: Erzsébet was soon prevailed upon by her family to marry another Erdődy, György, the cousin of her first husband. The only existing portrait of Erzsébet (Fig. 16) is a nineteenth-century copy of poor quality of a lost original which may have been painted at the beginning of the 1670s, not long after her second marriage.

Erzsébet's second marriage was a failure from the very beginning; György Erdődy was primarily interested in building his own career and spent most of his life at the court in Vienna where Erzsébet never visited him. They lived apart for most of their lives, and they were in contact mainly by correspondence. The ideals of the young girl were her father and first husband, two heroes who in their twenties gave their lives to defend the country. In her letters written to others Erzsébet mocked her courtier husband calling him "Servusko". She took him to be a coward and, hence, was scornful of him. The events of the year 1684 demonstrate the couple's very different habits. In that year the army of Imre Thököly,[8] leader of an uprising against the Habsburgs, marched towards Vienna and wanted to attack Erzsébet's castle at Makovicza. György Erdődy and his wife, hearing the news of the advancing army fled to Vienna. Erzsébet however turned back on the road in order to secure her property kept in the

---

[6] Ludiková, Mikó and Pálffy 2007, 327-8.

[7] Galavics 1986, 85-8; Galavics 1992.

[8] Imre Thököly (1657-1705) was prince of Upper Hungary between 1682 and 1685, in 1690 he became prince of Transylvania and leader of an anti-Habsburg uprising (1678-1690) in alliance with the Turks. In June 1682 he married Ilona Zrínyi, the widow of prince Ferenc I Rákóczi; therefore he was the stepfather of Erzsébet Rákóczi's nephew, Prince Ferenc II Rákóczi.

castle and to defend her estate with arms against the uprising. When Thököly's army occupied the castle and Erzsébet was captured, it was the king of Poland rather than György Erdődy to procure her release. Since Erzsébet did not have confidence in her husband's ability to defend her and her property, she retreated into voluntary exile in Poland.[9]

The most important factor to embitter their relationship might have been that György Erdődy handled his wife—and all her possessions—as if he were her guardian. Without asking for her permission or approval, he mortgaged and sold some of the Rákóczi estates. He was entitled do so, since Erzsébet had signed a marriage contract that gave full authority to her husband concerning her estates. The young wife reacted, however, with surprising force and determination.[10] In 1685 she left her husband and started divorce proceedings, which was considered a scandalous act in the predominantly Catholic kingdom of Hungary. Erzsébet persisted in her decision even though she was threatend by the archbishop of Esztergom entrusted with the re-conciliation, Lipót Kollonich, to spend the rest of her life in a convent. While the Viennese court and public opinion supported clearly the case of the husband, Erzsébet had her own supporters as well. She was backed by her friend, the Palatine Pál Esterházy and Ferenc II Rákóczi. While having reached an agreement as a conclusion of a long and desperate fight in 1696, nevertheless she still continued to live separated from her husband. Erzsébet was finally able to achieve relative independence in that she managed to handle her own possession freely. Managing her landed estates with an iron hand, she tried to overcome the difficulties caused by the rebellion led by Imre Thököly.

Nevertheless, the independence she finally gained, was soon lost due to the War of Independence (1703-1711) conducted by her dearly beloved nephew, Ferenc II Rákóczi. As the former wife of a court official loyal to the emperor, Erzsébet had to flee once more from Upper-Hungary and from 1704 onwards she lived in Croatia. Much as she longed to do so, she was never going to be able to leave Croatia again and died in exile in November 1707.

From the reality of her personal tragedy, Erzsébet Rákóczi fled into the past; she escaped to her memories. Her collecting activity and art patronage can be understood as a form of commemoration; namely, the cultivation of the memory of her beloved relatatives, whom she had lost far too early.

---

[9] Erzsébet Rákóczi's letter to Imre Erdődy (father of her first husband), dated: Cracow, 12 May 1684. HHStA, FAE, Lad. 101. fasc. 19. without pagination.

[10] Benda and Várkonyi 2001, 12.

She was only nine years old when she lost her mother, Erzsébet
Bánffy. Two decades after her mother's death, however, she commemorated
her befittingly by commissioning a large posthumous funerary painting in
the Carmelite chapel of the Kistapolcsány mansion. It has several
inscriptions and verses in Hungarian and Latin. Erzsébet Bánffy is portrayed
as lying on the tomb between two angels, and her soul is personified by
the figure of a young woman being carried towards Our Lady of Mount
Carmel by another angel.[11]

The depiction of Our Lady of Mount Carmel in the painting must have
been very important for Erzsébet Rákóczi, since the Chapel in which it
hung was the place where she herself had founded a Carmelite
confraternity in 1687. On the altar of the chapel, a painting of Our Lady of
Mount Carmel was placed—allegedly a personal gift from Pope Innocent
XI. Only a year after founding the confraternity, pilgrims were making
their way to the Kistapolcsány chapel and the tradition of pilgrimages is
continues today.

The other important point of reference in her life may have been her
father, László Rákóczi, whose personality, despite his early death, had a
huge effect on the small child. László Rákóczi was known as a talented
commander, whose political career had been interrupted by his unexpected
death at an early age. A short period of his life is well documented in his
diary (1653-1658).[12] His *memoires*, sketch the portrait of a Hungarian
nobleman, who spent his time mainly hunting, gambling or managing his
estates, but at the same time one can also follow his inquisitive and
receptive attitude to the arts.

Erzsébet inherited the inexhaustible, wild character of her father as
well as his passion for hunting. The big game trophies hunted by her, were
still exhibited in the castle of Kistapolcsány in the nineteenth century. She
loved her horses so much that she even wrote a poem about them. This is
the reason why she was given the title of "Diana of Kistapolcsány" in later
literature. As well as the passionate character of her father, she inherited
his versatility and his interest in the fine arts. Although this part of her life
is not well known, she seems to have continued her father's patronage of
the arts.

This can be observed especially in the formation of her silver collection.
Her correspondence, as well as her inventories, contains information about
her regular commissions filled by goldsmiths in Vienna and Bratislava
—an example of following in the footsteps of her father. She preserved her

---

[11] Garas 1953, 121; Buzási 1975, 103, 117; Rusina 1998, 455. Cat. No. 194. (Jozef
Medvecký).
[12] Horn 1990a.

inherited valuables with great care and tried thereafter to complete the collection. Erzsébet provided every piece with a mark of ownership. But instead of using her own name, she put the monograms of her parents László Rákóczi and Erzsébet Bánffy (C.L.R.D.F.V.—C.E.B.D.N. = Comes Ladislaus Rákóczi de Felső-Vadász—Comitissa Elisabetha Bánffy de Nagy-Mihály) on her silver dishes.

As these examples testify, the art patronage and commissions of Erzsébet Rákóczi were basically connected to the commemoration of the deceased members of her family. There was, however, a living person as well who had an enormous effect on her: Prince Pál Esterházy. He was her friend and patron, and at the same time, he can be considered as her model in art patronage as well as in piety. Based on their correspondence, one can assume that the Palatine Esterházy was Erzsébet's most important confidant until her death. Their friendship started when Erzsébet was 16-17 years old and their correspondence lasted to the final years she spent in exile in Croatia.

Although the scale of her art patronage can not be compared with that of the palatine of the country, one can detect some elements characteristic of his art patronage programme in Erzsébet's own commissions. For example, similar to Pál Esterházy perpetuation of the memory of the heroic death of his brother in the battle at Vezekény, Erzsébet raised a monument to her heroic first husband. As count Esterházy had done, Erzsébet Rákóczi linked the commemoration of her husband to the cult of St. Ladislaus, a Hungarian saint famous for his fight against the pagans.

On his estates, Pál Esterházy created several places for pilgrimages. Thus it may have been his example that led Erzsébet to found a place of pilgrimage in Kistapolcsány. She went several times on pilgrimage to Mariazell and donated together with her husband a statue of the Virgin Mary to the shrine. In 1691 she erected an altar in the chapel of the Holy Blood of the Benedictine abbey of Garamszentbenedek (Hronský Beňadik, Slovakia).[13] Unfortunately, none of these donations have survived. She may have visited the castle of Pál Esterházy in Frakno (today: Forchtenstein, Austria) several times during her life, and she certainly knew and admired the legendary treasury of the prince. The treasury could have provided a model for her collecting activity as well. Although her treasury was dispersed soon after her death, its inventories prove that she had a great and important collection.

---

[13] Koptik s.d.; Haiczl 1913. 128-9.

Documentary Evidence

Erzsébet Rákóczi made several inventories listing her own jewellery and tableware during her lifetime. There are seven extant inventories in the archive of the Erdődys. The fact that she prepared so many inventories of her wealth, tells much of her tumultuous life full of pain, complicated by the controversies with her second husband. Although she had to leave her estates during Thököly's uprising and Rákóczi's War of Independence and although, as a result, her estates were ruined, leaving her without income, she managed to save her valuables on both occasions and to take them with her on her peregrinations. Her treasures remained all she owned and, after leaving her estates, these objects remained the last tangible links to her family. This may be the reason why her silver and jewellery were inventoried again and again with every precious stone counted with meticulous care. She made notes about the weight and the size of her precious objects; moreover, she noted how each item had been acquired, whether she had commissioned it, received it as a gift or inherited the object in question. These exact notes of provenance attest to her very individual attitude toward art collecting: In the inventories of other families—or other members of her own family—the provenance has never had any importance, only the value of the objects counted. Others considered the collectibles as mere parts of the active capital: valuables that could easily be moved or be converted into cash. They made no efforts to keep them together and sold them in case of necessity. But there is no evidence of Erzsébet having ever sold any piece inherited from her parents, even though she was often pressed for money.

The first inventory was drawn up in January, 1694.[14] It contains only jewellery that could be documented before the death of Erzsébet. There are some additional notes in the list and some objects are deleted, signaling that these were not in her possession anymore. These notes were done soon after the death of Erzsébet, in November, 1707. The fate of the jewels can be followed by three other lists drawn up in Croatia, but unfortunately the objects can not be identified and their whereabouts are unknown today.

The inventories listing silver dishes date from the period of her Croatian journeys. Earlier she had kept her treasury in the castle of Hrussó (Hrussov, now Slovakia) belonging to the Rákóczi estates but later moved it to Croatia. One of them was drawn up in December, 1704.[15] She listed in it all those items that she took with herself from her Upper Hungarian estates. This inventory is not complete, since it cited "a previous general

---

[14] ÖStA, HHStA, FAE, Lad. 82. fasc. 3. No. 3/1.
[15] ÖStA, HHStA, FAE, Lad. 82. fasc. 3. No. 3/2.

inventory" made in Hrussó. The original, unfortunately, has not survived. Two years later, in 1706, she made a new inventory, listing only those objects that she inherited from her parents or commissioned to be made from the silver she inherited.[16] A third inventory survives as well, which listed all movable properties remaining in Hungary after her death, made in January 1708.[17]

The history of the objects once in the possession of Erzsébet Rákóczi can be documented for a few years after her death. According to the contract of marriage entered with her husband in 1672, all of her movable and immovable properties were inherited by her husband. Two years after her death, in 1709, György Erdődy made an inventory of these objects.[18] This list contains almost all of the tableware of Erzsébet. Four years later, after the death of György Erdődy in 1713, some of the most beautiful objects left the Erdődy collection, since they were inherited by different aristocrats, according to the Will of György Erdődy.[19] For example, a gilded mother-of-pearl cup decorated with a pelican belonging to Erzsébet, went into the possession of the Pálffy family, and after a long and adventurous journey and several auctions, it came into the collection of the Museum für Kunst und Gewerbe, Hamburg.[20] The cup bears the monogram of the parents of Erzsébet (C.L.R.D.F.V.—C.E.B.D.N.M); it is not mentioned, however, in the 1706 inventory of the interitance from her parents. It can be identified, nonetheless, in the other inventory of 1704. This would suggest that this cup will have been an object bought by Erzsébet to complete her parents' collection.

The less valuable silverware, candlesticks and silver dishes for everyday use have gradually disappeared from written sources. It is difficult to identify them even if they have remained in the Erdődy family's houses. But we can trace the path of the valuable ones. A certain György Erdődy, nephew of her husband, established the Erdődy entail (*fideicommissum*) in personal property with the most valuable silver dishes and other objects and moved the newly created treasury to Galgóc (Hlohovec, Slovakia). From that time the Rákóczi objects shared the fate of the Erdődy treasury.

The art collection of the Erdődy counts, kept in the Galgóc castle until the beginning of the twentieth century, was one of the most prestigious in Hungary. Masterpieces, such as the throne carpet of King Matthias

---

[16] ÖStA, HHStA, FAE, Lad. 82. fasc. 3. No. 3/3.
[17] Szerémi 1878, 126-30.
[18] SNA, ÚAE, Lad. 82. fasc. 3. No. 6.
[19] ÖStA, HHStA, FAE, Lad. 3. fasc. 4. No. 1.
[20] Museum für Kunst und Gewerbe, Hamburg. Inv. 1957/55a-b; see Rückert 1960, 201; Grotte 2008, 381.

Corvinus, made in Florence in the second half of the fifteenth century (today in the Magyar Nemzeti Múzeum, hereafter Hungarian National Museum), or the late Gothic wooden sculpture from the main altar of St. Martin's cathedral in Bratislava, the so-called *Nativity of Galgóc*, today the pride of the Slovakian National Gallery, were once part of the collection.

The Dispersal of Erzsébet's Collection

While most of the aristocratic art collections begun to be dispersed in the nineteenth century as the members of impoverished families sold the pieces of their treasures, the Erdődy family succeeded in keeping the collection together until the beginning of the twentieth century. In the summer of 1911, the millionaire John Pierpont Morgan sent two agents to offer seven million *Kronen* for the whole Erdődy treasury, but the family insisted on keeping its art collection.[21] Nine years later, after the Erdődy family had lost its landed estate in Northern Hungary (as the whole territory became part of the newly created Republic of Cechoslovakia), a consortium—its identity remained unknown—offered one and a half million Swiss Francs for the collection, but did not reach a deal. The family preferred to exchange the silver objects for real estate in Hungary, therefore they offered the treasures to the Hungarian National Museum.[22]

Unfortunately, circumstances did not allow the Museum to buy the precious art collection, and ultimately, the family was forced to sell its silver dishes piece by piece. Finally, the last 21 pieces of the treasure, all that they still retained from the former inheritance in 1930, were auctioned off to the Ernst Museum. Although the Hungarian National Museum (with financial aid from the government as well as from private individuals) was one of the most important buyers, a few dishes ended up in the possession of private collectors. One of the dishes was recognised among the works of art acquired illegally and smuggled out of the country by the Soviets;[23] others are still missing.

The catalogue of the auction held at the Ernst Museum (Budapest) contains detailed descriptions and is illustrated with photographs so the lots can easily be identified. But we lack information about the pieces sold between 1911 and 1930, since there are no sale or purchase contracts and receipts. We have additional information, however, from nineteenth-

---

[21] Markó 1912, 2.
[22] Archive of the MNM, No. 40/1921.
[23] Mravik 1998, 331, Cat. No. 19944.

century exhibition catalogues, which include pieces coming from the Erdődy collection. Some of these pieces had originally belonged to the Rákóczi family, as is testified by the names (monograms) incised on them. Several objects of the Erdődy collection were described in the catalogue of the historical goldsmith's work exhibition by Károly Pulszky and Jenő Radisics, two excellent connoisseurs of the nineteenth century.[24] Some of the objects in this catalogue had once belonged to Ezsébet Rákóczi. There was a sixteenth-century double standing cup—today with its counterpart in the Thyssen-Bornemisza Collection in Zürich.[25] Both double cups bear the monograms of the Rákóczi-Bánffy family and both can be identified in the 1704 and 1706 inventories of Erzsébet and in all of the entail inventories. They bear an assay mark for Augsburg and the maker's mark of an anonymous goldsmith. Both pieces were on show at the Millennium Exhibition held at Budapest in 1896; they belonged accordingly to the Erdődy family at this date. Most probably, they left the Erdődy collection in the 1920s because in 1930 the cups were already exhibited as parts of the collection of Baron Heinrich Thyssen-Bornemisza.[26]

Another silver object, once in the possession of Erzsébet Rákóczi, also entered the Thyssen-Bornemisza collection. It is a ceremonial cup that was once created from several different objects made at different times.[27] Its foot bears an assay mark for Augsburg and the maker's mark of an anonymous goldsmith (maybe that of Gregor Bair). Its stem has again an assay mark for Augsburg but the maker's mark is of Elias I Drentwett. Its bowl was made in Nuremberg in about 1570 and bears the maker's mark of Martin Rehlein. On the rim of the cup one can see the monograms of the Rákóczi–Bánffy family. The cup, however, can be identified in none of Erzsébet's inventories.

A silver cup, with a cover but without a foot and stem appeared in the inventories of Erzsébet. A cup without a foot was also listed in the inventory drawn up after the death of György Erdődy, but there is no trace of it after that. The reason might be that the cup was completed as a pastiche by the Erdődys using salvable parts of damaged objects from their collections: The stem thus might come from one of the cups belonging to a series in the Erdődy collection. The stem of the Rákóczi cup was made in the workshop of Elias I Drentwett and he was the one who made the above

---

[24] Pulszky and Radisics 1884; Pulszky, Radisics and Molinier 1886.

[25] Thyssen-Bornemisza collection, Zürich. Inv. K 142-3.

[26] Történelmi Főcsoport 1896, No. 6798; Heinemann-Fleischmann and Drey 1930. No. 54-5; Müller 1986, 148-51.

[27] Thyssen-Bornemisza collection, Zürich. Inv. K 141. Lit.: Rosenberg 1925, 122, 137, 394, 3962; Seling 1980, 865, 1312b, Müller 1986, No. 40.

mentioned series for the Erdődys as well. The shape and the decoration of the stems are the same in both cases.[28]

There is a crystal wine vessel in the form of a cask known only from a reproduction in the catalogue of the goldsmith' exhibition edited in 1886.[29] It was in the possession of the Erdődys until 1930, but they sold it before the auction. Its location today is unknown. The vessel bears the coat of arms and monograms of the Rákóczi–Bánffys on its foiled foot. Beyond that, the coat of arms of King Sigismund of Luxemburg (1387–1437) appears on it as well, namely, on its two ends on a blue enamel ground. It means that the wine vessel originally might have belonged to the collection of the king. Bearing the coats of arms and the monograms of the Rákóczi-Bánffy family, one might easily conclude that the object came into the possession of Erzsébet Rákóczi via the parental line, but several archival data contradict this supposition. The crystal vessel was most probably not part of the heritage Erzsébet received from her parents, though it was in her possession without doubt. In her 1704 inventory, there is mention of a piece of ["high tableware in the form of a cask, gilded and made of rock crystal" ["kristál da montánya"]. The object, however, did not appear in the inventory she had drawn up in 1706, containing all the treasures she inherited from her parents. This is not by accident, since the vessel was a gift of her mother-in-law, Éva Forgách.[30] Originally, the wine vessel might have been received by a member in the Forgách family from King Sigismund as a precious gift, but it had never been in the possession of the parents of Erzsébet. It was she who stamped it with the coat of arms and monograms of the Rákóczis.

In the last printed source of the collection of the Erdődys, the auction catalogue of the Ernst Museum in 1930, there were four other objects once belonging to the Rákóczis. All of them can be identified in the inventories of Erzsébet and bear the monogram of the Rákóczi-Bánffy family. The first is a Renaissance silver-gilt cup, today in the Hungarian National Museum, Budapest.[31] Its form suggests that originally it might have been part of a double standing cup. It is marked by the monogrammist IE (Jobst Heberlein) from Nuremberg;[32] the bowl is embossed with lobes (Fig. 18). It can be found in Erzsébet's 1704 inventory, but it cannot be identified in

---

[28] Bubryák 2010.

[29] Pulszky, Radisics and Molinier 1886, 143.

[30] ÖStA, HHStA, FAE, Lad. 82. fasc. 3. No. 3/4.

[31] MNM, Inv. 1950.149.

[32] Tebbe, Eser and Timann 2007, I/2, No. 334. Erika Kiss called my attention to this book. Lit.: Pulszky and Radisics 1884. 51. (room 3, 3/42), Történelmi Főcsoport 1896. Cat. No. 6801.

the inventory listing the objects she received from her parents. Thus this is another object which did not come from the collection of her parents, although it bears their monograms.

Figure 18: Jobst Heberlein, one half of a double standing cup, Nuremberg, last quarter of the sixteenth century, Hungarian National Museum, Budapest.

The second object is another cup with a cover. It must have been made in the workshop of Hermann Plexen in Augsburg, in the first half of the seventeenth century. Both inventories of Erzsébet Rákóczi mentioned and described it, today it is in the collection of the Hungarian National Museum, Budapest.[33]

The third object is a silver-gilt jug (Fig. 19), decorated with medals commemorating one of the most tragic moments in Hungarian history, that of the Battle of Mohács in 1526. From that time, Turks ruled over the larger part of the country for the next 150 years. On the top of the jug three medals are inserted, all being copies of medals commemorating the lost battle. Otherwise the jug is marked by Master Matthäus Seutter (1574-1632) from Augsburg; it must have been made at the beginning of the

---

[33] Today: Rákóczi Múzeum, Sárospatak, Deposit of the MNM, Inv. 1930.100.

seventeenth century. It can be identified in both inventories of Erzsébet and it bears the monograms of the Rákóczi-Bánffys as well.[34]

The fourth object was not auctioned, but it was mentioned in a list sent to the Hungarian National Museum containing those objects that the family intended to sell. The silver bowl's upper part has the shape of a shell held up by the splendid figure of a nymph; on its top the figure of a Roman soldier stands holding a shield and a spear (Fig. 20). The monograms of the Rákóczi-Bánffys appear on the bowl, as well. It bears the assay mark for Augsburg and the maker's mark of Johannes Lencker (1570-1637).[35] The work of art can be identified in the inventory of Erzsébet made up in 1706, listing the objects she inherited from her parents.

Figure 19: Matthäus Seutter, silver-gilt jug, ornamented with medals commemorating the Battle of Mohács (1526), Augsburg, early seventeenth century, Hungarian National Museum, Budapest.

---

[34] MNM, Inv. 1930.101.
[35] MNM, Inv. 1950.146; Falke 1928, 18; Seling 1980, No. 1128, 1157.

Figure 20: Johannes Lencker, silver-gilt cup decorated with a nymph, Augsburg, first quarter of seventeenth century, Hungarian National Museum, Budapest.

Conclusion

In sum, only these few gilded items of tableware listed above are still known today as examples of the rich treasury once owned by Erzsébet Rákóczi. Nevertheless, on the basis of the monograms and the coat of arms, further works of art can perhaps in future be identified as formerly belonging to this collection. Given the above-mentioned examples, it is highly possible, that Erzsébet put the monograms of the Rákóczi-Bánffys on all the silverware in her possession, not only on those once in the collection of her parents. The inventory drawn up at the death of her husband hints at this possibility as well: she might have stamped not only her splendid tableware but the more modest silverware as well, such as her plain silver plates and candlesticks. As has been demonstrated, she put her parents' monograms not only on the pieces inherited from them but on those that she herself acquired or received as gifts from others as well. Stamping the artworks with the monograms of her parents can be understood as a gesture by Erzsébet in honour of her parents.

But she might have had a more practical goal in mind as well. There is a clear distinction between the properties inherited or acquired under historical Hungarian inheritance law. Only a relative by blood could become beneficiary of inherited property; hence an object with Rákóczi provenance should have been inherited only by a member of that family. If there were no direct descendants among the heirs, the testator's family would have obtained the property. Acquired property on the other hand could have been inherited by the spouse. Since Erzsébet Rákóczi did not have children, all of her inherited property should have gone back to her family, namely to her nephew Ferenc II Rákóczi and her niece Julianna Rákóczi. But the properties acquired by her under the terms of the marriage contract signed by both parties in 1672, should have been inherited by her husband. Since she had signed the marriage contract, she could not dispose of her movable property otherwise.

I do not wish to exclude the possibility that Erzsébet had her parents' names incised in all of her silver dishes, so that the pieces acquired by her should seem to be heirlooms and hence be solely inheritable by her collateral Rákóczi relatives. That her plans were thwarted is due to the fact that Ferenc II Rákóczi, leader of the War of Independence (1703-1711) against the Habsburgs had fallen into disgrace with the Viennese court and the entire fortune of the family had been confiscated. Hence he was deprived of his heritage. György Erdődy to the contrary, who was familiar with the imperial court, could easily have made provisions that allowed him to hold on to those pieces of the Rákóczi treasure that had remained in his property.

Erzsébet's Posthumous Revenge

In a sense, however, Erzsébet Rákóczi reached her goal. Announcing the auction of the entire Erdődy collection in 1930, the Ernst Museum entitled the catalogue: "The Treasures of the princes Rákóczi".[36] By placing the name "Rákóczi" in the title, the organisers surely hoped to attract the attention of possible purchasers. As we have seen, in reality, the gorgeous meat dishes had never been in the possession of the prince and out of the 21 pieces, only four had once belonged to Erzsébet Rákóczi. It is quite ironic, therefore that her objects "eclipsed" those Erdődy pieces grouped together with Erzsébet's silverware. Thus the representative gilded tablewares of the Erdődy treasury—due to the auction of the Ernst Museum in 1930—became famous as being part and parcel of the fabulous

---

[36] Ernst Múzeum 1930.

art patronage of the Rákóczi family. The Erdődy silverware auctioned off in 1930 and bought by the Hungarian National Museum is known and exhibited up to this day as part of the "Rákóczi treasures".

CHAPTER FIVE

THE *MUSAEUM* OF THE 1ST DUCHESS OF NORTHUMBERLAND (1716-1776) AT NORTHUMBERLAND HOUSE IN LONDON: AN INTRODUCTION

ADRIANO AYMONINO

The private collection of Elizabeth Seymour Percy, 2nd countess and later 1st duchess of Northumberland, constitutes one of the most interesting assembled during the eighteenth century in Britain for many reasons.[1] First of all, it is one of very few independently assembled by a woman in the Georgian period. Secondly, for its extension and variety, covering almost the whole spectrum of the *naturalia* and *artificialia* collectibles, it is one of the largest—but today mostly unknown—private collections of the second half of the century. Finally, in its organisation and display it represents the collision of two principles and conceptions of collecting, coexisting at the time: on one hand the "new" methods of scientific taxonomy advanced by the British Enlightenment; on the other the culture

[1] This Chapter is an adapted extract from my Ph.D. dissertation: *Aristocratic Splendour: Hugh Smithson Percy (1712–1786) and Elizabeth Seymour Percy (1716–1776), 1st Duke and Duchess of Northumberland. A case study in patronage, collecting and society in eighteenth-century England* (University of Venice, School of Advanced Studies, 2009), under the supervision of Bernard Aikema and Edward Chaney, to whom I am deeply indebted. This research was partly funded by a research grant from the Paul Mellon Centre for Studies in British Art in London. My research would not have been possible without the help of Chris Hunwick, Clare Baxter and Lisa Little of the Archives of the Duke of Northumberland at Alnwick Castle and without the facilities of the Photographic Survey of the Courtauld Institute and the immense knowledge and kindness of Jane Cunningham.

of an aristocratic amateur collector, with its old-fashioned fascination for the rare, the precious and the marvellous. This essay provides an introduction to and an overview of the duchess's expansive collection— her *Musaeum* as she called it—and the nine-volume *Musaeum Catalogue* she personally compiled to accompany it.[2]

Elizabeth Seymour Percy (1716-1776) and Hugh Smithson Percy (1712-1786)

Not only the collection, but also the life and character of Elizabeth Percy were extraordinary in the context of Georgian high society (Fig. 21).[3] She was born on 26 November 1716, the daughter of Algernon Seymour, earl of Hertford and later 7th duke of Somerset, and his wife, Frances Seymour, daughter of the Hon. Henry Thynne, eldest son of the 1st viscount Weymouth.[4] On her paternal side she descended from two of the most influential aristocratic families of England: the Seymours, dukes of Somerset and the Percys, earls of Northumberland until the late seventeenth century, when their male line became extinct. However, as a woman, she was not destined to inherit the family title and fortunes, a privilege granted to her younger brother George. When in 1740 she married Sir Hugh Smithson (1712-1786), an ambitious young baronet of rather humble origins—his grandfather having been a haberdasher in London—she was therefore prepared to spend her life in the comfortable but provincial setting of Stanwick Hall, the Smithsons' seat in the North Riding of Yorkshire.

---

[2] A comprehensive description and analysis of the actual contents of the collection, the principles on which it was assembled and organised and the physical disposition of the objects at Northumberland House, is intended for publication as part of a forthcoming monograph on the collecting and patronage of the 1st duke and duchess of Northumberland. The two most comprehensive studies on the duchess's collection published so far are Baird 2004, 147-168 and French 2009, 59-82; 273-281. The former covers all of the patronage activities of Elizabeth, while the latter is more concentrated on her continental tours.

[3] For an updated bibliography on the duchess and her husband see Aymonino 2010, 289, notes 4 and 7; Baird 2004, 147-68. For the portrait of Elizabeth by Allan Ramsay see Smart 1999, no. 410, 167.

[4] On Algernon Seymour see Bucholz 2004; on Frances Seymour see Sambrook 2004.

Figure 21: Allan Ramsay, *Lady Elizabeth Seymour Percy, later 2nd Countess and later 1st Duchess of Northumberland*, oil on canvas, 72.4 x 52.7 cm, 1739, Collection of the Duke of Northumberland, Alnwick Castle.

Everything changed in 1744 with the death of Elizabeth's brother, an event that set the couple on the path of one of the most impressive social ascents in Georgian Britain. Their progression began with the inheritance of the earldom of Northumberland in 1750 and culminated in 1766 when the couple was elevated to the dukedom (third creation) by George III. Their social life and political achievements were equally successful. While the duke held some of the nation's most important posts over the course of his political career, Elizabeth came to be an immensely popular figure in eighteenth-century London. A constant presence at social events, she held the prestigious title of Lady of the Bedchamber to Queen Charlotte during the 1760s, while Northumberland House provided the setting for huge parties and official receptions. As a result, by the end of their lives

Elizabeth and her husband were ranked among the richest and most influential couples of the kingdom.

This striking social progression was supported from the beginning by patronage and collecting at the most extravagant level and the choices made by the couple often influenced British artistic and architectural trends in the second half of the century. They possessed a large collection of Old Masters as well as supporting contemporary artists such as Canaletto, of whom Hugh Smithson was one of the most faithful patrons during the painter's long London residence. Furthermore, the couple systematically reshaped the great houses of the Percys, which lay in neglected, if not ruinous condition, when they were inherited by Elizabeth in 1750. Northumberland House, the London mansion, was transformed according to neo-Palladian and contemporary continental standards and updated into a fashionable urban residence. Alnwick Castle, the ancestral baronial seat of the Percys, was rebuilt principally by Robert Adam in Gothic Revival style, in an attempt to restore its medieval glory. Syon House, just outside London, was refurbished by Adam as an ancient suburban Roman villa, one of the very first expressions of his neo-classical language in architecture and decoration.[5] After the death of Elizabeth in 1776, her husband crowned these lifelong efforts by commissioning from Robert Adam a huge funerary monument to her memory in Westminster Abbey, the most prestigious burial ground of the nation.[6] This extensive and concerted policy of patronage was clearly a quintessential part of a strategy to reaffirm the Percys as one of the most powerful families in the English aristocracy. If this patronage campaign was conducted by the couple together, the duchess exerted her judgement in complete autonomy over two spheres: Alnwick Castle, whose Gothic decoration she personally chose, and her huge collections displayed at Northumberland House, which she assembled throughout the course of her life.

Elizabeth's Milieu and the Background to her Collection

Her passion for collecting, an activity usually reserved for men, was supported and motivated by Elizabeth's education and by the rich cultural environment she lived in. Her mother, Lady Hertford, was a well known bluestocking with a deep interest in literature, while her father, Lord

---

[5] On Northumberland House, Alnwick Castle and Syon House see Harris 2001, 65-103 (with bibliography). On the patronage and collections of the duke and duchess, see Aymonino 2009.

[6] Aymonino 2010.

Hertford, was president of the Society of Antiquaries between 1724 and 1749, as well as a patron of architecture and a collector of antiquities, gems, medals, prints and books, a fixation that he transmitted spiritually and physically to his daughter.[7] Elizabeth's husband, Hugh Smithson, was a highly educated man and connoisseur: a collector himself and a great patron of architecture, he was also a member of the Society of Antiquaries, of the Royal Society, of the Society of Dilettanti and, with his wife, of the Society for the Encouragement of Arts, Manufacturers and Commerce. More importantly, in 1753 he became one of the members of the first board of trustees of the British Museum—having been appointed personally by Sir Hans Sloane in his will—and his role in organising and displaying Sloane's collections at Montague House must have had a huge influence on Elizabeth's choices in terms of collecting, classification and display.[8] Her personal cultural life was likewise substantial. Over an extended period of time, she patronised literary figures such as James Boswell and Thomas Percy and constantly shared with her husband, if not personally controlled, all the choices in terms of architecture, decoration and taste. Her role as Lady of the Bedchamber from 1761 to 1770 brought her into contact with Queen Charlotte's cultural circle, composed of other great woman collectors and intellectuals.[9] The Queen herself was an eager collector, had a strong interest in natural history and owned cabinets of butterflies, shells, ores and minerals. She also possessed a huge library and a collection of prints, coins, medals and ivories.[10] Other relevant figures included Margaret Cavendish-Bentinck, 2ⁿᵈ duchess of Portland, one of the greatest collectors of natural specimens of the eighteenth century, whose immense collections at Bulstrode, Buckinghamshire, were very well known to Elizabeth, and Mary Delany, an inseparable friend of the 2ⁿᵈ duchess of Portland, keen naturalist and creator of the famous paper mosaics of flowers.[11]

---

[7] Hughes 1940; Aymonino 2009, 15-7. Lord Hertford left his collections to his wife and, at her death, to Elizabeth. For his will of 22 Feb 1750 see: Prerogative Court of Canterbury, Prob/11/777 fol. 109 v ("Will of The Most Noble Algernon Baron Percy commonly called Earl of Hartford late Duke of Somerset", available online on the website of The National Archives:
http://www.nationalarchives.gov.uk/documentsonline/details-result.asp?Edoc_Id=3543012&queryType=1&resultcount=4, accessed 2 Dec 2010).
[8] Miller 1973, 48; Caygill 1994, 61-2.
[9] Campbell Orr 2005.
[10] Queen's Gallery 1974, 11, 13; Hedley 1975; Campbell Orr 2001; Roberts 2004, in particular 154-67, 385-7.
[11] On the duchess of Portland's collection as a whole, surprisingly, there are no detailed scholarly studies. See Festing 1986; Huxley 2003, 85-88; Rogers 2004;

The Collections and their Display
at Northumberland House

Elizabeth's fervour for collecting started early: already in 1741, when she was twenty-five and well before Hugh would take his place on the board of the British Museum, she remarked in a letter to her mother that her "rage of medals" was hourly increasing; by 1761 the "repository of curiosities" in her closet at Northumberland House, contained "so fine a collection of pictures, as to afford a most pleasing and almost endless entertainment to a connoisseur", as reported by Robert and James Dodsley in their famous description of London.[12] At the end of her life the collection, from being confined to the "closet" mentioned by Dodsley in 1761, had grown so much in size as to occupy almost all of Elizabeth's apartments at the first floor of Northumberland House, as testified by an inventory of the house compiled at the death of the duke in 1786.[13] The private and semi-private "Prayer Room", "Crimson Damask Room", "Small Crimson Room", "Her Grace's Sitting Room" and a series of 4 rooms in which the old Jacobean small gallery had been divided by the couple, gravitated around a room significantly called the "Museum Room". Unfortunately Northumberland House was pulled down in 1874, but these spaces can all be located by comparing the 1786 inventory with a plan of the first floor of the house of c.1749 (Fig. 22).[14] This double set of

---

Stott 2006; Sloboda 2010. Elizabeth visited Bulstrode in 1760, describing in her diaries the house and mentioning the "thousand curiositys" of the duchess. See Archives of the Duke of Northumberland, Alnwick Castle (cited hereafter as Alnwick Castle), DNP: MS 121/4, 29 May 1760. The passage is published in Greig 1926, 15-17. Elizabeth also listed many of the duchess's objects in a list of English collections that she wrote in the 1760s (see below note 15). On Mary Delany see Laird and Weisberg-Roberts 2009 (with extensive bibliography).

[12] Elizabeth's letter is kept in Alnwick Castle, DNP: MS 24, fol. 64 r: Stanwick, 8 September 1741; Dodsley and Dodsley 1761, V, 58.

[13] Alnwick Castle, SY: H/VI/2d, fols 13-44. The full transcription of the 1786 inventory will be soon available on the Provenance Index Database of the Getty Institute: http://piprod.getty.edu/starweb/pi/servlet.starweb.

[14] This "Plan of the one pair of stairs floor" (first floor), is part of a series of plans "about the time of Algernon, Duke of Somerset" (c. 1749), covering all the floors of Northumberland House: Alnwick Castle, SY: B/XV/2/K. They have been reproduced in Guerci 2007, figs XXXIII A-D, catalogued in vol. II, 284-85. Only the "Plan of the Ground Floor" (Alnwick Castle, SY: B/XV/2/K/2) has been published: Owsley-Rieder 1974, 26, fig. 29; Guerci 2010, 28, fig. 18. The disposition of the rooms as shown in these c. 1749 plans was slightly changed by the 1st duke and duchess in the works of alteration and refurbishment of the house

rooms was the realm of Elizabeth, a space where she could express a taste complementary to but different from the classicising one displayed by her husband in the state rooms at the ground floor of the house.

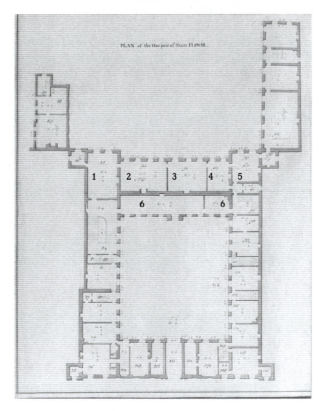

Figure 22: Plan of the first floor of Northumberland House, c. 1749, Alnwick Castle, SY: B/XV/2/K/4: 1. Prayer Room; 2. Crimson Damask Room; 3. Museum Room; 4. Small Crimson Room; 5. Her Grace's Sitting Room; 6. Rooms in the Gallery.

started in 1750. In the case of the first floor, for instance, the plan shows that at that time the old Jacobean gallery had been divided in two rooms (fig. 22, no. 6), while we know from the 1786 inventory (see above note 12) that they became four during the 1st duke's and duchess's lifetime. On the refurbishment of Northumberland House begun by Algernon, 7th duke of Somerset (the father of the duchess) in 1748-50 and continued by Elizabeth and Hugh in 1750-58 and in 1770-75 see Aymonino 2009, 59-81 and Aymonino and Guerci forthcoming.

Elizabeth constantly enriched her sources of inspiration in terms of collecting with hectic journeys around Britain and the continent, especially in Holland, Flanders and France. Everything she thought worth of notice was reported in her numerous diaries, notebooks, and letters.[15] Her obsession with ordering and cataloguing provides us with lists of all sorts, many of which reported collections she saw at home or abroad, plus the details of her own collection, or the places and sources where she personally acquired objects and works of art. Among the most illuminating with regards to her own collecting are a list of paintings, statues, busts, bas-reliefs, cameos, intaglios and miscellaneous curiosities taken from the most famous English collections of the time and a concise list of some celebrated contemporary European collections: a system of reference against which Elizabeth's must be placed.[16]

---

[15] The 56 diaries of the duchess are kept in Alnwick Castle, DNP: MS 121/1-59. A small selection of extracts from them was published by Greig 1926; Percy-Jackson-Stops 1974; French 2009, 65-70. Notebooks and miscellaneous material of the duchess are preserved in Alnwick castle, DNP: MS 121/60-192. For lists of objects in her collection see esp. DNP: MS 121/60; 121/63; 121/87; 121/88; 121/90. See also DNP: MS 692-694. The correspondence of Elizabeth is scattered throughout the general correspondence of the family: the class of material chronologically covering her years is DNP: MS 24-45.

[16] For the former see Alnwick Castle, DNP: MS 121/88. This list was compiled between 1760 and 1766: see Aymonino 2009, 160, note 623. It constitutes an exceptional document on English collections of the time, giving additional information in respect to what had already been published in Dodsley and Dodsley 1761 and what would subsequently be published in Martyn 1766. The thousands of objects reported come mostly from some of the most renowned collections of the time: Dr Richard Mead; Thomas Newton, bishop of Bristol; Horace Walpole at Strawberry Hill; the earl of Orford at Houghton Hall; the earl of Egremont at Petworth House; the earl of Pembroke at Wilton House; the earl of Exeter at Burghley House; the duchess of Portland at Bulstrode; the duke of Bedford at Woburn Abbey; the duke of Marlborough at Blenheim Palace; the king at St James's Palace, Windsor Castle, Kensington Palace and Hampton Court. For the latter list see Alnwick Castle, DNP: MS 121/60, fol. 286. The date of this list is probably later, being 1770 and 1771 the most recurring dates in the notebook containing the list. Unfortunately, only the names of the collections appear in it, without the contents being listed. Among the continental collections appear those of Gerrit Braamcamp in Amsterdam, of Griffier Hendrick Fagel in The Hague and of Charles Theodore Wittelsbach, elector palatine, in Düsseldorf. A transcription of the two lists will be published in a future study (see above, note 2). For an introduction to British collecting in the eighteenth century see Sutton 1981-85, III-V; Haskell 1985.

The *Musaeum Catalogue*

The various lists regarding her own objects were eventually consolidated to form what is an extraordinary example of the taxonomical principles on which many cabinets of the eighteenth century were based: a *Musaeum Catalogue* in nine volumes, which she personally wrote in the 1770s, listing all the items of her collection—and some of her husband's—and dividing them into specific categories (see Appendix).[17] This enormous cataloguing effort was very likely intended for publication, following a general trend among British collectors of the eighteenth century. Recently published catalogues included the British Museum's of 1761 and 1762 and the ongoing work of Horace Walpole for his Strawberry Hill catalogue, eventually published in 1774, must have been prominent among contemporary inspirations.[18] Elizabeth's death in 1776 seems to have left her plan unfulfilled, which would explain the various gaps in the *Musaeum Catalogue* and the absence in it of prestigious classes of items, such as the "Clock Work", the "Drawings" or the ancient "Imperial Medals" annotated elsewhere in her notebooks.[19]

What she assembled throughout her lifetime was a typical English cabinet of the eighteenth century, embracing the whole spectrum of the manmade and natural worlds.[20] Unlike the more scientific collections of Hans Sloane and the 2nd duchess of Portland, that of Elizabeth was nevertheless largely devoted to works of art and *artificialia* in general and it was more the product of a dilettante than the research tool of a scholar. In the *Musaeum Catalogue*'s division into categories, she likely followed a system of classification similar to that adopted by Hans Sloane and then formalised in the early arrangement of the British Museum.[21] Some of these categories, however, are merged together in an eclectic way which reveals the amateur character of their arrangement. Furthermore, the disposition of the objects in the various rooms and especially in the

---

[17] Alnwick Castle, DNP: MS 122-127. A transcription of the *Musaeum Catalogue* will be soon available on the Provenance Index Database of the Getty Institute: http://piprod.getty.edu/starweb/pi/servlet.starweb.
[18] Powlett 1761; Powlett 1762; Walpole 1774.
[19] For the "clock work" and "drawings" see Alnwick Castle, DNP: MS 693, 9 and 27. For the "Imperial Medals in the collection of Elizabeth Duchess of Northumberland" see DNP: MS 121/90/A.
[20] As introduction to the cabinet tradition in England and its evolution in the eighteenth century, see MacGregor 1994; MacGregor-Impey 2001, in particular 147-168; Anderson-Caygill-MacGregor-Syson 2003; Sloan-Burnett 2003; MacGregor 2007, in particular 11-69.
[21] Powlett 1761; Powlett 1762; MacGregor 1994; Caygill 2003; Sloan 2003.

"Museum Room" still bore memories of the old fashioned cabinet of marvels, with its juxtaposition of different classes of objects inside the same space, if not inside the same physical wooden cabinet.

By comparing what is listed in the *Musaeum Catalogue* with the 1786 inventory of Northumberland House and with the first-floor plan (Fig. 22), it is possible to get a clearer idea of the disposition of the collections in the 1st duchess's rooms.

The Contents of the *Musaeum*

The first three volumes of the *Musaeum Catalogue* gather some of the most recurrent objects in seventeenth- and eighteenth-century European cabinet collections: pictures (including pastels, miniature and wax portraits), prints, medals and coins. The great majority of her paintings were Dutch or Flemish canvases of medium if not small size, whose dimensions and unpretentious themes were traditionally considered more apt to intimate spaces of retirement, as private or semi-private rooms and cabinets, while larger Old Masters were paraded in the public rooms.[22] Elizabeth's were mainly maritime views, landscapes or genre paintings (Fig. 23) and were closely hung throughout the rooms, apart from the "Museum Room" which did not display paintings, being crammed with tables, commode tables and mahogany glass cases containing the bulk of the small objects.[23] Included in the general class of "Pictures", among other categories, were also the miniatures of the family, a series of wax portraits by Isaac Gosset (Fig. 24) and a collection of 86 full length miniatures of European aristocrats and English and French actors, commissioned by the duchess from the Swiss artist Jean Louis Fesch (Fig. 25).[24]

---

[22] Alnwick Castle, DNP: MS 122A, fols 1-5, 30-31, 87-91 and 115-116. On the taste for Dutch art in England see Jackson-Stops 1985, esp. 146-173, 354-75 and Russell 1989.

[23] Alnwick Castle, SY: MS H/VI/2d, fols 21-24. The painting by David Ryckaert the younger is unpublished. See Haute 1999. It was listed by the duchess in the *Musaeum Catalogue* as "Physician examining urinal by Ryckaert": see Alnwick Castle DNP: MS 122/A, fol. 89r. Many of these paintings still remain in the "Duchess' Sitting Room" at Syon House but a large section of them was sold at Sotheby's 26 March 1952, lots 39-146. For the duchess's personal acquisition of the Dutch and Flemish paintings during her tours in Holland and the Flanders see French 2009, 65-70 and my forthcoming study (see above note 2).

[24] Alnwick Castle, DNP: MS 122/A, fols 135, 152-154, 157v-158, 173. The miniatures of the Percy family are still preserved at Alnwick Castle: see Foster 1921. Of the original wax portraits of Isaac Gosset–the most famous English wax

Figure 23: David Ryckaert the younger, *An Interior with an Alchemist, a Woman and a Child* (*Vanitas*), oil on canvas, 67.9 x 94 cm, signed, l.l., D. Rÿckaert and dated 1644 [?], Collection of the Duke of Northumberland, Syon House.

Elizabeth's enormous collection of prints was organised across many albums and fixed to their sheets with tabs of unfolded papers.[25] The core of the collection was a large group of albums of Netherlandish masters of the late sixteenth or early seventeenth century. Almost all the great figures of Antwerp print production were present, especially Collaert, Goltzius, Galle, Passe, Sadeler, Stradanus, de Vos and Wierix—a choice reflecting her taste for Dutch and Flemish painters and her frequent travels in the region. This makes Elizabeth one of the few recorded female print collectors of the eighteenth century and the only one who listed them in an inventory. The 1786 inventory reveals that the majority of the prints was very likely kept in a "wainscot press" in the "third room in the gallery" with maps, portraits and other unspecified objects.[26]

---

engraver of the eighteenth century–listed by the duchess, only a few remain at Alnwick Castle, mounted in a later frame and with no author's attribution. For Isaac Gosset see Craske and Craske 2004. The 86 miniatures by Jean Louis Fesch are also still preserved in the castle: Alnwick Castle, DNP: MS 762. On them see Aymonino forthcoming. On Fesch see Treydel 2003.

[25] Alnwick Castle, DNP: MS 122/B. The collection of prints was entirely sold in 1951. See Sotheby's 11 April 1951, lots 164-350. For the current location of many of the volumes of prints in libraries throughout the world see Griffiths 2001.

[26] Alnwick Castle, SY: MS H/VI/2d, fol. 41.

Figure 24: Isaac Gosset, Series of wax portraits of British worthies and aristocrats, from top clockwise: *John Manners, Marquess of Granby*, 12 x 15 cm, c. 1765; *Mary Maxwell, later 18th Countess of Sutherland*, 15 x 17 cm, c. 1760; *George II*, 15 x 18 cm, c. 1750; *Princess Charlotte of Mecklenburg-Strelitz*, 15 x 18 cm, c. 1760; *Inigo Jones*, 11.5 x 13.2 cm; *Lady Mary Coke*, 15 x 18 cm, c. 1750; *Hugh Smithson Percy, 1st Duke of Northumberland*, 15 x 18 cm, c. 1770; *William, 18th Earl of Sutherland*, 15 x 17 cm, c. 1760. In the centre: *Elizabeth, 1st Countess Brooke of Warwick*, 12 x 15 cm, c. 1750, Collection of the Duke of Northumberland, Alnwick Castle.

The next category, medals and coins, was the real point of excellence of the entire collection.[27] Building on her father's collection, either autonomously or through the services of Louis Dutens, a French diplomat and numismatist, Elizabeth managed over time to amass one of the largest numismatic collections of Georgian Britain, particularly strong in north European medals.[28] As the inventory reports, they were kept in medal cases distributed between the "Museum Room" and the "second room in the gallery".[29]

---

[27] Alnwick Castle, DNP: MS 122.

[28] All of her coins and medals, including some pieces made by the greatest medallists of the post-Renaissance period, were sold at Sotheby's, 3 December 1980 and Sotheby's, 17 June 1981. It was considered at that time "the most important auction of Continental medals ever held" in England, as the introduction to the 3 December 1980 catalogue reported. On Louis Dutens see Luard 2004.

[29] Alnwick Castle, SY: MS H/VI/2d, fols 21, 36, 37.

Figure 25: Jean Louis Fesch, *Lady Carry, Lord Carry, Lord Russborough*, pen, pencil and watercolour on vellum, 10 x 8 cm, c.1770, Collection of the Duke of Northumberland, Alnwick Castle.

The fourth volume lists her ethnographic collection, based on similar contemporary examples and especially, again, on a specific section of the British Museum devoted to the "variety of utensils that each nation in each century has produced"[30] Most of these items, as is the case for the majority of the objects listed in following volumes, being of poor economic value, seem to have disappeared during the last two centuries. This section of the collection was limited but varied and included, among others, items from the Americas and China, the badge of "the Order of the K[ing] of Siam form'd of precious Stones" and many costumes of European religious orders kept in a large mahogany glass case in the "Museum Room".[31]

---

[30] Alnwick Castle, DNP: MS 123. The quotation is from Powlett 1761, 18. See also Powlett 1762, 37, 54-58, 64-66; King 1994; Mack 2003.
[31] Alnwick Castle, SY: MS H/VI/2d, fol. 22.

The fifth category groups in an eccentric way everything carved or sculpted.[32] It mixes together different classes of objects such as gems and intaglios—another very widespread category of objects in antiquarian collections—with little statues and bas-reliefs. Apart from a series of supposedly antique cameos and intaglios, also listed were "Cameos" by James Tassie, the period's most famous English producer of casts after ancient engraved gems.[33] Other categories included small bas-reliefs and statues in ivory and marble and to these one must add a set of bronze statuettes from the Zoffoli workshop, the Roman suppliers of reduced copies of celebrated ancient statues, which are only partially listed in the *Musaeum Catalogue* but are fully registered in the 1786 inventory.[34] Several of these still survive, distributed between Alnwick Castle and Syon House—among them the *Venus de Medici*, the *Dying Gaul*, the *Hercules Farnese*, the *Apollo Belvedere*, the so-called *Menander and Agrippina*. Originally they were displayed in the "Crimson Damask Room" "on the mantle piece" and in the "Museum Room", also here almost certainly above the chimney piece, as traditional in English eighteenth-century cabinets and interiors in general.[35]

The following sixth volume, the last section of the *artificialia*, covers a miscellaneous category in which she evidently grouped together, haphazardly, everything that could not be included in other volumes, from miscellaneous curiosities to manuscripts, to "Japan", porcelain and glass.[36] There were also "antiquities", such as a "lachrymatory" or a "small brass Mercury with a bag of money", given to her by her father, and historical curiosities, such as the supposed "Queen Elisabeths gloves" or a "cap made of the hair of Mary Queen of Scots" that she bought at the sale of the collection of Ebenezer Mussell in 1765, plus various missals, some Japanese items and a long list of porcelain.[37]

---

[32] Alnwick Castle, DNP: MS 124.

[33] Ibid, fols 3r 4r. On James Tassie see Smith 1995; Thomson 2004. The cameos are listed in the *Catalogue* as by Dr Quin, the original partner of Tassie.

[34] Alnwick Castle, DNP: MS 124, fol 83r; SY: MS H/VI/2d, fols 17, 22. Some of these Zoffoli statuettes have been published in Wilton-Bignamini 1996, 280-281; French 2009, 74. On the Zoffoli bronzes and their display see Haskell and Penny 1981, esp. 93-98; Teolato 2010.

[35] See, as an example of display of Zoffoli's bronzes, the celebrated portrait of *Sir Lawrence Dundas and his grandson in the pillar room at 19 Arlington Street*, painted by John Zoffany in 1769 and now at Aske Hall (N. Yorks): Jackson-Stops 1985, 356-57, n. 281.

[36] Alnwick Castle, DNP: MS 125.

[37] Ibid., fols 2v, 27v-28r, 85v-86r, 120v, 140v-141v. Mussell 5-6 June 1765, lot 77. See Baird 2004, 163.

The seventh volume is missing, probably lost during the course of the last two centuries or never completed by the duchess before her death. It almost certainly listed, or intended to list, the "natural curiosities" that do not appear in other parts of the *Musaeum Catalogue* but that were listed in one of her notebooks, such as "the skeleton of a sea horse", some "sea eggs", "the rattle of a rattle snake", "scallops", "cockles", "trumpets", "specimens of all the kinds of small shells", etcetera.[38] The shells appear furthermore in the "Museum Room" together with a collection of stones.[39]

These "stones" were listed in the eighth volume, together with—rather eccentrically—a huge collection of specimens of woods from all over the world.[40] The volume lists various sorts of mineral specimens divided according to genres—ores, spars, crystals, earths, marbles and gems— once again reflecting more or less Sloane's division of his collection of minerals.[41] She also possessed a small collection of "petrifactions" —mostly petrified vegetable specimens—and fossils, a growing passion among English collectors and naturalists, whose efforts led in time to the birth of the modern science of palaeontology.[42] All of these items were kept by Elizabeth in the "Museum Room" or in boxes and cabinets in the "second room in the gallery".[43]

Finally the last volume indexed the books, an essential part of every collection of the eighteenth century and earlier.[44] The main strengths of Elizabeth's private library were in literature, history, theology and natural history, all of which were well diffused genres of eighteenth-century libraries.[45] Furthermore, the contents of her library strongly resemble that of Queen Charlotte', testifying once more to the close connection of the duchess to the queen and her cultural circle.[46]

---

[38] Alnwick Castle, DNP: MS 693, 1.
[39] Alnwick Castle, SY: MS H/VI/2d, fol. 24.
[40] Alnwick Castle, DNP: MS 126.
[41] Thackray 1994.
[42] Ibid.; Cook 2003a; Cook 2003b.
[43] Alnwick Castle, SY: MS H/VI/2d, fols 22, 24, 36.
[44] Alnwick Castle, DNP: MS 127.
[45] Paintin 1989; Jervis 1999.
[46] Queen's Gallery 1974, 11.

Conclusions

As a whole, Elizabeth's *Musaeum* constitutes one of the largest private British collections of the second half of the eighteenth century. Certainly, it was one of the very few amassed by a woman. The unusual separation of the spheres of influence with her husband, unambiguously marked by the physical disposition of the collections in Northumberland House, demonstrates the cultural independence of Elizabeth and her powerful and active role in the activity of the couple. What she gathered over time shows perfectly the variety and vastness of interests of an educated woman of the highest ranks of the English aristocracy during the central decades of the century. More specifically, the activity of Elizabeth must be placed beside that of the other educated and independent women who surrounded Queen Charlotte, on whose circle a specific scholarly study is still wanting. Yet Elizabeth's collection is outstanding in its own right both for its breadth and for the quality of some of its objects.

However, the collection was also marked by contradictions. Elizabeth's taste as a collector was inconsistent. For some categories, such as coins, medals and indeed prints, she clearly showed a high level of discernment. For others, such as paintings, she followed established trends more passively, probably choosing the pictures more for their subjects than for their intrinsic artistic value. These variations in taste were echoed by tensions within the general structure of her collection. This was an odd combination of new scientific principles and old fashioned display, a tangible expression of the absorption and reuse of the new 'enlightened' notions by a private amateur. After her death in 1776 the duke almost certainly did not continue the collecting activity of his wife. Nevertheless he preserved her rooms untouched, as the 1786 inventory testifies, certainly as homage to the activity and passions of his wife.

In 1874 Northumberland House was pulled down to make space for a connection between Trafalgar Square and the newly-created Victoria Embankment. The collections were packed up and redistributed mainly between Syon House, Alnwick Castle and 17 Princes Gate, London, in a context completely different from that originally intended.[47] Subsequently,

---

[47] 17 Princes Gate was bought by the family after the destruction of Northumberland House. At Alnwick Castle can be found six typewritten and handwritten volumes compiled in 1930-33, covering most of the works of art still kept in the various residences of the Percy family at that date (Alnwick Castle, library, uncatalogued material). See esp.: "Catalogue of contents. Albury Park; 17 Princes Gate; in the collection of the Duke and Duchess of Northumberland; 1930"; "Catalogue of the pictures in the collection of the Duke and Duchess of Northumberland at Syon

during the course of the twentieth century, most of Elizabeth's objects were sold at auction and this contributed even further to the loss of the memory of the collection as a whole. Only through written testimonies is it possible to resuscitate the duchess' collection from oblivion and to give back to it the place that it deserves as one of the most interesting British private collections of the late Georgian era.

House, Albury Park, Alnwick Castle, 17 Princes Gate, compiled by W. Collins Baker of the National Gallery, 1930"; "Catalogue of the pictures in the collection of the Duke and Duchess of Northumberland, 1933 [compiled by W. Collins Baker]".

Appendix

1st Duchess of Northumberland's *Musaeum Catalogue*, c.1770s (Archives of the Duke of Northumberland, Alnwick Castle, DNP: MS 122-127).*

I. PICTURES [122a]: Oil Colour Pictures: Shipping and Landskips; Miscellaneous; Portraits; Works of Gosset; Enamels, Miniatures and Water Colours; Fesch; Crayons.

II. PRINTS [122b]: Fables, Emblems and Metamorphoses; Sacred Subjects; Statues, Medals, Antiquities; Architecture, Views and Landskips; Natural History; Miscellaneous Prints; Works of Devos; Habits; Works of Galle; Works of Stradanus; Portraits; Works of Collaert; Works of Wierx; Works of De Pass; Works of Hollar; Works of Goltzius; Works of Callot; Works of Teniers; Works of Sadeler.

III. MEDALS AND COINS [122]: English Gold Medals; Foreign Gold Medals; English Silver Medals; Foreign Silver Medals; English Gold Coins; English Silver Coins.

IV. ARMS, HABITS, UTENSILS, ORNAMENTS, CURIOSITIES OF DIFFERENT NATIONS [123].

V. CAMEO'S, INTAGLIAS, BAS RELIEFS, BRONZES, BUSTS, STATUES [124].

VI. ANTIQUITIES, HISTORICAL CURIOSITIES, MISCELLANEOUS DITTO, MANUSCRIPTS, JAPAN, PORCELAIN, GLASS etc. [125].

VIII. PETRIFACTIONS, FOSSILS, ORES, SPARRES, CHRISTALS, EARTHS, WOODS, MARBLES, GEMS etc. [126].

---

* I transcribed here only the headings of the general classes and sub-classes in which the *Musaeum Catalogue* is divided. The original spelling has been maintained. The full transcription will soon be available on the Provenance Index Database of the Getty Institute: http://piprod.getty.edu/starweb/pi/servlet.starweb.

IX. BOOKS: Poetry and Plays; Letters; Miscellanies; History and Lives; Divinity; Novels and Romances [127].

CHAPTER SIX

THE PRINCELY MOTHER AS COLLECTOR: BETWEEN MATERNAL LOVE AND DYNASTIC REPRESENTATION

HEIKE ZECH

Many mothers are collectors; they treasure pictures and objects of and by their children. This phenomenon sparked my interest when an unusual jewel was brought to my attention.[1] The piece itself is a comparatively simple nineteenth-century amethyst and gold cross pendant in its original fitted case.[2] It is remarkable because of its provenance and the fact that it is accompanied by a handwritten note explaining its history: the cross was originally given to Queen Marie of Bavaria (1825-1889) by her son, Prince Otto (1848-1916) on the occasion of his Catholic confirmation. The queen in turn presented the jewel to her lady-in-waiting, countess von der Mühle, when she converted to Catholicism in 1874.

A second object, originally owned by the queen had appeared on the market two years earlier: its style is somewhat sweeter, more romantic, and reflects the personality of the donor, Marie's first-born son, Ludwig II (1845-1886), the highly eccentric king of Bavaria: it is a miniature gold

---

[1] Many colleagues and friends helped and supported me during the preparation of this article which is based upon my paper on the subject held at the conference *Women Collectors* organised by Andrea M. Gáldy, Susan Bracken and Adriana Turpin in 2008. I would like to thank them for giving me the opportunity to share these observations, and would like to extend my thanks to Carmen Holdsworth-Delgado, Thorsten Eichhorn, Regina Gerisch, Florent Heintz, Angela McShane, Britta Olenyi-von Husen, Corinne Thépaut-Cabasset and Friederike Wolf-Südmeyer.
[2] The pendant was sold through Sotheby's Amsterdam 30 October 2007, AM1031, lot 615.

pill box in the shape of a book.[3] Again a handwritten label with the history of the box was carefully placed inside the fitted case. According to family tradition the label was written by Queen Marie herself. The coincidence of two such items, presumably labelled by the queen herself seemed to deserve more attention, since it suggests that she did not only form a maternal collection but also actively curated, interpreted and reviewed it in a rather personal and meticulous fashion. What was her motivation? Only many years after having received it, the cross jewel was passed on to somebody very close to her.

Collecting Memorabilia of Motherhood: Maternal Collecting as Part of the *Conditio Humana*?

Before looking at Queen Marie's maternal memorabilia in more detail, it is worth exploring the conditions of maternal collecting in general and evidence for earlier examples at the Munich court. The two objects suggest a specific style of sentimental, intimate acquiring of memorabilia that could be called maternal collecting, and is very different from the material-, place- or date-based types of collecting that are the natural focus of our discipline. This type of collecting could be considered a set of behaviours,[4] motivated by a biological fact that at early modern princely courts was linked to a specific role within society.[5] It has been argued that women, even in the highest parts of society, had fewer opportunities to form collections of art in the same ways as their male counterparts because of a relative lack of independence and spending power.[6] Consequently, collections formed by women would have a tendency to express their roles in their environment. Gere and Vaizey state on documented cases of collecting interests of women: "Sometimes their roles as collectors, particularly the royal mistresses and consorts, were complementary to the

---

[3] The gold box was also sold through Sotheby's Amsterdam 1 November 2005, AM0966, lot 1956.
[4] Susan M. Pearce for example argued that personality and motives inform the choice and perception of objects in what she calls "behavioural interaction with objects"; Pearce 1994, 38-40.
[5] The question of gender and roles at court has been addressed by several authors over the last decades, for example Bastl 1995, with further references. The project *Briefe adeliger Frauen* at the University of Vienna explores the roles of women at courts in the Holy Roman Empire between the sixteenth and eighteenth century. http://www.univie.ac.at/Geschichte/Frauenbriefe.
[6] For example Gere and Vaizey 1999, 10 with further references.

central relationships in their lives."[7]

Maternal collecting, as we witness it today, seems to be a part of the *conditio humana*, possibly more a form of behaviour in response to a "maternal instinct". One is tempted to assume by default that it had to exist in previous centuries in very much the same way that we see today. But is this really true, given the very different set-up of female lives up to the nineteenth and even twentieth century? The following aspects appear relevant in this context: which works of art and memorabilia did women collect in relation to their role as mothers? Why were these objects collected? What was their function in relation to other roles assumbed by their respective female collectors in a courtly environment? The most obvious problem in this matter is that of the collections' survival.[8] In addition, the following two questions also beg an answer: to what degree can we speak of collections and how were these displayed? My primary interest is to understand the reasons and the nature of the self-representation of the maternal role within a courtly context in the age of absolutism. Therefore my understanding of collecting is as follows: a collector is someone who gathers works of art to form a group of objects related to a certain subject matter over a long period of time and who brings them together in one place.

Several disciplines are concerned with similar questions, sociological and historical gender studies regarding the role of the mother, as well as art history and related fields—in other words, they investigate context, persons, images and even a specific iconography of the mother as collector. Using the above-mentioned nineteenth-century objects as a starting point, several eminent women associated with the court of Munich from the late seventeenth century were studied. The goal was to establish whether there is any evidence for the collection of works of art or maternal memorabilia, and the motivation behind their acquisition.

At times observations on sentimental collections can be more revealing about the author and the time in which the analysis was made rather than the piece in question. The most obvious challenge in this respect is the ultimately unanswerable question as to whether, in the periods studied here, maternal love was felt and expressed by forming maternal

---

[7] Ibid., 14.

[8] Collections are often dispersed after the death of collectors. Britta Jürgs states in the introduction to an anthology of essays on female collectors: "In den seltensten Fällen blieben die Sammlungen tatsächlich nach dem Tod der Sammlerinnen über mehrere Generationen hinweg in deren Familie oder wurden an einem Ort aufbewahrt, an dem sie ihren geschlossenen Charakter bewahren konnten."; Jürgs 2000, 9.

collections. In 1980 the feminist philosopher Élisabeth Badinter even argued that maternal love is a myth created in modern times. She presents material on the reality of motherhood in France from the seventeenth century in evidence of her hypothesis that maternal love is not an instinct.[9] Women and children were frequently separated very early so that emotional bonding rarely occurred.[10] Badinter's point of view highlights the difficulties in reconstructing and understanding the emotions of individuals who lived in an era in which the expression of emotions was suppressed or ritualised. We fail to understand these individuals' psychological complexity; every interpretation necessarily will be tainted by our own experiences. The only way out of this dilemma is to study the material within the context of its own time and not from our point of view, or simply to admit the limitations of the study.

Daughter, Wife and Mother: the Roles of Women at Princely Courts in the Eighteenth Century

Court ceremonial served as a corset that made it often difficult for women to be the masters of their own lives and emotions. Virtually all the roles of a woman's life were predetermined from her birth: from daughter to wife and mother. Even the *maitresse-en-titre* was a clear-cut role within the social hierarchy of the court.

In 1715 Johann Gottlieb Corvinus published his *Frauenzimmer-Lexicon*.[11] It covers a wide range of subjects, from recipes and instructions on household management to biographies of historical, contemporary and legendary women and, for want of a better word, self-help chapters. The volume is a *vade mecum* that rarely fails to give information on any aspect

---

[9] Badinter offers a close study of the principles underlying the perception of children up to early modern times. Based upon Augustinus' *De civitate dei* it was not uncommon to see children as symbol for the power of evil in need of education and salvation. Consequently maternal affection was not only an inappropriate means to help children to overcome their sinful nature; it was considered a sin in itself. Badinter admits that opposed to the theological point-of-view, common practice was different. She also cites sociological studies to prove that from around 1600 onwards in France it became more and more common among all classes to send their children to nurses directly after birth; Badinter 1982, 36-42.

[10] Kevill-Davies for example states in her history of childhood: "Indeed, the maternal instinct, that visible commodity which we nowadays assume all mothers automatically possess, appears to have been in short supply two or three hundred years ago."; Kevill-Davies 1988, 8.

[11] Corvinus (Amaranthes) 1715.

Figure 26: Frontispiece of Johann Gottlieb Corvinus's (Amaranthes) *Frauenzimmer-Lexicon*, Wolfenbüttel, 1715.

of aristocratic female life in the early eighteenth century.

The frontispiece of the volume shows the private room of a lady (Fig. 26). It is lavishly decorated with a frescoed ceiling, wallpaper and textiles. The lady of the house is depicted on the left, seated at her dressing table and busy with the finishing touches of her *toilette*. A maid helps her to arrange her hair and a little girl watches them. The status and education of the lady are revealed by her possessions: books, a globe, a map, a lute on the side table next to a tray with playing cards. Their reflection on the tray allows us to determine its material as silver. Six sconces or candleholders are distributed in the room, all fitted with lit candles, an extremely expensive way of lighting the room. No bed is visible, but a door in the background is left open and grants a glimpse into the next room, the kitchen where a servant is shown in front of the hearth. This somewhat unlikely sequence of rooms demonstrates that the frontispiece is to give the reader a flavour of the range of subjects addressed in the book. With regard to the subject-matter explored here, it is worth noticing that the woman is depicted as the mother of a girl who is part of her world and spends time with her during the day. The toilet service on the dressing table with two mirrors, in a period when mirror glass was extremely expensive, is another clue. Large, expensive toilet services, often in silver, were a typical gift to a bride, "a perquisite of the married woman"[12] and sometimes given after the birth of the first son.[13] The ceiling fresco depicts three classical goddesses: Venus, Minerva and Diana—three sides of the various roles a woman of the early eighteenth century would have been expected to follow. No portraits are shown on the walls; the maternal role is not expressed by a collection of maternal memorabilia, but by depicting a daughter and the toilet service as evidence of her status and possibly also of the fact that the woman depicted here has given birth to an heir.

Henriette Adelaide of Savoy (1636-1676): the Childless Spouse

The pressure to give birth to an heir can be sensed in many biographies of women from the eighteenth century, among them Henriette Adelaide of

---

[12] Toilet services came into fashion in the mid seventeenth century. By the end of it Augsburg had become the main provider of luxury silver toilet services in the Holy Roman Empire, often acquired on the occasion of a marriage; Blair 1987, 108-9; Glanville 1990, 360.
[13] Maria Leczinska, queen consort of Louis XV, for example was given a toilet service by Henri-Nicolas Cousinet in 1729 to celebrate the birth of the dauphin; Blair 1987, 129.

Savoy, the wife of Elector Ferdinand Maria of Bavaria (1636-1679). In 1665 she moved into the apartment of her late mother-in-law and subsequently refurbished the rooms. Only a fraction of the ensemble survived the bombing of 1944, but the original composition is still legible in the reconstructed apartment. The clergyman Ranuccio Sforza developed a complex iconographical programme related to the subjects of the Wittelsbach dynasty and love.[14]

The first few years following the marriage of Henriette and Ferdinand in 1650, were overshadowed by the fact that no heir to the throne was born. After ten long years, Henriette Adelaide gave birth to her first child, Princess Maria Anna of Bavaria (1660-1690). And only in 1662, twelve entire years after the marriage, she gave birth to Prince Max Emanuel (1662-1726). The enormous relief felt upon the arrival of an heir,[15] shows how important the function of a princely wife as a mother was. In fact, giving birth to a future ruler was the crucial goal of this female role in a princely household. The decoration of Henriette Adelaide's apartment dates back to the time when the pressure on a young wife, who failed to become a mother, kept mounting. It was impossible for her to present herself as mother, which might possibly be the explanation for the unusual iconography chosen for her apartment.

The main cabinet is nowadays known as *Herzkabinett*, Heart Cabinet, referring to the importance of hearts in the iconographic programme of the ceiling. It consists of a series of *quadri riportati* that depict hearts in various contexts. The room has survived without any dramatic changes and thus provides an important example of the self-representation of a woman who failed to be a mother for some time, even though her position was defined by her status as legitimate mother of a dynasty. She could not collect and display images of her children and therefore had to look for an alternative and more subtle means of defending her position. Hearts and love knots are the two main symbols of the ceiling, at the same time they are the armorial devices of the Order of the Annunciate of the House of Savoy. Love and dynastic representation are thus fused into one: the central panel shows the arrow-pierced hearts of the princely couple surrounded by a corona of *amoretti*. All other depictions in the room add to the message of the central panel, that is the promise that love overcomes all obstacles, even a childless marriage.

---

[14] Neumann 2007[2], 63.

[15] The enormous relief felt by Elector Ferdinand Maria upon the birth of his first son and heir was expressed by lavish commissions, including the construction of the church and monastery of Saint Cajetan, nowadays known as *Theatinerkirche* opposite the Residenz in Munich; Kaiser 2008.

Figure 27: Johann Jakob Kleinschmidt after Cosmas Damian Asam, *Therese Kunigunde in Exile surrounded by Portraits of her Children and Husband*, in: Anonymus, *Fortitudo Leonina*, 1715, Munich, Bayerische Staatsbibliothek.

Therese Kunigunde (1676-1730): the Mother in Exile

Eventually Electress Henriette Adelaide gave birth to a male heir, Prince Max Emanuel who was to become one of the most fascinating electors of Bavaria. In 1695 he married the Polish princess Therese Kunigunde. The Austrian War of Succession hit the Duchy of Bavaria with unexpected violence and destroyed all dreams of Bavarian dominance in Europe; after the battle of Höchstadt in 1704 Munich was plundered and Elector Max

Emanuel fled to France. His wife Therese Kunigunde acted on behalf of her husband as Princess Regent. In 1705 she was denied re-entry into Bavaria after a visit to Venice, and remained not only virtually without any political power but also separated from her children and husband for over a decade. Any contact with the children who were raised in Klagenfurt under Austrian supervision—perceived as imprisonment by the Bavarian party—was denied her by the Austrian occupants. She spent several years of exile in Venice. This tragic life as political refugee is commemorated in a print (Fig. 27) after a design by Cosmas Damian Asam (1686-1739). It was issued by the Jesuit order in Munich as part of a series of prints published on the occasion of the triumphal return of Elector Max Emanuel to Munich in 1715.[16]

The print shows the electress seated at a desk in a small cabinet. Through a window the Punta della Dogana in Venice is visible. Therese Kunigunde is shown writing the words "Penelope Ulysii" in a book, thus identifying herself with Ulysses' wife Penelope, who for two decades patiently awaited her husband's return from the Trojan battlefields. A small dog, sign of marital fidelity, supports the reading of the print as celebration of Therese's exemplary virtue during the exile of the family. In front of her a group of portraits of her husband and children decorate the wall. They form a shrine-like virtual collection of a mother who in real life could not form a material collection due to the historical circumstances: the portraits take the place of the sitters who were separated from their mother. Each portrait is inscribed with the name and the position of the sitter, e.g. "Carolus Albert. Pr.[inceps] El.[ectoralis]" or "Maria Anna Primogenita" for her oldest surviving child who was born in 1696. The age of each child is given on the frame of the respective portraits. Two portraits are reflected in the overmantle mirror behind the princess: her husband, Elector Max Emanuel, and her oldest son, Karl Albrecht (1697-1745), heir to the throne. Attached to the mirror frame we find Latin mottoes. In combination with the portraits they translate into a political message: we can read "Semper idem" ("Always the same") and underneath "Constantia in adversis" ("Constancy in adverse conditions") amongst other mottoes.[17] On the base under the mirror, an inscription

---

[16] Anonymus 1715. The reproduction shown here is taken from the volume preserved at the Bayerische Staatsbibliothek, München (BSB: Res/2 Bavar. 297 c), which is available online through the library homepage: www.bsb-muenchen.de.

[17] On ribbons: "Fides coniungalis" (marital faithfulness) and "Pietas Exemplaris" (exemplary piety), directly underneath in cartouches: "Non fallit" (She does not deceive) and "Movet Aspectu" (She moves with a glance). Attached to the lower part of the frame: "Accepta refundit" (She gives back what she received) and

underlines the interpretation of the princess regent as the modern typology of heroic women in the Old Testament who defended their people, e.g. "beautiful Rachel" or "strong Judith". "Rachel was both beautiful and pious, Susanna beautiful and chaste, Judith was strong, and Sarah was generous, but it is she, the ruler who holds the reins of Bavaria, Theresa only, who possesses all these [virtues] assembled."[18] The comparisons firmly root Therese Kunigunde not only in a classical but also in a Christian tradition and underline her possession of the classical princely virtues such as *pietas* and *fortitudo* in combination with typically female virtues, such as chastity and beauty.

None of the portraits is meant to depict the likeness of the sitter, but their respective position in relation to Therese Kunigunde as Princess Regent of Bavaria and as mother of a dynasty. The reference to Penelope and biblical heroines does imply that maternal love was not the major impetus, but rather faithful promotion and protection of the family as a dynasty. This print is not the only instance of a portrait of Therese Kunigunde with pictures of members of her family. A portrait of Therese Kunigunde at the age of twenty-five (Fig. 28) depicts her holding up a portrait miniature of her eldest son, then seven years of age.[19] The portrait dates from 1704 directly after she was proclaimed Princess Regent by her husband. Therese Kunigunde herself is not wearing insignia of power apart from the ermine trimmings indicating her status as electress. The portrait of Karl Albrecht is mounted as a so-called *boîte à portrait*, a form of jewel introduced as diplomatic gift by Louis XIV of France. The form was soon used throughout Europe in similar ways.[20]

One cannot help but compare this example of a female regent with other women temporarily in power as Princess Regent, such as Marie de' Medici (1575-1642) or Markgravine Sibylla Augusta of Baden (1675-1733).[21] Both of them acted on behalf of their infant sons, not their exiled

---

"Munificentia principalis" (princely generosity). Some of the mottoes can be traced in Jesuit publications, for example: "Dona accepta in deum refundit". See Masen 1681, 602.

[18] "PVLCHRA RACHEL SIMVL ET PIA / PVLCHRA ET CASTA SVSANNA / EST FORTIS IUDITH / MVNIFICENSQUE SARA / EST QUAE BOICAS / PRINCEPS MODERATUR HABENAS / HAEC COLLECTA SIMVL / SOLA TERESA TENET".

[19] I would like to thank Corinne Thépaut-Cabasset, Paris, for drawing my attention to this portrait.

[20] An example of a *boîte à portrait* with the portrait of an Elector is in the Gilbert Collection on loan to the Victoria & Albert Museum, London: Loan: Gilbert.294-2008. See also Coffin and Hofstetter 2000, 81-2, cat. n. 34.

Sibylla Augusta also represented herself in the company of her offspring; a most

husbands. Thus the period of their reign was clearly defined and limited from the very outset until the coming of age of the heir. The motif of a collection of portraits of her children within portraits of Therese Kunigunde is used as a symbol of the nature of her status as mother and leader of a dynasty; she represents her family. The display replaces the actual process of collecting.[22] All pictures within the picture underline the dynastic dimension and show the children as uniform group of princes and princesses. This virtual maternal collection is not about affection, it is about the struggle for survival as a dynasty.

Figure 28: Johan Andreas Wolff, *Electress Therese Kunigunde with a Miniature Depicting her Son Karl Albrecht*, oil on canvas, 1704, Munich, Schloss Nymphenburg.

---

remarkably lifelike wax group of her and her children survives at the Badisches Landesmuseum in Karlsruhe, Germany, online catalogue entry on www.tuerken beute.de. For a detailed biography see Esser 1983; Kaack 1983; Vetter 2007.

[22] This is not to say that Therese Kunigunde did not collect, but there seems to be no surviving documentation of her possessions during her time in Venice. She lived in comparatively simple circumstances during her Venetian exile; Kägler 2009, no pagination.

The Court of Elector Karl Albrecht of Bavaria
(1697-1745): Wife and Mistress as Mothers

Kunigunde Therese's first-born son was Karl Albrecht, later Emperor Karl VII. His first son was born on 4 October 1723, not to his wife, but to his mistress, Carlotta von Ingenheim (born 1703). The prince accepted the child and made him count Holnstein (1723-1780). The year before, in October 1722, Karl Albrecht had married archduchess Maria Amalie of Austria.[23] The mother of the illegitimate first son was presented with a state-of-the-art town house designed by the leading architect of the time, François Cuvilliés, and was married to one of Karl Albrecht's chamberlains. But as far as we are able to tell from archival records, Carlotta von Ingenheim, refused to accept her role as a mother, reputedly because of the associated shame.[24] It is difficult to tell from a chronological distance of almost three hundred years if such feelings were really involved.

Carlotta von Ingenheim's portrait survives in a private collection and shows her in exactly the same pose and against the same background as one of the official portraits of Electress Maria Amalie, now on display in the Residenz of Munich, in an unusually daring attempt to imitate the modes of representation reserved for her rival, that is as spouse rather than mother.[25] The legitimate spouse, Maria Amalie, added to this a maternal collection: two pendants of double-portraits of the four eldest children were probably displayed in her private quarters.[26]

---

[23] After a first ceremony in Vienna on 5 October 1722, the marriage was celebrated in Munich after the couple's arrival on 17 October. We are informed of the unusual pomp of the wedding and the generous gifts of jewellery presented by the young husband to his wife. Only in 1727 did Maria Amalie give birth to a son, the future Elector Max III Joseph; Haller 1988, 48 and 54.

[24] Ibid., for a detailed biography.

[25] Joseph Vivien, *Portrait of Maria Amalia of Bavaria* (1701-1756), 1722, Munich, Bayerische Staatsgemäldesammlung, inv. n. 2488; circle of Joseph Vivien, *Portrait of Baroness Carlotta von Ingenheim*, 1722, Munich, Private Collection; illustrated in: Haller 1988, 51.

[26] Workshop George Desmarées, *Portraits of Princesses Maria Antonia Walburgis and Theresia Benedikta of Bavaria*; *Portraits of Princes Joseph and Joseph Ludwig of Bavaria*, circa 1740, Munich, Residenz, inv. nn. G0057 and G0058.

Figure 29: Porcelain cup with a portrait of the future King Maximilian II of Bavaria as a baby, c.1813-1814, Munich, Bayerisches Nationalmuseum.

Queen Therese of Bavaria (1792-1854): Mother of Angels, not Princes

The Age of Enlightenment marks a change regarding the status of children within society and as a result acceptable forms of parenting which also allowed for a more open expression of maternal love.[27] Queen Therese of Bavaria, née princess of Saxe-Hildburghausen is an example of this new generation of mothers. She became the wife of Ludwig I of Bavaria (1786-1868, king from 1825-1848) in 1810.[28]

The changes to family life in the late eighteenth and early nineteenth century are reflected in the arts, particularly in portraiture. Informal family portraits are an invention of this time, as opposed to official portraits

---

[27] Jean-Jacques Rousseau's novel *Emile*, published in 1762, advocated a more compassionate approach to childcare and education, and initiated the revolutionary changes to the perception and protection of children; Kevill-Davies 1988, 8-9 with further references.

[28] Bavaria was created a kingdom by Napoleon Bonaparte in 1806.

including symbols of the rank and status of the sitter. The representation of the children of the future Queen Therese is a particularly interesting and daring example of depicting royal children simply as children, and not small adults decorated with sashes and orders. Decorations of royal commissions included pieces with portraits of the royal children based upon portraits by court painters. Several examples survive, such as a cup (Fig. 29) in the Bayerisches Nationalmuseum in Munich, which is decorated with the portrait of the future King Maximilian II (1811-1864) as a baby, probably around 1813/1814.[29] It is unmarked but considered a Nymphenburg piece because of its quality and provenance from the royal household.[30] The cup depicting the baby prince is of a somewhat more intimate character than the examples discussed so far: the child is shown without any royal insignia, which was not a universal practice as the comparison with a portrait miniature of François Joseph Charles Bonaparte, king of Rome (1811-1832), as a baby proves.[31]

Several comparable portraits of children of the Bavarian royal family without symbols of their status were commissioned and are in line with other such portraits of the period, including children's heads as cherubim by court painter Joseph Karl Stieler (1781-1858).[32] These portraits were not kept in a private room, but hung in semi-public rooms of the palaces.[33]

---

[29] Bayerisches Nationalmuseum, Munich, inv. n. Ker 2207/2372; Hantschmann 1995, 292, cat. n. 133, ill.

[30] The cup was given to the Bayerisches Nationalmuseum as a bequest of King Ludwig I of Bavaria, thus the sitter is very likely a member of the royal family. Hantschmann identified the sitter based upon the date of the cup, contrary to an earlier identification. This proves how difficult, nearly impossible it is to identify portraits of children without attributes or symbols of status; Hantschmann 1995, 292.

[31] The miniature is part oft he Gilbert Collection on loan to the Victoria and Albert Museum. Loan: Gilbert.255-2008; Coffin and Hofstetter 2000, 68-9, cat. n. 20.

[32] For example a portrait of Josephine, princess of Leuchtenberg, aged three from 1810, illustrated in: v. Hase-Schmundt, 1971, 120, cat. n. 23. This type of portrait was also repeated on a Nymphenburg ecueille, 1818/1821, from the royal collection, now property of the Wittelsbacher Ausgleichsfond; Hantschmann 1995, 306, cat. n. 164.

[33] For example see v. Hase-Schmundt 1971, 121, cat. no. 34, 122, cat. no. 37-42 and, most importantly, 127, cat. no. 83. The latter is a full-length portrait of Princess Maximiliane Josepha Caroline (born 1810) who died in 1821 that is inspired by Raphael's *Transfiguration*. She was the daughter of King Maximilian I and his second wife Caroline, née princess of Baden (1776-1841)—the stepmother of Queen Therese's spouse. Watercolours of interiors of aristocratic homes became fashionable during the *Biedermeier* period. Franz Barbari's depictions of the salons and studies of Austrian aristocrats, such as the one owned by Princess Karolina

Additionally they were reproduced on luxury items and thus shared with a wider public very much in the fashion of modern royal memorabilia.

Queen Marie of Bavaria (1825-1889):
the Mother as Curator

The changes of attitude towards maternity and therefore the objects collected in relation to it were slow and are difficult to measure. Let us return to Queen Marie whose presumably handwritten notes inspired this essay. Née princess of Prussia (1825-1889), she was married to King Maximilian II, the very same whose portrait as a baby is depicted on the Nymphenburg cup discussed above.

Cross pendant and pill box were gifts of sons to a princely mother and as such different from the other works discussed in this article which were initiated by the respective mother herself to express her role and, possibly, affection. One of the items was, in turn, presented by the mother after a considerable time span to a lady-in-waiting. Again the question of collecting cannot be separated from the question of iconography and symbolism. Though the Bavarian royal family is of Roman Catholic denomination, the queen remained Protestant until 1874. The gift of the cross to a member of her household on the occasion of her conversion constitutes in itself a symbolic act of intimacy, of allowing somebody into the inner circle of the royal family.

The pill box is of a rather different quality: whereas the amethyst cross has a high value as a symbolic present with a long-standing tradition, the pill box is an object of vertu with seemingly minor symbolic significance. It was presented to Queen Marie by Ludwig II on her 54th birthday on 15 October 1879. The *putto* does not only echo the angelic portraits of the children of King Ludwig I and Queen Therese of Bavaria, Ludwig II's grand parents, its meaning can be traced back even further. The posture of the figure is taken from the famous angels on Raphael's *Sistine Madonna*, now in the Gemäldegalerie Alter Meister in Dresden.[34] Today often reduced to the depiction of cute, unruly boys with wings, their iconography goes back to the tradition of *giochi di putti* as a mirror of adult life. The angel supporting his chin with his arm can be seen as an

---

Maria Kinsky, show the typical crowded interiors of the period. The fashion of filling rooms with small objects resulted in a more freequent display of family portraits, for example, on a lady's writing desk; Stangler and Leindl 1997, cat. n. 1.234.16-7, 6.15, 7.13.

[34] Raphael, *Sistine Madonna*, 1512/1513, Dresden, Gemäldegalerie Alter Meister. The painting entered the Saxon Royal Collection in 1753.

allegory of melancholy.[35] The choice seems very suitable for Ludwig II, the melancholic fairy tale king.[36]

The choice of a miniature box with a miniature angel is in itself significant: it has a toy-like quality and on a superficial level evokes a romantic childhood world. It is the precious token of a child to a mother, even though the child was 34 years old in 1879. In contrast the grown-up gift of a religious jewel was presented by the teenage Otto to his mother. Queen Marie did not only collect these items, she apparently also made sure they were labelled with a description and short account of the occasion upon which they were received; their provenance was supposed to be preserved. Family tradition has it that Queen Marie wrote these labels herself. The objects of the collection are charged with symbolism referring to important moments in the relationship between mother and child or evoking the childhood of one of the donors. It seems that Queen Marie felt it appropriate to pass on the religious, semi-official gift of the cross, while the pill box as the more sentimental, intimate offering remained in her collection until her death.

Maternal Collecting: Tracing the Untraceable

It has to be admitted that the research on this subject has turned into an exercise of working around gaps of evidence and losses, while also withstanding the great temptation to project personal experiences and judgments on historic material. Only very few traces of maternal collections as described at the beginning were found during the research for this essay. The focus on one particular dynasty certainly limited the chances of finding relevant objects relating to this area of collecting which is very much in flux and very vulnerable to voluntary or accidental dispersal by future generations, especially when the objects are not of particular material value, such as children's' drawings.

Maternal collections are not necessarily visible, official collections with a dedicated shrine-like space within an architectural setting or a cabinet. By their very nature they tend to be informal, undocumented,

---

[35] Dürer's famous woodcut *Melenconia I* from 1514 is the best known example of the symbolic gesture. Panofsky 1923.

[36] Ludwig II might not have been aware of this tradition of the motif. No other Bavarian aristocrat has been the subject of so many studies and biographies since his mysterious death in 1886—one day after being declared unfit to reign due to mental illness. His brother Otto also suffered from mental illness. The relationship with their parents has been investigated and made responsible for the fate of the two brothers; Richter 1997 and Richter 2001.

ever-changing and often easy to move from one place to another. This mobility of maternal collections can reach the point where they are closer to virtual collections than a group of real objects gathered in one physical space. Regardless of this very fluid, dynamic character, they remain crucial for the self-identification of the respective collecting mother, especially in the absence of her children. It is significant in this context that the best evidence for mothers' gathering their children around them through memorabilia before the nineteenth century is Electress Therese Kunigunde, who was separated from her children and her people. Where it was impossible to fulfil the maternal role in reality, its representation became crucial. Her loss is our gain, because the results of this propaganda, i.e. portraits of Therese Kunigunde not with her children but with their pictures, survive to the present day as a virtual maternal and dynastic *Schatzkammer*. It is not a collection of intimacy as far as we can tell, for her claims to power and the status of her children are clearly connected and visible in the portraits. Only in the early nineteenth century do the presentations focus on the children as individuals, not as princes and heirs to the throne. Gifts by children to their mothers seem to vary according to occasion and to the character of the donor, as the two gifts to Queen Marie seem to indicate. Her use of the objects in later life was probably informed by the character of the respective gift and its giver.

If maternal, sentimental collections were formed before the nineteenth century by women of the court in Munich, either the actual memorabilia do not survive, the objects have lost their history or they are hidden in private collections, such as the two discoveries related to Queen Marie. The material gathered here relates to a group of extraordinary women and mothers in sometimes very difficult, challenging circumstances. The role as mother was of utmost importance for all of them. Even though the material traces of their collections are few, there are other sources and other dynasties that could be studied in relation to maternal collections, for example wills and inventories. The picture that emerges from the material presented here may be that of a very common development, it might also be an exception. It is my hope that this article might inspire further research in this area of the history of collecting.

CHAPTER SEVEN

THE DUCHESSE DE BERRI AND THE AESTHETICS OF ROYALISM: DYNASTIC COLLECTING IN NINETEENTH-CENTURY FRANCE

PHILIP MANSEL

Marie Caroline, duchesse de Berri, asserted her politics and her personality not only through her charities, her entertainments, and her attempted uprisings against Louis-Philippe in 1832, but also through her collections. She has been called both "la Marie Stuart de la Vendée" and "the Queen of the Troubadour style".

The Collector

Marie Caroline (Fig. 30), princess of the Two Sicilies, was born in the palace of Caserta on 5 November 1798. A grand-daughter of King Ferdinand IV of Naples (after 1816 Ferdinand I of the Two Sicilies), she spent most of her youth in Palermo, during the royal family's retreats to Sicily in 1799-1800 and 1806-16, caused by the French occupations of Naples. In the Capella Palatina of Palermo, and later in Notre Dame de Paris on 17 June 1816, she was married to her cousin, a nephew of Louis XVIII, Charles-Ferdinand, duc de Berri. He was heir to the throne of France, as his elder brother the duc d'Angoulême showed no signs of producing children. The Berris' first duty was to do so (Fig. 31). In the meantime one of their occupations was to expand the picture collection begun by the duke in London. Like many Frenchmen, Berri had his cultural horizons broadened by emigration. Living on a British pension, he had frequented sale rooms and Colnaghi's, buying works by Wouvermans among others.[1]

Collecting reflected the competitive dynasticism which, as well as nationalism, revolution, and class conflicts, shaped nineteenth-century France. Because they were competing to win or secure the throne, in order to improve their political credentials, the three rival dynasties, Bourbons, Orléans and Bonapartes had to be more active in the arts, as well as in other public spheres. Their patronage took two forms. First all monarchs took a personal interest in expanding and improving the national (then called imperial or royal, depending on the dynasty in power) collections in the Louvre and Versailles, with the help of their respective artistic advisers—Baron Denon under the Empire, the comte de Forbin under the Restoration, the comte de Nieuwerkerke under the Second Empire. In response to this massive monarchical patronage, many of the most famous painters of the age—including David (Premier peintre de l'Empereur), Ingres, Baron Gérard (Premier peintre du roi), Isabey (Dessinateur de la chambre under both the Empire and the Restoration), Horace Vernet, Prud'hon, and Ary Scheffer—were also court painters, painting dynastic portraits and events.

Second, each dynasty also had members who, helped by the generous annual incomes all received from the civil lists of the period, made large private collections. During the Empire the Empress Josephine's taste for historical subjects and Redouté flower paintings anticipated that of the duc and duchesse de Berri. In all she owned 362 pictures, some of which can be admired in her château of Malmaison today.[2] A shared artistic influence was her chamberlain, Count Lancelot Turpin de Crissé, who later painted views of Naples for the duchesse de Berri, and of Paris for the duc de Bordeaux. Napoleon I's brother, Lucien, made an impressive collection of paintings, while his half-uncle Cardinal Fesch accumulated the phenomenal total of 16,000 pictures, in the course of his career as Grand Aumonier and archbishop of Lyon, and later during his exile in Rome. Most were sold after his death; some are now in the Musée Fesch in Ajaccio.[3]

In accordance with Orléans family tradition (before the revolution the picture gallery of the Orléans' palace, the Palais Royal, had been one of the most famous in Paris), both as duc d'Orléans and king of the French, Louis-Philippe made a collection of pictures, both French and Spanish.[4] They included the Horace Vernet scenes of the battles of Valmy and

---

[1] Castelot 1951, 58.
[2] Pougetoux, 2005.
[3] Edelein-Badie 1997; Bonnet Saint-Georges 2010, 30-9.
[4] Cabanis 1985.

Jemappes, in which Louis-Philippe had fought for the first Republic, now in the National Gallery, London. He also founded the French national portrait collection, the Musée de l'Histoire de France, which opened in the château de Versailles in 1837.

The duc and duchesse de Berri were the principal collectors of the elder branch of the Bourbons. Their collection reflected not only the competing dynasticism of the period but also their personal taste, and the aesthetics of royalism. Like all official patrons of the Restoration, the duc and duchesse de Berri tried to appropriate or celebrate the Bourbon past, in particular the patron of the French Restoration, Henri IV. Henri IV was the warrior king who fought his way to the throne in 1589-1596, reconciled Frenchmen after horrific civil conflicts, and died under an assassin's knife in 1610. Already there had been a revival of interest in this popular royal hero in the eighteenth century and under the Empire: the Empress Josephine had hung pictures of Henri IV in her gallery at Malmaison. After 1814 parallels with the restored Bourbons, who had also come to the throne after years of conflict, increased his appeal. The duc and duchesse de Berri bought a picture by Revoil of Henri IV playing with his children in front of the Spanish ambassador, another by Crépin of Henri IV's former minister, the duc de Sully, showing his grandson the monument containing the heart of his murdered master.

In addition they acquired a version of Baron Gérard's *Entry of Henri IV into Paris*, the triumph of the salon of 1817. Commissioned by Louis XVIII from his Premier peintre, Baron Gérard, it was a pictorial expression of the hopes and fears of the Restoration. The painting shows rebels, e.g. former revolutionaries and Bonapartists—such as Gérard himself—being granted pardon as foreign troops leave Paris: an echo of the situation in France in 1817. Anticipating the 1820 picture by Alexandre Menjaud showing Berri's death-bed agony, witnessed by his illegitimate children whose mother was his English mistress Amy Brown, the king's mistress and illegitimate children are shown in the corner: the Bourbons were no prudes. Berri also began to buy modern French pictures such as, in a gesture to French nationalism, two battle scenes, *Le Trompette mort* and *Le chien du régiment* by the Bonapartist Horace Vernet, both now in the Wallace Collection. They were among the nineteen pictures he purchased at the salon in 1819.[5] As well as reflecting their love of the arts, the Berris' collection had a political purpose, to popularise the Restoration.

Before his wife's eyes on 13 February 1820, however, the duc de Berri

---

[5] Bonnemaison, 1822.

was fatally stabbed by a Bonapartist fanatic called Louvel, outside the
Paris opera. During his long death-bed agony in an antechamber of the
Paris opera, the groans of the dying prince mingled with the sounds of the
opera-singers, as the royal family and the ministers gathered round the
death-bed. "Killed on the field of battle," said Paris wits, referring to
Berri's many affairs with opera-singers.

Eight months later his widow did her dynastic duty, by bearing a son,
the duc de Bordeaux. Her courage and originality are revealed by a scene
at the birth on 29 September 1820. As leader of the Bonapartists in Paris,
Maréchal Suchet had been chosen to be one of the witnesses to the birth,
with a former émigré, the Maréchal de Coigny. In the corrosive distrust
prevailing in Paris, only a Bonapartist could be trusted to guarantee the
veracity of a Bourbon birth. The birth was so rapid that the duchess could
barely keep the umbilical cord attached to the child long enough for
Suchet to see it with his own eyes. According to the British ambassador,
Sir Charles Stuart, the princess urged the marshal to pull on her cord
himself with the words "Prenez, Mr. le Maréchal! Tirez!" Upon the
marshal showing some repugnance to do so, she repeated "Mais tirez
donc, Mr. le Maréchal!"[6]

Despite this incontrovertible evidence, the venom of party passions and
personal ambitions led the Bourbons' liberal cousins the duc and duchesse
d'Orléans, whose place in the order of succession had been diminished by
Bordeaux's birth, to spread doubts about it in the pages of the duchess's
private diary, her *journal*. Royalists, however, hailed him as "l'enfant du
miracle, Henri Dieudonné". The regime seemed assured.[7]

The marriage of the duc and duchesse de Berri had been exceptionally
happy. To commemorate her murdered husband, on his saint's day the
feast of Saint Charles, on 4 November 1820, the duchesse founded the
elegant neoclassical Hospice Saint Charles at Rosny beside her château of
Rosny in Normandy, formerly owned by the minister of Henri IV, the duc
de Sully. The architect was the Swiss Joseph Antoine Froelicher.[8]
Underneath the chapel altar, she buried Berri's heart, his blood-stained
clothes and a copy of Chateaubriand's commemorative panegyric,
Memoires historiques sur le Duc de Berri, bound in black leather, of
which all witnesses of the murder had been given a copy.[9] Thereafter, with
an income of 1,500,000 francs a year from the civil list—about £75,000,

---

[6] Mansel 2001, 167-9, 179.

[7] Ibid., 179.

[8] Macé de Lépinay 1976, 367-83.

[9] Sothebys's London sales catalogue, 14 April 2011: item 200, contains the
reproduction of a painting of the scene by Hilaire Thierry.

over twice what Prince Albert would obtain in the United Kingdom in 1840—the widowed duchesse de Berri was a leader of taste, fashion and entertainment in Paris until the revolution of 1830. In order to keep her out of politics, to fulfill a traditional royal function and to make Paris tradesmen happy, both Louis XVIII and Charles X were glad for her to devote her time and her income to the arts. With the possible exception of Marie Antoinette (who owned far fewer pictures), she would be more active as a patron of the arts than any woman of the French royal family since Anne of Austria.

The Collection

The curator of her collection was another émigré, the Chevalier Bonnemaison. To advertise his patron's taste and status, in 1822 he published a catalogue in which he hailed the duc de Berri as "le protecteur des artistes". He dedicated it:

> A SON ALTESSE ROYALE MADAME LA DUCHESSE DE BERRY.
> MADAME,
> C'est à VOTRE ALTESSE ROYALE qu'est due l'heureuse pensée de multiplier et de faire connaitre plus généralement par la lithographie les productions remarquables des peintres de genre de l'école actuelle....
> Le très humble et très obéissant serviteur, Le cher BONNEMAISON.[10]

After her husband's murder, the duchesse de Berri had moved to the Tuileries palace. While the Dutch old masters liked by her husband stayed in their previous residence, the Elysée, she continued his project of making a modern French collection. Other contemporary collections, for example those of the duke of Hamilton, the marquess of Hertford or the Rothschilds, represent attempts to appropriate the past for self-aggrandisement in the present. They asserted their status by the purchase of objects with royal provenance. The Bourbons' dynastic rivals the Bonapartes and the Orléans preferred pictures showing national scenes, of battles and heroic deeds.[11] The collection of the duchesse de Berri reflected the aesthetics of royalism, as well as her personal taste. It concentrated on family life, good works and provincial landscapes. The reasons for these aesthetic choices were in part political. The family and the provinces were two bases of the restored Bourbon monarchy. It tried to heal, through charities, family life and the provinces, the damage inflicted

---

[10] Bonnemaison, 1822, unpaginated.
[11] Chaudonneret, 1999, 141.

by revolution, nationalism and Paris.

Indeed the first city to declare for Louis XVIII, on 12 March 1814, while Napoleon I was still in control of Paris, had been a provincial city, Bordeaux—hence the duchesse de Berri's son's title of duc de Bordeaux. Throughout the 1820's she made official tours of the provinces, often with a charitable purpose (visits to churches, hospitals, and memorials), accompanied by members of her household. She regularly summered in Dieppe, a sea-side resort which she helped to make fashionable.[12] She also spent months at her château of Rosny. It was packed with books and pictures, and had a garden filled with rare plants and animals including giraffes.[13] Both Dieppe and Rosny represented new departures. They were in Normandy, outside the gilded circle of the Bourbons' traditional residences in the Île de France.

Figure 30 (left): Print by M. Delpech from a portrait by Robert Lefevre, *Portrait of the Duchesse de Berri*, c.1825, Philip Mansel collection.

Figure 31 (right): James Pradier. *The Duchesse de Berri with her two Children, Mademoiselle and the Duc de Bordeaux*, c.1825, Philip Mansel collection.

---

[12] Mansel 1978, 381.
[13] Guibal 2007, 49-59.

Family Life

The 1821 portrait by Louis Hersent, formerly in her collection, of her two children, Bordeaux and his elder sister Louise, later duchess of Parma, is in complete contrast to Gérard's portrait of the young king of Rome—and to portraits of Marie-Antoinette's children, by Madame Vigée-Lebrun and Adam Wertmuller. Showing the prince in his cradle, watched by his sister, it is entirely domestic and familial. As the entry in the catalogue of her collection boasted, there are no signs of grandeur, no trace of militarism. In contrast to portraits of Marie Antoinette with her children, the mother is not represented. The focus is on the children.

For every historical picture, such as Taunay's *La mort de Bayard*, Destouches's *Marie Stuart à Lochleven* or Revoil's *Henri IV with his children*, we find many more scenes of contemporary domesticity. The present predominates over the past. Here is a list of some of the pictures the Berris bought before 1822. Many represent women and children:

La chambre des petits savoyards by M. Bonnefond;
Une scène des boulevards and
L'entrée du Théatre de l'Ambigu Comique
by M. Boilly;
Martin Drolling *Maison à vendre*
and *Interieur d'une salle à manger*;
M.Danloux's *Le petit gourmand* and
La petite boudeuse;
Mlle Gérard *Une mère de famille entourée de ses enfants*
and *L'heureuse mère*;
Une distribution d'aumones by M. Taunay;
A Scheffer's *La bonne vieille*;
M. Destouche's *Une jeune dame visitant son père en prison*;
Louis Hersent's *Louis XVI distribuant ses bienfaits aux pauvres.*
M. Duval Camus *Les Frères de la doctrine chretienne.*[14]

---

[14] Bonnemaison 1822, no pagination; paintings from the duchess's collections can be found in many French museums, including the Louvre. Her 1828 portrait by Alexandre Dubois-Drahonnet is in the Musée de Picardie, Amiens. *Sully montrant a son petit-fils le monument renfermant le Coeur d'Henri IV* (1819) by Marie-Philippe Coupin de la Couperie is in the Musée national du château de Pau. The *Messe de relevailles de la Duchesse de Berri* (1828) by Louis-Nicolas Lemasle is in the Musée Antoine-Lecuyer in Saint Quentin. Despite so many sales, her descendants still own some of her pictures. A few French royal portraits still hang on the walls of her palace in Venice, now the municipal casino.

Figure 32: Auzou, like Pradier and many other contemporary painters, also tried to link French family feelings to the restored Bourbons.

Directly linking the family and the Restoration, Madame Auzou's *Une des croisées de Paris le jour de l'arrivée de S.M. Louis XVIII* (1814) is one of the most political of the Berri's pictures (Fig. 32). A young and beautiful mother, surrounded by her children, is shown returning to health after a long illness with "a smile of happiness on her colourless lips", as she watches the entry into Paris on 3 May 1814 of Louis XVIII, the king who "has given the Charte to his peoples and commanded them to forget hatreds and sufferings". Pictures, by Mlle Gérard, Bonnefond, Danloux (another royalist émigré who had exhibited at the Royal Academy in London) and many others also concentrate on family life and children: for example *La Bonne Mère* by M. Genod, showing a mother feeding her daughter; *Une famille malheureuse* by Prud'hon portrays a family facing poverty as the father is mortally ill.[15] The family was the basis of royalism: blessed by the church, it was naturally opposed to the revolution's wars and legalisation of divorce. Children were believed to be less corrupt, therefore more loyal, than adults. A favourite song of the period, taken from a play by Colle, *La partie de chasse d'Henri IV*, was called "Où peut-on etre mieux, qu'au sein de sa famille?"

Yet the collection was not escapist. Scenes of prison, poverty and illness also hung on the duchesse de Berri's walls. The collection was also full of views—of Rosny, Italy, Switzerland and Greece. Paris was not excluded. Pictures by Boilly of the boulevards and the theatre of the Ambigu-Comique are a tribute to the Bourbons' post-revolutionary reengagement with Paris. The duchesse de Berri lived there for half the year and made the capital the centre of her entertainments.

The subscribers' list to the printed catalogue of the collection confirms the European character of Restoration Paris. It includes names like Galignani, the European bookseller in Paris, happily still with us; the great printer Didot; bankers like Casimir Perier and two barons de Rothschild; Talleyrand; the publisher Treuttel and Wurtz; Pugin and Liszt; booksellers in Paris, Brussels, Rotterdam, Saint Petersburg, Berlin and Warsaw; the earls of Essex and Yarmouth, the dukes of Wellington and Bedford; the king and queen of the Two Sicilies and the empress mother of Russia.[16]

The Patron

How much the duchesse de Berri was involved in particular decisions to buy or commission is unknown. But she loved pictures at least as much as her husband. She had a drawing-master from Piedmont, the Chevalier Storelli and herself frequently painted views of Rosny and Dieppe. Contemporaries were impressed; even the acid Orleanist Madame de Boigne remarked on the intelligent tact with which she talked to artists.[17] She also visited the great flower painter Redouté in his atelier, bought the originals of his drawings of roses, became one of his pupils and helped him get a job at the Muséum d'histoire naturelle; he dedicated his *Album*

---

[15] Bonnemaison 1822, no pagination.
[16] Ibid.
[17] Kremers 2002, 63, 102, 114 and 129.

des roses, one of which is named after her, to the duchess in 1825.

The duchesse de Berri's collecting was not restricted to paintings. She loved books, particularly the novels of Walter Scott and the plays of Victor Hugo. The bindings of the books in her library, one of the most admired of the day, are masterpieces from the golden age of French book-binding: a black mourning binding decorates Chateaubriand's tribute to her husband. All bindings bear her coat of arms, pairing Berri and the Two Sicilies.[18] Books too reveal the aesthetics of royalism, in this case hyper-sacralisation of the dynasty. In Hugo's early royalist poems he compared the duchess to the Virgin Mary and the birth of the duc de Bordeaux to that of Jesus Christ: both were saviours of the world. She helped him get a pension and watched his daring Romantic play *Hernani*.

Her *Bal Marie Stuart* in the Tuileries on 2 March 1829 was a Franco-British celebration, commemorating in the spirit of Walter Scott an imaginary visit of Marie de Guise (represented by the wife of the British ambassador, Lady Stuart de Rothesay) to her daughter Mary Queen of Scots (the duchesse de Berri herself) and Francois II (the duc de Chartres, son of the duc d'Orléans) in France. Guests went to the royal library in search of accurate illustrations on which to base their magnificent 1560s historical costumes.[19] Contemporaries write that the duchess at parties was in extraordinarily high spirits. "Balls are starting, above all at court; the duchesse de Berri loves them and is inexhaustible," wrote the comte de Castellane. Thanks to her, the Bourbon court again became a social and artistic magnet.[20]

She was as avant-garde in taste as she was reactionary in politics. Operas were dedicated to her. She helped to popularise the music of Beethoven in Paris and to launch the career of Eugène Scribe, the most popular French dramatist of the nineteenth century. His plays, such as *Avant, Pendant et Après* about the French revolution and its consequences, were performed in a theatre called, after her, le Théatre de Madame. Fascinated by dress, she also patronised a new fashion magazine called *La Mode*, edited by Emile de Girardin, which published early articles by Balzac and George Sand.[21]

Her collecting, or desire to accumulate, was multi-dimensional, as befitted a princess, confident of her rank and importance, who read, drew and sang with equal energy. In addition to books and pictures, she also

---

[18] The sales catalogue of the library at Rosny (1837) contains 2,578 lots; many collections of novels, manuscripts and prints were sold as single lots.

[19] Lami 1829, passim.

[20] Mansel 1989, 103, 138.

[21] Grenville 1861, 20; Mansel 2001, 324 n.

collected ivory, porcelain, miniatures, musical scores and elegant Restoration furniture in light-woods, which can be seen in a famous drawing by Auguste Garneray of her apartment in the Tuileries. She led and formed taste.[22] Her collection of musical scores included operas by Rossini, Bellini and Donizetti.[23] Part of her collections of stones, agates, shells, fossils and geological specimens was housed in a twelve-drawer birch and ebonised cabinet: she is also said to have owned 1,400 stuffed animals.[24]

The July Revolution and the Collection's Dispersion

The revolution of July 1830 occurred, just after a visit by her father Francis I, king of the Two Sicilies, to Paris. Parisians had rioted in the garden of the Palais Royal as guests danced in the state apartment above, at a ball given by Louis-Philippe, duc d'Orléans in honour of his brother-in-law. "C'est une fête toute napolitaine, Monseigneur", Narcisse de Salvandy whispered to Orléans: "we are dancing on a volcano". The duchess's only criticism of the coup by her father-in-law Charles X, attempting to restrict the freedoms given by the Charte, was its feebleness of execution. The best French troops were away fighting in Algiers. Fighting in defence of the Charte, Parisians defeated the Royal Guard.[25]

The July revolution was a harsh awakening. It showed that, despite the Bourbons' dedication to good works and the provinces, most of France followed the leadership of Paris, and wanted a liberal constitution. The royal family departed into an exile which proved definitive. To their disgust their cousin, the duc d'Orléans, ascended the throne as Louis Philippe, king of the French. His son the duc de Chartres, the duchess's dancing partner in 1829, became Prince Royal. Both royalists and their enemies agreed that the Restoration had been "une comédie courtisanesque de quinze ans".

Like Empress Marie-Louise, who moved her collection to the Duchy of Parma after 1814, from 1830 the duchesse de Berri was able to move the bulk of her collection outside France, since it belonged to her and not to the Crown. Books, paintings, furniture left Rosny, the Tuileries and the Elysée for her massive eighteenth-century castle of Brunnsee outside Graz in Austria, where she lived after 1835. In a further sign of the close connections between pen and sword in French history, two of her favourite

---

[22] Sotheby's 14 April 2011, 75 and items 187-257.
[23] Music, Continental and Russian Books and Manuscripts, Sotheby's catalogue, London 8 June 2011, items 186-212.
[24] Sotheby's (14 April 2011), lot 248.
[25] Mansel 2001, 235.

writers continued to write on her behalf. For Chateaubriand, she was the only Bourbon with a strong character. He wrote legitimist pamphlets in favour of 'Henri V' (the duc de Bordeaux) and his mother, often ending with the cry "Madame, votre fils est mon roi!" He also acted as her agent in her negotiations with the royal family, after the failure of her insurrection and the birth of an illegitimate child in 1832, known as *l'enfant de la Vendée*.[26] Victor Hugo, whose books the duchess collected and to whose plays she went, supported the July revolution. The duchesse de Berri's taste in literature had evidently been more romantic and radical than her politics. Eventually, Hugo paid his debt to his former patron with a vitriolic poem attacking the Catholic convert, Monsieur Deutz, "paien infame", who in 1832 had betrayed the duchesse de Berri's hiding-place in Nantes to Louis-Philippe's police: *A l'homme qui a vendu une femme* (1835).[27]

In order to finance her family and household in exile, the duchesse de Berri had to sell many of her books, paintings and manuscripts, and her late husband's Flemish pictures from the Elysée palace, not always for high prices. Sales took place in Paris in 1830, 1831, 1836, 1837, and 1863.[28] 40 pictures were sold in 1830, 235 in 1836, 97 in 1837, 409 in 1863. In all, she had probably owned 1,000 pictures. Royalists could help her financially by buying her pictures. The Paris Rothschilds, for example, semi-legitimists keen on royal provenances, bought four Wouvermans at her 1836 sale.[29]

The duchesse de Berri died in 1870 at Schloss Brunnsee in Austria. She had lived long enough to know that her son, the last French Bourbon of the elder line, the comte de Chambord (as the duc de Bordeaux was known after 1830) would remain without direct heirs, as his wife Marie Therese of Modena had born him no children. This was not the Bourbons' only disaster. In 1861 her nephew, the last king of Naples, Francesco II, had been exiled, her family's kingdom of the Two Sicilies annexed to Piedmont. The Bourbon duchy of Parma had also been annexed to Piedmont; the duchesse de Berri's daughter Louise Marie, duchess of Parma, widow of the last reigning duke, had died in exile in 1864.

Until 2011, however, the duchesse de Berri's collections enjoyed a prolonged after-life in Austria. They remained at Brunnsee, belonging to her descendants by her second marriage, in 1832, to Count Lodovico

---

[26] Clement 2002, 66-83.

[27] Degout 2002, 114.

[28] Sale catalogues with prices are in the British Library, shelfmark 7862, f. 9. The duke's collection included 14 Wouvermans and 8 Teniers: 118 lots in total.

[29] Ferguson 1998, 360; Dupont-Logié 2007, 75 and 82.

Lucchese Palli, son of a viceroy of Sicily. A time-capsule of Restoration France, Brunnsee contained drawings by Isabey of the duchess and her household reading, playing billiards and attending chapel at Rosny; portraits of the duchess's ladies-in-waiting by Alexandre-Jean Dubois Drahonet, author of one of the finest portraits of the duchess, wearing early examples of French neo-gothic jewellery, now in the Musée de Picardie in Amiens; and her diaries and letter-books. Even the bedrooms were furnished with exceptional Restoration furniture. In an unusual gesture of dynastic piety and personal affection, perhaps intended to assert the royal connections of the non-royal Lucchese Palli family, the bedroom and apartment of the duchesse de Berri were preserved as she had left them, for over a hundred years—longer than were Prince Albert's in Windsor Castle. They contained portraits of the French and Neapolitan Bourbons, book-shelves packed with royalist works (some of which advocated a return to the ancien regime), the duchess's manuscripts, and the Vienna coffee porcelain service "with which she had her last coffee half an hour before her death at 9 am on 16 April 1870", as a hand-written note in Italian attests.[30] I was lucky enough to be able to consult the manuscripts in 1976, during research for my thesis on the Restoration court. These collections, however, have since been divided among family members. Most surviving objects were dispersed at sales at Sotheby's in London, on 14 April and 8 June 2011.[31]

The duchesse de Berri's son, the comte de Chambord, also had a magnificent collection and archive, coming from royalist families in France as well as the French royal family itself. Until his death in 1883, they made his Schloss Frohsdorf south of Vienna into a Versailles in exile, a cultural challenge to the regimes in power in France (as if the "Old Pretender" had maintained a collection of English royalist art in exile in Rome).[32] On his widow's death in 1886, they were left to the head of the Spanish Bourbons of the Carlist line, Don Carlos. One of his descendants, Countess Wurmbrand, told me in 1988 that before the war, so many pictures were hanging in the Schloss that you could not touch the walls. However, sales began. The Frohsdorf library, with signed first editions by royalist writers such as Balzac, was sold at Maggs in 1936. The castle itself was sold in 1942 to the postal authorities. The collections and archives, like those at Brunnsee, have been dispersed.[33]

---

[30] Sotheby's (April 2011), lot 105, item 233.

[31] Ibid.

[32] Arsac 1884, 165-85 describes some of the works of art, mainly dynastic portraits, then in Frohsdorf. I am grateful for this reference to Patrick Guibal.

[33] Montplaisir 2008, 625-6. Some archives are now in the Archivio di Stato of Lucca.

A few pictures and pieces of porcelain remain with Don Carlos's descendants, the Wurmbrand family, in the Jagdhaus of Frohsdorf and with other descendants elsewhere. The only Restoration collection on public view, apart from some grand royal objects in the Département des objets d'art of the Louvre and the Paris Musée des Arts Décoratifs, is the Jeanvrot collection in the Musée des Arts Décoratifs in Bordeaux.[34] The later Bourbons have no equivalent, as centres of a dynastic collection, of Malmaison, the Musée Napoleon Ier in Fontainebleau and the Museo Napoleonico in Rome for the Bonapartes or the Musée Louis-Philippe at his château of Eu in Normandy and the château d'Amboise for the Orléans. Even the residences of the later Bourbons have gone. The palaces of the Tuileries and Saint-Cloud were burnt in 1870-1, and their remains demolished by the Third Republic, in a symbolic act of destruction, in 1883. The duchesse de Berri's château and hospice at Rosny, vandalised by subsequent owners, are now abandoned.

The French Bourbons failed on three levels: biologically, historically, and politically. They failed to perpetuate themselves, to memorialise themselves, and to keep their throne. However, until Chambord's death in 1883, in collecting as in politics and literature, they remained among the driving forces of nineteenth-century France. The dynamism of the duchesse de Berri's collection and patronage was confirmed in 2007 by a magnificent exhibition organised by Patrick Guibal, "Entre cour et jardin. Marie-Caroline, duchesse de Berri", at Sceaux, as that of her son the comte de Chambord will be, at an exhibition to be held in 2013 at Chambord.

***

For a few years after 1870 that provincial France which the duchesse de Berri had courted so energetically returned a royalist majority to the Chamber of Deputies. Chambord, however, turned down an offer of the throne in 1873, refusing to accept the Tricolour for the sake of "the white flag of Henri IV". Perhaps, had he not done so, both his own and his mother's collections might have survived intact, to be admired today in France.

---

[34] du Pasquier 2007, passim.

BIBLIOGRAPHY

Manuscript Sources

Archives Nationales Paris, *Archives Privées*, series AN371AP, papers of the Maison de la Duchesse de Berri.

Archives of the Duke of Northumberland, Alnwick Castle, DNP: MS 24-45; 121/1-192; 122-127; 692-694; 762.

—. SY: B/XV/2/K

—. SY: H/VI/2 d

Archivio di Stato, Florence, *Mediceo del Principato* 2941 folio; entries 4859, 4866, and 4878 in the Medici Archive Project Documentary Sources database.

Archivio di Stato, Florence *Depositaria Generale*, Parte Antica 391.

—. *Fabbrica Medicea* 1, 2, 19, 20.

—. *Guardaroba Medicea* 28.

—. *Mediceo del Principato* 4068.

Ham House Archive (The National Trust), which includes key seventeenth-century inventories of Ham House, may be consulted on application to the National Trust. These inventories will be published in full in Rowell 2013

HMC 1979 *Report on family and estate papers of the Tollemache Family Earls of Dysart and Baronets 16th–20th centuries including correspondence and papers of John Maitland, Duke of Lauderdale (1616-1682)* RCHM 1979, Buckminster Park (NRA 23003).

HMC 1987 & 1992 *Catalogue of the Family and Estate Papers in the possession of Timothy 5th Baron Tollemache at Helmingham Hall, Suffolk*, RCHM 1987 & 1992, Helmingham Hall & Suffolk Record Office (NRA 6277).

Koptik, Odo. *Enumeratio illustrium familiarum juxta serium alphabeticam, quae imagini miraculosae B. M. V. in Cella Styriensi asservatae dona votiva sacraverunt*. Wien, ÖNB, *Hss*. Cod. 8329.

Maitland Family Papers (Thirlestane Castle Trust) may be ordered and consulted at the National Archives of Scotland, Edinburgh. A catalogue of the entire archive can be consulted at Thirlestane, at the National Library of Scotland in Edinburgh, or via the website of the National Register of Archives for Scotland.

http://www.nas.gov.uk/onlineRegister/, reference NRAS832.
ÖStA, HHStA, *FAE*, Lad. 3. fasc. 4. No. 1. Testament of György Erdődy, dated: Bratislava, 2. September, 1710. 09. 02. and its execution, Ibid. No. 14. dated: Szomolány, 23. March, 1713.
—. Lad. 82. fasc. 3. No. 3/1. Erzsébet Rákóczi's inventory of her jewellery, dated: Kistapolcsány, 1. January-8. June, 1694.
—. Lad. 82. fasc. 3. No. 3/2, Erzsébet Rákóczi's inventory of her silverware, dated: Szávaújvár, 10. December, 1704.
—. Lad. 82. fasc. 3. No. 3/3, Erzsébet Rákóczi's inventory of her silverware inherited from the parents, dated: Szávaújvár, 10. May, 1706.
—. Lad. 82. fasc. 3. No. 3/4. Bequest of Éva Forgách, dated: Brumov, 23. November, 1672.
—. Lad. 101. fasc. 19. (without No.) Letter of Erzsébet Rákóczi to Imre Erdődy, dated: Cracow, 12. May, 1684.
SNA, *ÚAE*, Lad. 82. fasc. 3. No. 6. György Erdődy's inventory of his silverware, dated: Bratislava, 31. August, 1709.
The Diary of the Duchesse de Berry, Schloss Brunnsee, Styria, Austria.
The National Archives, London: *Prerogative Court of Canterbury*, Prob/11/777. http://www.nationalarchives.gov.uk/documentsonline/details-result.asp?Edoc_Id=3543012&queryType=1&resultcount=4, accessed 2 Dec 2010)

Printed Sources

Alberti, Leon Battista. *The Family in Renaissance Florence*. Translated by Renée Neu Watkins. Columbia, SC: University of South Carolina Press, 1969.
Aldrich, Megan. "The Countess of Dysart's Backstools." In *Understanding Art Objects: Thinking Through the Eye*, edited by Tony Godfrey, 30-41. Aldershot: Ashgate 2009.
Allegri, Ettore and Alessandro Cecchi. *Palazzo Vecchio e i Medici: Guida storica*. Florence: SPES, 1980.
Alpers, Svetlana. *The Art of Describing: Dutch Art in the Seventeenth Century*, Chicago: University of Chicago Press, 1983.
Álvarez, Mari-Tere. "The *Almoneda*; the Second-hand Art Market in Spain." In: *Auctions, Agents, and Dealers: the Mechanisms of the Art Market, 1660-1830*," edited by Jeremy Warren and Adriana Turpin, III, 33-9. Beazley Archive and Studies in the history of collections in association with the Wallace Collection: Oxford and London, 2008.
Anderson, Jaynie. "Rewriting the History of Art Patronage." *Renaissance*

Studies 10, 2, *Women Patrons of Renaissance Art, 1300-1600* (1996): 129-38.

Anderson, Robert Geoffrey William, Marjorie Caygill, Arthur MacGregor and Luke Syson, eds. *Enlightening the British: Knowledge, Discovery and the Museum in the Eighteenth Century.* London: British Museum Press, 2003.

Angyal, Dávid. "Rákóczi Erzsébet és Zrínyi Miklós." *Századok,* 35 (1901): 359-60.

Anonymus. *Fortitudo Leonina In Utraque Fortuna Maximiliani Emmanuelis V. B. Ac Sup. Palat. Ducis [...] Secundum Heroica Majorum suorum Exempla Herculeis Laboribus Repraesentata. Eidemque Post Felicissimum Suum, Suorumque in Patriam Reditum demissißime D. D. D. Ab Universa Societatis Jesu per Superiorem Germaniam Provincia.* Munich: Maria Susannah Jäcklin/Sebastian Hauser, 1715.

Arminjon, Catherine ed. *Quand Versailles était meublé d'argent,* exhibition catalogue, Paris: Versailles 2007.

Attenborough, David, ed. *Amazing Rare Things,* London: Royal Collection Publications/Yale University Press 2007.

Avery, Charles. "Hubert le Sueur, The 'Unworthy Praxiteles' of Charles I." *Walpole Society,* XLVIII, (1980-82): 135-209.

Aymonino, Adriano. *Aristocratic splendour: Hugh Smithson Percy (1712–1786) and Elizabeth Seymour Percy (1716–1776), 1st Duke and Duchess of Northumberland. A case study in patronage, collecting and society in eighteenth-century England.* PhD dissertation, University of Venice, School of Advanced Studies, 2009.

—. "Decorum and Celebration of the Family Line: Robert Adam's Monuments to the 1st Duchess of Northumberland." *Burlington Magazine* 152, 5 (2010): 288-96.

—. *The Miniatures by Jean Louis Fesch in the Collection of the Duchess of Northumberland: a Portrait of Late Georgian Society.* London: Roxburghe Club, forthcoming.

Aymonino, Adriano and Manolo Guerci. *"The Grandest of the Palaces of the Strand:" The House of the 1st Duke and Duchess of Northumberland in London, 1749-1786,* forthcoming.

Baarsen, Reinier. "Wilhelm de Rots and Early Cabinet-Making in The Hague." *The Burlington Magazine,* CL, June 2008, 372-80.

Badinter, Élisabeth. *L'Amour en plus. L'histoire de l'amour maternel du XVIe au XIXe siècle.* Paris: Flammarion, 1980.

—. *Die Mutterliebe. Geschichte eines Gefühls vom 17. Jahrhundert bis heute.* Munich: Piper, second edition, 1982.

Baia, Anna. *Leonora di Toledo, Duchessa di Firenze e di Siena*. Todi: Z. Foglietti, 1907.

Baird, Rosemary. *Mistress of the House. Great Ladies and Grand Houses 1670-1830*. London: Phoenix, 2004.

Barnes, Susan J., Nora De Poorter, Oliver Millar and Horst Vey. *Van Dyck: A Complete Catalogue of the Paintings*. New Haven and London: Yale University Press, 2004.

Barta, Ilsebill. *Familienporträts der Habsburger. Dynastische Repräsentation im Zeitalter der Aufklärung (Museen des Hofmobiliendepots 17)*. Wien: Böhlau, 2001.

Bary, Roswitha von. *Henriette Adelaide. Kurfürstin von Bayern*. Regensburg: Pustet, 2004.

Bastl, Beatrix. "Zur Sozialen Identität der Adeligen Frau. Ihre Ausdrucksformen an kleinen Höfen". In *Adelige Hofhaltung im österreichisch-ungarischen Grenzraum vom Ende des 16. bis zum Anfang des 19. Jahrhunderts. Schlaininger Gespräche*, edited by Rudolf Kropf and Gerald Schlag, 21-38. Eisenstadt, 1995.

Benda, Borbála and Gábor Várkonyi eds. *Rákóczi Erzsébet levelei férjéhez 1672–1707*. (Milleniumi Magyar Történelem, Források.). Budapest: Osiris Kiadó, 2001.

Bencard, Mogens. *Silver Furniture*. Copenhagen: Rosenborg 1992.

Berglar Schroer, Hans-Peter. *Maria Theresia in Selbstzeugnissen und Bilddokumenten*. Reinbek/Hamburg: Rowohlt, 1980.

Bergvelt, Ellinoor and Renee Kistemaker, eds. *De wereld binnen handbereik. Nederlandse kunst- en rariteitenverzamelingen, 1585-1735*. Zwolle: Waanders Ungevers and Amsterdam: Amsterdams Historisch Museum, 1992.

Biblioteca Apostolica Vaticana, ed. *Cristina di Svezia a Roma, 1655-1689—Queen Christina of Sweden at Rome, 1655–1689* (Exhibition Catalogue). Rome, Vatican: Biblioteca Apostolica, 1989.

Blair, Claude, ed. *The History of Silver*. London-Sydney: Macdonald & Co, 1987.

Bonnemaison, Féréol. *Galerie de Son Altesse Royale Madame la Duchesse de Berry*. Paris: Impr. de J. Didot, l'ainé,1822.

Brafman, David. *Insects and Flowers: the Art of Maria Sibylla Merian*. Los Angeles: J.Paul Getty Museum 2008.

Brett, Cécile. "Antonio Verrio (c.1636-1707): His Career and Surviving Work." *The British Art Journal* (Winter/Spring 2009-10): 4-17.

Brewer, John and Roy Porter, eds. *Consumption and the World of Goods*. London. Routledge, 1993.

Brewer, John and Frank Trentmann, eds. *Consuming Cultures, Global*

Perspectives: Historical Trajectories, Transnational Exchanges. Oxford and New York: Berg, 2006.

Brink, Claudia and Andreas Henning, eds. *Raffaels Sixtinische Madonna. Geschichte und Mythos eines Meisterwerks.* Munich: Deutscher Kunstverlag, 2005.

Brown, Jonathan. *Kings & Connoisseurs: Collecting Art in Seventeenth-Century Europe.* Princeton: Princeton University Press, 1995.

Bubryák, Orsolya. "Erdődy Anna serlegsorozata a források tükrében." In *"Ez világ, mint egy kert..." Tanulmányok Galavics Géza tiszteletére.* Edited by Orsolya Bubryák, 187-204. Budapest: MTA Művészettörténeti Kutatóintézet–Gondolat Kiadó, 2010.

Burnet, Gilbert. *Bishop Burnet's History of His Own Time,* Oxford: Clarendon Press, 1823.

Buzási Enikő. "17th Century Catafalque Paintings in Hungary." *Acta Historiae Artium,* 21 (1975): 87-119.

Cabanis, José. *Goya: Le musée espagnol de Louis-Philippe.* Paris: Gallimard, 1985.

Campbell Orr, Clarissa. "Queen Charlotte as Patron: some Intellectual and Social Contexts." *Court Historian* 6, 3 (2001), 183-212.

—. "Queen Charlotte and Her Circle". *The Wisdom of George the Third,* edited by Jonathan Marsden, 162-78. London: Royal Collection Publications, 2005.

Castelot, André. *Le duc de Berry et son double mariage.* Paris: Sfelt, 1952.

Cavazzini, Patrizia. *Painting as Business in Early Seventeenth-Century Rome.* University Park: The Pennsylvania State University Press, 2008.

Caygill, Marjorie. "Sloane's Will and the Establishment of the British Museum." In *Sir Hans Sloane: Collector, Scientist, Antiquary, Founding Father of the British Museum,* edited by Arthur MacGregor, 45-68. London: British Museum Press in association with Alistair McAlpine, 1994.

—. "From Private Collection to Public Museum. The Sloane Collection at Chelsea and the British Museum in Montague House". *Enlightenment: Discovering the World in the Eighteenth Century,* edited by Kim Sloan and Andrew Burnett, 18-28, London: British Museum Press, 2003.

Cellini, Benvenuto. *The Autobiography of Benvenuto Cellini,* edited and abridged by Charles Hope and Alessandro Nova from the translation by John Addington Symonds. Oxford: Phaidon, 1983.

Chadwick, Whitney. *Women, Art and Society,* London: Thames & Hudson, 2007.

Chaplin, Helen. Matilda, Countess of Radnor, and William Barclay Squire. *Catalogue of the Pictures in the Collection of the Earl of*

Radnor. Privately printed at the Chiswick Press: London, 1910.

Chaudonneret, Marie Claude. *L'état et les artistes 1815-1833*. Paris: Flammarion, 1999.

Checa, Fernando, ed. *The Inventories of Charles V and the Imperial Family*. Madrid: F. Villaverde Editores, 2010.

Chew, Elizabeth. "The Countess of Arundel and Tart Hall." In *The Evolution of English Collecting: Receptions of Italian Art in the Tudor and Stuart Periods,* edited by Edward Chaney, 285-314. Yale University Press, Studies in British Art 12: New Haven and London, 2003.

Ciletti, Elena. "An 18ᵗʰ-Century Patron: the Case for Anna Maria Luisa de' Medici." *Woman's Art Journal* 5 (1984): 23-7.

Cinelli, Carlo. "Il Quartiere di Eleonora." In: *Palazzo Vecchio: officina di opere e di ingegni*, edited by Carlo Francini, 240-5. Cinisello Balsamo, Milano: Silvana Editoriale, 2006.

Clement, Jean-Paul. "Chateaubriand et la duchesse de Berry." In *Marie Caroline de Berry. Naples, Paris, Graz. Itinéraire d'une princesse romantique*. Paris: Somogy, 2002, 66-83.

Coffin, Sarah and Bodo Hofstetter. *The Gilbert Collection. Portrait Miniatures in Enamel*. London: Philip Wilson Publishers in association with the Gilbert Collection 2000.

Colvin, Howard and John Newman, eds. *Of Building: Roger North's Writings on Architecture*. Oxford: Clarendon Press, 1981.

Coniglio, Giuseppe. *I viceré spagnoli di Napoli*. Naples: Fausto Fiorentino, 1967.

Conti, Cosimo. *La prima reggia di Cosimo I de' Medici nel Palazzo già della Signoria di Firenze descritta ed illustrata: coll'appoggio d'un inventario inedito del 1553 e coll'aggiunta di molti altri documenti*. Florence: Giuseppe Pellas, 1893.

Cook, Jill. "The Nature of the Earth and the Fossil Debate." In *Enlightenment: Discovering the World in the Eighteenth Century*, edited by Kim Sloan and Andrew Burnett, 92-9. London: British Museum Press, 2003a.

—. "Rocks, Fossils and the Emergence of Palaeontology." In *Enlightenment: Discovering the World in the Eighteenth Century*, edited by Kim Sloan and Andrew Burnett, 100-5. London: British Museum Press, 2003b.

Coppens, Thera "Agnes Block, vriendin van Vondel, op de Vijverhof aan de Vecht." In *Petite Histoire*, edited by Thera Coppens, 19-23. Baarn 1997.

Corvinus, Johann Heinrich. Amaranthes *Frauen-Zimmer-Lexicon*.

Leipzig: Johann Friedrich Gleditsch und Sohn, 1715.

Cowan, Brian. "Arenas of Connoisseurship: Auctioning Art in Later Stuart England." In *Art Markets in Europe, 1400-1800*, edited by Michael North and David Ormrod, 153-66. Aldershot: Ashgate, 1998.

Cox-Rearick, Janet. *Dynasty and Destiny in Medici Art: Pontormo, Leo X. and the Two Cosimos*. Princeton NJ: Princeton University Press, 1984.

—. *Bronzino's Chapel of Eleonora in the Palazzo Vecchio*. Berkeley/Los Angeles/Oxford: University of California Press, 1993.

Cripps, Doreen. *Elizabeth of the Sealed Knot: a Biography of Elizabeth Murray, Countess of Dysart*. London: Roundwood Press, 1975.

Curti, Francesca. *Committenza, collezionismo e mercato dell'arte tra Roma e Bologna nel Seicento: La quadreria di Cristiana Duglioli Angelelli*. Rome: Gangemi Editore, 2007.

Czarkowski-Golejewski, Kajetan. "Die Kurfürstin Therese Kunigunde." *Zeitschrift für Bayerische Landesgeschichte* XXXVII (1974): 843-70.

Daston, Lorraine and Katherine Park. *Wonders and the Order of Nature, 1150-1750*. New York: Zone Books, 1996.

de Beer, Esmond S. ed. *The Diary of John Evelyn*, Oxford: Oxford University Press, 1959.

de Bray, Lys. *The Art of Botanical Illustration: A History of Classic Illustrators and their Achievements*. London: Quantum Publishing Ltd., 2001.

Degout, Bernard. "Victor Hugo et la Duchesse de Berry." in *Naples, Paris, Graz. Itinéraire d'une princesse romantique*, edited by Marie Caroline de Berry, 110-23. Paris: Somogy, 2002.

di Gioia, Stefania, ed. *Cristina di Svezia: le collezioni reali*. Milano: Electa, 2003.

Dillmann, Edwin. *Maria Theresia*, Munich: Deutscher Taschenbuch Verlag, second edition, 2006.

Dodsley, Robert and James Dodsley. *London and its Environs Described. Containing an Account of whatever is most remarkable for Grandeur, Elegance, Curiosity or Use, in the City and in the Country twenty Miles round it* [...], 6 vols. London: R. and J. Dodsley in Pall-Mall, 1761.

Duerloo, Luc and Werner Thomas, eds. *Albert & Isabelle: 1598-1621*. Turnhout: Brepols, 1998.

Dunbar, John. *Sir William Bruce*, exhibition catalogue, Edinburgh: Scottish Arts Council, 1970.

Dunbar, John. "The Building Activities of the Duke and Duchess of Lauderdale, 1670-82." *Archaeological Journal* CXXXII (1976): 202-30.

Earenfight, Theresa. "Two Bodies, One Spirit: Isabel and Fernando's Construction of Monarchical Partnership." In *Queen Isabel I of Castile: Power, Patronage, Persona*, edited by Barbara E. Weissberger, 3-18. Woodbridge and Rochester, NY: Tamesis, 2008.

Edelein-Badie, Beatrice. *La collection de tableaux de Lucien Bonaparte, prince de Canino.* Paris: Editions de la Reunion des Musees Nationaux, 1997.

Edelstein, Bruce L. *The Early Patronage of Eleonora di Toledo: The Camera Verde and Its Dependencies in the Palazzo Vecchio.* Ph.D. thesis, Harvard University, 1995.

—. "Nobildonne napoletane e committenza; Eleonora d'Aragona ed Eleonora da Toledo a confronto." *Quaderni storici* 35:2, no. 104: Committenza artistica femminile (2000): 295-329.

—. "Bronzino in the Service of Eleonora di Toledo and Cosimo I de' Medici: Conjugal Patronage and the Painter-Courtier." In *Beyond Isabella: Secular Women Patrons of Art in Renaissance Italy*, edited by Sheryl E. Reiss and David G. Wilkins, 225-61. Kirksville, MO: Truman State University Press, 2001.

—. "The Camera Verde: a Public Center for the Duchess of Florence in the Palazzo Vecchio." *Mélanges de L'École Française de Rome: Italie et Méditerranée* 115, no. 1 (2003): 51-87.

—. "La fecundissima Signora Duchessa: the Courtly Persona of Eleonora di Toledo and the Iconography of Abundance." In *The Cultural World of Eleonora di Toledo: Duchess of Florence and Siena*, edited by Konrad Eisenbichler, 71-97. Aldershot: Ashgate, 2004.

—. "Eleonora di Toledo e la gestione dei beni familiari: una strategia economica?" In *Donne di potere nel Rinascimento*, edited by Luciano Arcangeli and Susanna Peyronel, 743-64. Rome: Viella, 2008.

Eichberger, Dagmar. "Margaret of Austria's portrait collection: female patronage in the light of dynastic ambitions and artistic quality." *Renaissance Studies* 10 (1996), 259-79.

—. *Leben mit Kunst, Wirken durch Kunst: Sammelwesen und Hofkunst unter Margarete von Österreich, Regentin der Niederlande.* Turnhout: Brepols, 2002.

—. "A Noble Residence for a Female Regent: Margaret of Austria and the 'Court of Savoy' in Mechelen." In *Architecture and the Politics of Gender in Early Modern Europe*, edited by Helen Hills. Aldershot: Ashgate, 25-46, 2003.

Eichberger, Dagmar and Lisa Beaven, "Family Members and Political Allies: The Portrait Gallery of Margaret of Austria." *The Art Bulletin* 77 (1995): 225-48.

Eichberger, Dagmar and Yvonne Bleyerveld. *Women of Distinction: Margaret of York, Margaret of Austria.* Leuven: Davidsfonds and Turnhout: Brepols, 2005.

Eidelberg, Martin. "'Landskips...Dark and Gloomy': Reintroducing Henry Ferguson." *Apollo* (September 2000): 27-36.

Eisenbichler, Konrad, ed. *The Cultural Politics of Duke Cosimo I de' Medici.* Aldershot: Ashgate, 2001.

—, ed. *The Cultural World of Eleonora di Toledo.* Aldershot: Ashgate, 2004.

Engel, Hendrik *Alphabetical List of Dutch Zoological Cabinets and Menageries,* Amsterdam: Editions Rodopi V. V. 1986.

Ernst Múzeum ed. *A Rákóczyak ötvösműkincsei/ Die Goldschmiedekunstschätze der Fürsten Rákóczy* (Az Ernst Múzeum aukciói, XLIV.) Budapest: Ernst Múzeum, 1930.

Esser, Saskia. *Leben und Werk der Markgräfin Franziska Sibylla Augusta,* exhibition catalogue. Rastatt: Stadt Rastatt, 1983.

Falke, Otto von. "Der Augsburger Goldschmied Johannes Lencker." *Pantheon,* 1 (1928): 12-22.

Fantoni, Marcello, Louisa C. Matthew, and Sara F. Matthews-Grieco, eds. *The Art Market in Italy, 15th-17th Centuries/Il mercato dell'arte in Italia, secc. XV.* Ferrara: ISR and Modena: Franco Cosimo Panini, 2003.

Ferguson, Niall. *The World's Banker. The History of the House of Rothschild.* London: Weidenfeld and Nicolson, 1998.

Ferino Pagden, Sylvia. *Isabella d'Este: Fürstin und Mäzenatin der Renaissance: "La Prima Donna del Mondo."* Vienna: Kunsthistorisches Museum, 1994.

Férnandez de Córdova Miralles, Álvaro. *La Corte de Isabel I - Ritos y ceremonias de una reina* (1474-1504), Madrid: Dykinson, 2002.

Festing, Sally. "Rare Flowers and Fantastic Breeds. The 2nd Duchess of Portland and her Circle, I-II." *Country Life,* 167 (1986): 12 June, 1684-86 (I) and 19 June, 1772-74 (II).

ffolliott, Sheila. "Wife, Widow, Nun, and Court Lady: Women Patrons of the Renaissance and Baroque." In *Italian Women Artists, Renaissance to Baroque,* edited by Jordana Pomeroy and Claudio Strinati, 31-40. Milan: Skira, 2007.

Filangieri, Riccardo. *Castel Nuovo: Reggia angioina ed aragonese di Napoli.* Naples: E.P.S.A., 1934.

—. *Rassegna critica delle fonti per la storia di Castel Nuovo.* Naples: A Miccoli, vol. 4, 1940.

Förster, Elborg, ed. *A Woman's Life in the Court of the Sun King: Letters of Liselotte von der Pfalz*. Baltimore and London: The Johns Hopkins University Press, 1984.

Foster, Joshua James. *A Catalogue of Miniatures, the Property of His Grace the Duke of Northumberland*. London: Privately printed at the Chiswick Press, 1921.

Franceschini, Chiara. "Los scholares son cosa de su excelentia, como lo es toda la Compañia: Eleonora di Toledo and the Jesuits." In: *The Cultural World of Eleonora di Toledo: Duchess of Florence and Siena*, edited and with an introduction by Konrad Eisenbichler, 181-206. Aldershot: Ashgate, 2004.

French, Anne. *Art Treasures in the North. Northern Families on the Grand Tour*. Norwich: Unicorn Press, 2009.

Fuchs, Rudolf Herman. *Dutch Painting*, London: Thames & Hudson 1978.

Gadessi-Fleming, Touba. *Identity and Physical Deformity in Italian Court Portraits 1550-1650: Dwarves, Hirsutes, and Castrati*. Ph.D. diss., Northwestern University, 2007.

Galavics, Géza. *Kössünk kardot az pogány ellen. Török háborúk és képzőművészet*. Budapest: Képzőművészeti Kiadó, 1986.

— "Fürst Paul Esterházy (1635–1713) als Mäzen. Skizzen zu einer Laufbahn." *Wiener Jahrbuch für Kunstgeschichte* 45 (1992): 121-41.

Gáldy, Andrea M. "Con bellissimo ordine": *Antiquities in the Collection of Cosimo I de' Medici and Renaissance Archaeology*. Ph.D. thesis, University of Manchester, 2002.

—. "'Che sopra queste ossa con nuovo ordine si vadiano accommodando in più luoghi appartamenti'-Thoughts on the Organisation of the Florentine Ducal Apartments in the Palazzo Vecchio 1553." *MKIF*, 46, 2/3 (2002): 490-509.

—. "The Scrittoio della Calliope, a Tuscan Museum." *Renaissance Studies* 19, 5 (2005): 699-709.

—. "Tuscan Concerns and Spanish Heritage in the Decoration of Duchess Eleonora's Apartment in the Palazzo Vecchio." *Renaissance Studies* 20, 3 (2006): 293-319.

—. "The Collector as Master: Duke Cosimo de'Medici's *museo* in the Palazzo Vecchio." In *Sammeln als Institution*, edited by Barbara Marx and Karl-Siegbert Rehberg, 13-21. Munich: Deutscher Kunstverlag, 2006.

—. "L'appartamento di Eleonora di Toledo in Palazzo Vecchio: la scena della nuova Isabella la Cattolica." In *Le donne Medici nel sistema europeo delle corti: XVI-XVIII secolo*, edited by Giulio Calvi and Riccardo Spinelli, 615-26. Florence: Edizioni Polistampa, 2008.

—. "Moving House-Moving Courts: How Palazzo Pitti became the main

Medici Residence in Florence." *Medicea* 4 (2009): 24-42.

—. "Lost in Antiquities: Cardinal Giovanni de' Medici." in *The Possessions of a Cardinal: Art, Piety, and Politics*, 1450-1700, edited by Mary Holingsworth and Carol Richardson. University Park: Pennsylvania State University Press, 2010.

Garas, Klára. *Magyarországi festészet a XVII. században*, Budapest: Akadémiai Kiadó, 1953.

Gaston, Robert. "Eleonora di Toledo's Chapel: Lineage, Salvation and the War against the Turks." In *The Cultural World of Eleonora di Toledo, Duchess of Florence and Siena*, edited by Konrad Eisenbichler, 157-80. Aldershot: Ashgate, 2004.

—. "Untangling the Mannerist Narrative: Bronzino, Moses, and Eleonora of Toledo in the Palazzo de' Signori, Florence." *Melbourne Art Journal* 9-10 (*Art, Site and Spectacle: Studies in Early Modern Visual Culture*, ed. by David R. Marshall) (2007): 62-77.

Gere, Charlotte and Marina Vaizey. *Great Women Collectors*. London and New York: Philip Wilson Publishers in association with Harry N. Abrams, 1999.

Glanville, Philippa. *Silver in Tudor and Early Stuart England. A Social History and Catalogue of the National Collection 1480-1660*. London: Victoria and Albert Museum, 1990.

Goldthwaite, Richard. *Wealth and the Demand for Art in Italy, 1300-1600*. Baltimore: The Johns Hopkins University Press, 1993.

Greig, James, ed. *The Diaries of a Duchess: Extracts from the Diaries of the 1st Duchess of Northumberland*. London: Hodder and Stoughton, 1926.

Grenville, vicomte E. [Arthur Barbat de Bignicourt] de. *Histoire du Journal La Mode*. Paris: Bureau du Journal La Mode nouvelle, 1861

Griffiths, Antony. "Elizabeth, Duchess of Northumberland and her Albums of Prints." In *Dear Print Fan: a Festschrift for Marjorie B. Cohn*, edited by Craigen Bowen, Susan Dackerman, Elizabeth Mansfield, 139-44. Cambridge (MA): Harvard University Art Museums, 2001.

Grotte, András. "'Gyöngyházbul való pelikán forma': Rákóczi László csészéje Hamburgban." *Művészettörténeti Értesítő* 57 (2008): 377-86.

Guerci, Manolo. *The Strand Palaces of the Early Seventeenth Century: Salisbury House and Northumberland House*. Ph.D. dissertation, 2 vols., University of Cambridge, 2007.

—. "The Construction of Northumberland House and the Patronage of Its Original Builder, Lord Henry Howard, 1603-14". The *Antiquaries Journal*, 90, 2010, 1-60.

Guibal, Patrick. "Rosny au temps de la Duchesse de Berry." In *Entre Cour et Jardin. Marie-Caroline, Duchesse de Berry*, 49-58, edited by Cecile Dupont-Logié Musée de l'Île-de-France, Sceaux, 2007.

Haak, Bob. *The Golden Age*. Amsterdam: Meulenhoff/Landshoff, 1984.

Haiczl, Kálmán. *A garamszentbenedeki apátság története*. Budapest: "Élet" Irodalmi és nyomda részvénytársaság, 1913.

Haller, Elfi M. "Kurfürst Karl Albrecht—Kaiser Karl VII. Aufstieg und Niedergang." In *Palais Holnstein. Ein Münchner Adelspalais*, edited by Ilse Aechter, 9-70. Munich: Bayerische Vereinsbank, 1988.

Hantschmann, Katharina. *Nymphenburger Porzellan 1797-1847. Geschichte, Modelle, Dekore*. Munich: Klinkhardt & Biermann, 1996.

Hanzl-Wachter, ed. *Schloss Hof. Prinz Eugens tusculum rurale und Sommerresidenz der kaiserlichen Familie*, St. Pölten: Residenz-Verlag, 2005.

Harris, Eileen. *The Genius of Robert Adam. His Interiors*. New Haven and London: Yale University Press, 2001.

Hase- Schmundt, Ulrike von. *Joseph Stieler 1781-1858. Sein Leben und sein Werk. Kritisches Verzeichnis der Werke*. Munich: Prestel-Verlag, 1971.

Haskell, Francis. *Patrons and Painters: A Study in the Relations between Italian Art and Society in the Age of the Baroque*. London, Chatto & Windus, 1963.

—. *Rediscoveries in art: some aspects of taste, fashion, and collecting in England and France*. Ithaca, N.Y.: Cornell University Press, 1976.

—. *Patrons and Painters: A Study in the Relations between Italian Art and Society in the Age of the Baroque*, rev. ed., New Haven: Yale University Press, 1980.

—. "The British as collectors". In *The Treasure Houses of Britain: 500 Years of Private Patronage and Art Collecting*, edited by Gervase Jackson-Stops, 50-9. New Haven and London: Yale University Press, 1985.

Haskell, Francis and Nicolas Penny. *Taste and Antique: the Lure of Classical Sculpture, 1500-1900*. New Haven and London: Yale University Press, 1981.

Haute, Bernadette van. *David III Ryckaert: A Seventeenth-Century Flemish Painter of Peasant Scenes*. Turnhout: Brepols, 1999.

Hayward, Maria, ed. *The 1542 Inventory of Whitehall: the Palace and its Keeper*. London: Illuminata Publishers for The Society of Antiquaries of London, 2004.

Hearn, Karen. "A Question of Judgement: Lucy Harrington, Countess of Bedford, as Art Patron and Collector." In *The Evolution of English*

Collecting: the Reception of Italian Art in the Tudor and Stuart Periods, edited by Edward Chaney, 221-39. New Haven and London: Yale University Press, Studies in British Art 12, 2003.

Hedley, Olwen. *Queen Charlotte.* London: J. Murray, 1975.

Heinemann-Fleischmann, Rudolf and A. S. Drey ed. *Sammlung Schloss Rohoncz, Vols. I–II. Plastik und Kunstgewerbe.* (Ausstellungs Katalog, Neue Pinatkothek, München) München: F. Bruckman A.G., 1930.

Hernando Sánchez, Carlos José. "Poder y cultura en el Renacimiento napolitano: La biblioteca del virrey Pedro de Toledo." *Cuadernos de Historia Moderna* 9 (1988): 13-33.

—. "La vida material y el gusto artistico en la corte de Nápoles durante el Renacimiento: el inventario de bienes del virrey Pedro de Toledo." *Archivo Español de Arte* 66 (1993): 35-55.

—. *Castilla y Nápoles en el siglo XVI. El virrey Pedro de Toledo: linaje, estado y cultura (1532-1553).* Valladolid: Junta de Castilla y León, 1994.

—. "El *Glorioso Trivmfo* de Carlos V en Napoles y el humanismo de corte entre Italia y España." In *Carlo V, Napoli e il Mediterraneo. Atti del Convegno Internazionale* edited by Giuseppe Galasso and Aurelio Musi, 447-521. Naples: Società Napoletana di Storia Patria, 2001.

Herrmann, Frank, ed. *The English as Collectors: A Documentary Sourcebook.* London: John Murray, 1972.

Herzenberg, Caroline L. *Women Scientists from Antiquity to the Present.* West Cornwall CT: Locust Hill Press, 1986.

Hills, Helen. ed. *Architecture and the Politics of Gender in Early Modern Europe.* Aldershot: Ashgate, 2003.

Hjorst, Mette and Sue Laver, eds. *Emotion and the Arts.* New York-Oxford: Oxford University Press, 1997.

Holst, Niels von. *Creators, Collectors, and Connoisseurs.* New York: G.P. Putnam's Sons, 1967.

Hoppe, Ilaria. "A Duchess' Place at Court: the Quartiere di Eleonora in the Palazzo della Signoria in Florence." In *The Cultural World of Eleonora di Toledo: Duchess of Florence and Siena,* edited and with an introduction by Konrad Eisenbichler, 98-118. Aldershot: Ashgate, 2004.

Horn, Ildikó, ed. *Rákóczi László naplója.* With a postscript by Ágnes R. Várkonyi. Budapest: Magvető Kiadó, 1990a.

—. "Rákóczi László pályája (1663–1664)" *Hadtörténelmi Közlemények,* 103, 2 (1990b): 61-90.

Howarth, David. "The patronage and collecting of Aletheia, Countess of Arundel, 1606-54." *Journal of the History of Collections* 10 (1998),

125-38.

Hughes, Helen Sard. *The Gentle Hertford. Her Life and Letters.* New York: Macmillan Co., 1940.

Huxley, Robert. "Natural History Collectors and their Collections: 'simpling macaronis' and Instrument of Empire." In *Enlightenment: Discovering the World in the Eighteenth Century*, edited by Kim Sloan and Andrew Burnett, 80-91. London: British Museum Press, 2003.

Hyde, Melissa and Jennifer Milam, eds. *Women, Art and the Politics of Identity in Eighteenth-Century Europe.* Aldershot: Ashgate, 2003.

Impey, Oliver, and Arthur MacGregor, eds. *The Origins of Museums: The Cabinet of Curiosities in Sixteenth- and Seventeenth-Century Europe.* Oxford: Clarendon Press, 1985.

Jackson-Stops, Gervase, ed. *The Treasure Houses of Britain: 500 years of Private Patronage and Art Collecting*, New Haven and London: Yale University Press, 1985.

James, Susan. *The Feminine Dynamic in English Art, 1485-1603: Women as Consumers, Patrons and Painters.* Aldershot: Ashgate, 2009.

Jameson, Anna. *Companion to the Most Celebrated Private Galleries of Art in London. Containing accurate catalogues, arranged alphabetically, for immediate reference, each preceded by an historical & critical introduction, with a prefatory essay on art, artists, collectors and connoisseurs.* London: Saunders and Otley, 1844.

Jardine, Nicholas, James A. Secord and C. Spary. *Cultures of Natural History.* Cambridge: Cambridge University Press 1996.

Jauncey, James *Thirlestane Castle*, undated guidebook: Lynch McQueen Ltd, c.2005.

Jervis, Simon. "The English Country House Library." In *Treasures from the Libraries of National Trust Country Houses*, edited by Nicolas Baker, 13-33. New York: Royal Oak Foundation & The Grolier Club, 1999.

—. "The Baroque Exhibition in London." *The Burlington Magazine* CLI (June 2009): 370.

Johnson, Geraldine A. and Sara F. Matthews Grieco, eds. *Picturing Women in Renaissance and Baroque Italy.* Cambridge, Cambridge University Press, 1997.

Jordan, Annemarie. "Exotic Renaissance Accessories: Japanese, Indian and Sinhalese Fans at the Courts of Portugal and Spain."*Apollo* 150 (1999): 25-35.

—. "Mujeres mecenas de la casa Austria y la infanta Isabel Clara Eugenia." In *El arte en la Corte de los Arquiduques Alberto de Austria e Isabel Clara Eugenia (1598-1633)*, edited by Alejandro Vergara and

Ana Cabrera, 118-37. Madrid, 1999.

Jordan Gschwend, Annemarie and Johannes Beltz, eds. *Elfenbeine von Ceylon. Luxusgüter für Katharina von Habsburg.* Zurich: Museum Rietberg, 2010.

Jürgs, Britta, ed. *Sammeln, nur um zu besitzen? Berühmte Kunstsammlerinnen von Isabella d'Este bis Peggy Guggenheim.* Berlin: Aviva Verlag, 2000.

Kaack, Hans-Georg. *Markgräfin Sibylla Augusta. Die große badische Fürstin der Barockzeit*, Constance: Stadler, 1983.

Kägler, Britta. "Weibliche Regentschaft in Krisenzeiten. Zur Interimsregierung der bayerischen Kurfürsten Therese Kunigunde (1704/05)." *Zeitenblicke* VIII, 2, 2009 [15.10.2010].

Kaiser, Alfred. *München. Theatinerkirche St. Kajetan.* Regensburg: Schnell und Steiner, 2007.

Kevill-Davies, Sally. *Yesterday's Children. The Antiques and the History of Childcare.* Woodbridge: Antique Collectors' Club, 1988.

Kiefer, Carol Solomon, ed. *The Empress Josephine: Art and Royal Identity.* Amherst, Massachusetts: Mead Art Museum, Amherst College, 2005.

King, Catherine. *Renaissance Women Patrons: Wives and Widows in Italy, c. 1300-1550.* Manchester: Manchester University Press, 1998.

King, Jonathan C.H. "Ethnographic Collections." In *Sir Hans Sloane: Collector, Scientist, Antiquary, Founding Father of the British Museum*, edited by Arthur MacGregor, 228-44. London: Published for the Trustees of the British Museum by British Museum Press in association with Alistair McAlpine, 1994.

Klingensmith, Samuel John. *The Utility of Splendour. Social Life and Architecture at the Court of Bavaria. 1600-1800.* Chicago-London: University of Chicago Press, 1993.

Knecht, Robert J. *Catherine de' Medici.* London and New York: Longman, 1998.

Komaszynski, Michel. "Die politische Rolle der bayerischen Kurfürstin Therese Kunigunde." in: *Zeitschrift für Bayerische Landesgeschichte*, 45 (1982): 555-73.

Kovács, Sándor Iván. "'Veri a hab a kősziklát...' A költőnő Rákóczi Erzsébet." In *Eleink tündöklősége. Tanulmányok, esszék*, edited by Sándor Iván Kovács. Budapest: Balassi Kiadó, 1996.

Kremers, Hildegard. *Marie Caroline de Berry: Naples, Paris, Graz. Itinéraire d'une princesse romantique.* Paris: Somogy, 2002.

La France, Robert G. *Bachiacca: Artist of the Medici Court.* Fondazione Carlo Marchi: Studi. Florence: Leo S. Olschki, 2008.

Laing, Alastair and Nino Strachey. "The Duke and Duchess of Lauderdale's Pictures at Ham House", *Apollo* CXXXIX (May 1994): 3-9.

Laird, Mark and Alicia Weisberg-Roberts, eds. *Mrs. Delany and her Circle*. New Haven and London: Yale Centre for British Art, Sir John Soane Museum in association with Yale University Press, 2009.

Lamberini, Daniela. "Strategie difensive e politica territoriale di Cosimo I de' Medici nell'operato di un suo provveditore." In *Il principe architetto: atti del convegno internazionale (Mantua 21-23 October 1999)*, edited by Arturo Calzona, Francesco Paolo Fiore, Alberto Tenenti and Cesare Vasoli, 125-52. Florence: Leo S. Olschki, 2002.

Lami, Eugene. *Quadrille de Marie Stuart*. Paris: Imprimerie A. Fonrouge, 1829.

Lauts, J. and R. Stratmann, *Caroline Louise, Markgräfin von Baden, 1723–1783*. Karlsruhe, Badisches Landesmuseum, 1983.

Lawrence, Cynthia, ed. *Women and Art in Early Modern Europe: Patrons, Collectors, and Connoisseurs*. University Park, PA: The Pennsylvania State University Press, 1997.

Leone de Castris, Pierluigi, ed. *Castel Nuovo: il Museo Civico*. Naples: Elio de Rosa Editore, 1990.

Liss, Peggy K. "Isabel - Myth and History," *Isabel la Catolica, Queen of Castile*, ed. David A. Boruchoff, 57-78. Basingstoke/New York: Palgrave/Macmillan 2004.

Loconte, Aislinn. "The North Looks South: Giorgio Vasari and Early Modern Visual Culture in the Kingdom of Naples." In *Art and Architecture in Naples, 1266-1713: New Approaches*, edited by Cordelia Warr and Janis Elliott. 16-37 Chichester: Wiley-Blackwell, 2010.

Lombardi, Giancarlo. "Dalla Sala delle Carte Geografiche al Quartiere della Guardaroba: un'ipotesi di ricostruzione topografica." In *La Sala delle Carte geografiche in Palazzo Vecchio: "capriccio et invenzione nata dal Duca Cosimo"*, edited by Alessandro Cecchi and Paola Pacetti, 135-49. Florence: Edizioni Polistampa, 2008.

Ludiková, Zuzana, Árpád Mikó and Géza Pálffy. "A szepeshelyi Szent Márton-templom, egy felső-magyarországi katolikus központ késő reneszánsz és barokk sírkövei és halotti címerei." *Művészettörténeti Értesítő* 56, 2 (2007): 313-44.

Lunenfeld, Marvin. "Isabella I of Castille and the Company of Women in Power." *Historical Reflections/Reflexions Historiques* IV, 2 (1978): 207-29.

MacGregor, Arthur, ed. *Sir Hans Sloane: Collector, Scientist, Antiquary,*

Founding Father of the British Museum. London: Published for the Trustees of the British Museum by British Museum Press in association with Alistair McAlpine, 1994.

—. "From Private Collection to Public Museum. The Sloane Collection at Chelsea and the British Museum in Montague House". In *Enlightenment: Discovering the World in the Eighteenth Century*, edited by Kim Sloan and Andrew Burnett, 18-28. London: British Museum Press, 2003.

—. *Curiosity and Enlightenment: Collectors and Collections from the Sixteenth to the Nineteenth Century.* New Haven and London: Yale University Press, 2007.

MacGregor, Arthur and Oliver Impey, eds. *The Origins of Museums. The Cabinet of Curiosities in Sixteenth and Seventeenth-century Europe.* London: House of Stratus, 2001.

Macé de Lépinay, Francois. "Un témoignage de la tradition néo-classique sous la Restauration; l'hospice Saint Charles de Rosny sur Seine." *Bulletin de la Société de l'Histoire de l'Art francais* (1976): 376-85.

Mack, John. "'Ethnography' in the Enlightenment". In *Enlightening the British: Knowledge, Discovery and the Museum in the Eighteenth Century*, edited by Robert Geoffrey William Anderson, Marjorie Caygill, Arthur MacGregor and Luke Syson, 114-8. London: British Museum Press, 2003.

MacLeod Catharine and Julia Marciari Alexander, eds. *Painted Ladies: Women at the Court of Charles II*, exhibition catalogue. New Haven and London: National Portrait Gallery, London and the Yale Center for British Art, 2001.

Macray, W. D. ed. *Calendar of Clarendon State Papers*, III, Oxford, 1876.

Mansel, Philip. *The Court of France 1814-1830.* Ph.D. thesis, University of London, 1978.

—. *The Court of France 1789-1830.* New York and Cambridge: Cambridge University Press, 1989.

—. *Paris between Empires: Monarchy and Revolution 1814-1852.* London: St. Martin's Press. 2001.

Marcolin, Massimo, and Paola Paccetti. "I quartieri di Cosimo I e di Eleonora di Toledo nel Palazzo Ducale dal 1540 al 1562." *Medicea: Rivista intterdisciplinaria di studi medicei* 6 (2010): 20-31.

Markó, Miklós. "A galgóczi vár és műkincsei." *Vasárnapi Ujság* 59, 1 (1912): 2.

Martyn, Thomas. *The English Connoisseur: Containing an Account of whatever is Curious in Painting, Sculpture, &c., in the Palaces and Seats of the Nobility and Principal Gentry of England, both in Town and Country.* 2 vols. London: L. Davis and C. Reymers, 1766.

Masen, Jacob SJ. *Speculum Imaginum Veritatis Occultae. Ed. tertia prioribus correctior.* Cologne: J. A. Kinckius, 1681.

Matthews-Grieco, Sara F. and Gabriella Zarri. "Committenza artistica femminile." *Quaderni Storici* 104 (2000): 283-422.

Meoni, Lucia. *Gli arazzi della collezione fiorentina: le manifatture medicee da Cosimo I a Cosimo II, 1545-1621.* Florence: Sillabe, 1998.

—. "Le *Storie di Giuseppe.* Il capolavoro dell'arazzeria fiorentina." In *Giuseppe negli arazzi di Pontormo e Bronzino. Viaggio tra i tesori del Quirinale a Roma,* edited by Louis Godart, 193-265. Loreto: Tecnostampa Edizioni, 2010.

Miccio, Scipione. "Vita di don Pietro di Toledo." *Archivio Storico Italiano* 9, series I (1846): 1-89.

Middione, Roberto. "San Giacomo degli Spagnoli a Napoli: il sepolcro di Pedro de Toledo." *FMR* n.s. 3 (2004): 99-124.

Millar, Oliver. *Sir Peter Lely, 1618-80,* exhibition catalogue. London: National Portrait Gallery, 1978.

Miller, Edward. *That Noble Cabinet: a History of the British Museum.* London: Deutsch, 1973.

Montplaisir, Daniel de. *Le comte de Chambord, dernier roi de France.* Paris: Perrin, 2008.

Moore, Cathal, Nino Strachey and Christopher Rowell. *Ham House,* London: The National Trust, 1995 (and revised editions).

Mravik, László. *"Sacco di Budapest" Depredation of Hungary 1938–1949.* (Hungarian National Gallery publications 1998/2.) Budapest: Hungarian National Gallery, 1998.

Müller, Hannelore. *European Silver. The Thyssen–Bornemisza Collection.* London: Sotheby's publication, 1986.

Murdoch, Tessa ed. *Boughton House: the English Versailles,* London: Faber & Faber, 1992.

Murdoch, Tessa. "Jean, René, and Thomas Pelletier, Huguenot Family of Carvers and Gilders in England, 1682-1726 - I and II." *The Burlington Magazine* (November 1997): 732-42, and (June 1998): 363-72.

—, ed. *Noble Households: Eighteenth-Century Inventories of Great English Houses,* Cambridge: John Adamson, 2006.

Murphy, Caroline P. *Murder of a Medici Princess.* Oxford: Oxford University Press, 2008.

Neumann, Hermann. *Die Münchner Residenz.* Munich: Prestel, 2nd edition 2007.

North, Michael and David Ormrod, eds. *Art Markets in Europe, 1400-1800.* Aldershot: Ashgate, 1998.

Ogilvy, Brian W. *The Science of Describing.* Chicago: University of Chicago Press 2006.

Orsi Landini, Roberta. *Moda a Firenze* (1540 - 1580): *lo stile di Eleonora di Toledo e la sua influenza.* Florence: Pagliai Polistampa, 2005.

Oßwald-Bargende, Sybille. *Die Mätresse, der Fürst und die Macht. Christina Wilhelmina von Grävenitz und die höfische Gesellschaft,* Frankfurt-New York: Campus, 2000.

Owsley, David and William Rieder. *The Glass Drawing Room from Northumberland House.* London: Victoria & Albert Museum, 1974.

Paccoud, Stéphane and Sylvie Ramond, eds., *Juliette Récamier, muse et mécène.* Paris: Hazan, 2009.

Pagnini, Maria Camilla. "Giovanni Battista del Tasso legnaiolo e architetto a corte." In *Palazzo Vecchio: officina di opere e di ingegni,* edited by Carlo Francini, 122-25. Cinisello Balsamo: Banca Toscana and Silvana, 2006.

Paintin, Elaine. *The King's Library.* London: British Library, 1989.

Pane, Giulio. "Pietro di Toledo vicerè urbanista." *Napoli nobilissima* 14 (1975): 81-95.

Pane, Roberto. *Il Rinascimento nell'Italia meridionale.* 2 vols. Milan: Edizioni della Comunità, 1975-7.

Pangels, Charlotte. *Die Kinder Maria Theresias. Leben und Schicksal in kaiserlichen Glanz.* München: Callwey, 2nd edition, 1990.

Panofksy, Erwin. *Dürer Melenconia I. Eine quellen- und typengeschichtliche Untersuchung.* Berlin: B. G. Teubner 1923.

Parigino, Giuseppe Vittorio. *Il tesoro del principe: funzione pubblica e privata del patrimonio della famiglia Medici nel cinquecento.* Edited by Accademia Toscana di Scienze e Lettere "La Colombaria", Studi. Florence: Olschki, 1999.

Pasquier, Jacqueline du. *Raymond Jeanvrot. Une passion royaliste. Naissance d'une collection bordelaise.* Paris: Somogy Edition d'art, 2007.

Patton, H. M. ed. "Lauderdale Letters." *Scottish History Society, Miscellany,* VI, third series, XXXIII, 1939.

Pearce, Susan M., ed. *Interpreting Objects and Collections.* New York: Routledge, 1994.

—. *On Collecting. An Investigation into Collecting in the European Tradition.* London-New York: Routledge, 1995.

Peck, Linda Levy. *Consuming Splendour: Society and Culture in Seventeenth-Century England.* Cambridge: Cambridge University Press, 2005.

Percy, Victoria and Gervase Jackson-Stops. "The Travel Journals of the 1st

Duchess of Northumberland, I-III", *Country Life*, 155 (1974), 31 January, 192-5 (I); 7 February, 250-52 (II); 14 February, 308-10 (III).

Pita Andrade, José M. "The Dukes of Alba." In *Great Family* Collections, edited by Douglas Cooper, 265-88. New York: MacMillan, 1965.

Pointon, Marcia. "Intrigue, Jewellery, and Economics: Court Culture and Display in England and France in the 1780s." In *Art Markets in Europe, 1400-1800*, edited by Michael North and David Ormrod, 201-19. Aldershot: Ashgate, 1998.

Pougetoux, Alain. *La collection de peintures de l'imperatrice Joséphine.* Notes et documents des musées de France n. 37, Paris: Réunion des Musées Nationaux, 2005.

Powlett, Edward. *The General Contents of the British Museum: with Remarks. Serving as a Directory in Viewing that Noble Cabinet* [by Edmund Powlett]. London: R. & J. Dodsley, 1761.

—. *The General Contents of the British Museum: with Remarks. Serving as a Directory in Viewing that Noble Cabinet. The Second Edition, with Additions and improvements, and a Complete index* [by Edmund Powlett]. London: R. & J. Dodsley, 1762.

Preyer, Brenda. "The Florentine *casa.*" In *At Home in Renaissance Italy*, edited by Marta Ajmar-Wollheim and Flora Dennis, 34-49. London: Victoria and Albert Museum, 2006.

Pulszky, Károly and Jenő Radisics. *A magyar történeti ötvösmű kiállítás lajstroma*. Budapest: Franklin, 1884.

Pulszky, Károly, Jenő Radisics and Emile Molinier. *Chefs-d'oeuvre d'orfèvrerie ayant figuré à l'exposition de Budapest, Vols. I–II*. Paris: A. Levy, [1886].

Purcell, Mark. "The Private Library in Seventeenth- and Eighteenth-Century Surrey." *Library History* XIX (July 2003): 119-127.

Queen's Gallery, ed. *George III Collector & Patron: an Exhibition of Paintings, Drawings, Furniture, Clocks, Porcelain, Silver, Scientific Instruments, Books, Miniatures, Gems*. London: Queen's Gallery, Buckingham Palace, 1974.

Radisch, Paula Rea. "Lovisa Ulrike of Sweden, Chardin, and Enlightened Despotism." In *Women, Art and the Politics of Identity in Eighteenth-Century Europe*, edited by Melissa Hyde and Jennifer Milam, 46-63. Aldershot: Ashgate, 2003.

Rall, Hans. *Die Wittelsbacher in Lebensbildern*, Munich: Piper 2005.

Rebecchini, Guido. *Private Collections in Mantua, 1500-1630.* Rome: Edizioni di storia e letteratura, 2002.

Redondo, Augustin. "Emergence et effacement de la femme politique a la Renaissance: Isabelle la Catholique et Maria Pacheco." In *Images de la femme en Espagne aux XVIe et XVIIe siecles: Des traditions aux renouvellements et a l'emergence d'images nouvelle*, edited by Augustin Redondo, 291-304. Paris: Publications de la Sorbonne, 1994.

Reiss, Sheryl E. and David G. Wilkins, eds. *Beyond Isabella: Secular Women Patrons of Art in Renaissance Italy*, Kirksville, MO: Truman State University Press, 2001.

Reitsma, Ella. *Maria Sibylla Merian & Dochters, Vrouwenlevens tussen kunst en wetenschap*. Zwolle: Waanders, 2008.

Reresby, Sir John. *The Memoirs of the Honourable Sir John Reresby, Bart.*, London: Samuel Harding, 1734.

Réthelyi, Orsolya, and Beatrix Basics, eds. *Mary of Hungary: the Queen and her Court, 1521-1531*. Budapest: Budapest History Museum, 2005.

Richter, Arndt. *Die Geisteskrankheit der bayerischen Könige Ludwig II. und Otto. Eine interdisziplinäre Studie mittels Genealogie, Genetik und Statistik*, Neustadt an der Aisch: Degener & Co, 1997.

Richter, Werner. *Ludwig II., König von Bayern*, Munich: Stiebner Verlag, 14th edition, 2001.

Rieder, Heinz. *Maria Theresia. Herrscherin und Mutter*. Munich: Diederichs, 1999.

Robert, Herve et.al. *Le mécénat du Duc d'Orléans 1830-1842*. Paris: Delegation a l'action artistique de la ville de Paris, 1993.

Roberts, Jane, ed. *George III and Queen Charlotte: Patronage, Collecting and Court Taste*. London: Royal Collections, 2004.

Rohlmann, Michael. "Leoninische Siegverheißung und clementinische Heilserfüllung in der Sala di Costantino." *Zeitschrift für Kunstgeschichte* 57 (1994): 153-69.

Rosenberg, Marc. *Der Goldschmiede Merkzeichen*, vols. I–IV. Frankfurt am Main: Frankfurter Verlags-Anstalt A.G., 1922–1928.

Rothe, Carl *Die Mutter und die Kaiserin. Briefe der Maria Theresia an ihre Kinder und Vertraute*, Berlin: Hans von Hugo Verlag, 1940.

—. *Maria Theresia. Die Mutter und die Kaiserin. Briefe an ihre Kinder und Vertrauten*. Vienna-Munich: Herold Verlag, 1968.

Rousseau, Claudia. "The Pageant of the Muses at the Medici Wedding of 1539." In *"All the World's a Stage...": Art and Pageantry in the Renaissance and Baroque*, edited by Barbara Wisch and Susan Scott Munshower, 415-57. University Park, PA: Pennsylvania State University Press, 1990.

Rowell, Christopher. "'That Delightful and Magnificent Villa': Clive of India's Claremont and its Collections." *Apollo*, CLIII, no. 470 (April 2001): 14-22.

Rowell, Christopher ed. *Ham House: 400 Years of Collecting and Patronage*, New Haven and London: Yale University Press, 2013, forthcoming.

Rubinstein, Nicolai. *The Palazzo Vecchio (1298–1532): Government, Architecture, and Imagery in the Civic Palace of the Florentine Republic*. Oxford: Clarendon Press, 1995.

Rückert, Rainer. "Museum für Kunst und Gewerbe. Erwerbungen für die europäische Abteilung in den Jahren 1950-1959." Jahrbuch der Hamburger Kunstsammlungen, 5 (1960): 151-232.

Rusina, Ivan ed. *Barok. Dejiny slovenského výtvarného umenia*. Bratislava: Slovenská národná galéria, 1998.

Russell, Francis. "The Hanging and Displaying of Pictures, 1700-1850". In *The Fashioning and Functioning of the British Country House*, edited by Gervase Jackson-Stops, 133-53. Washington: National Gallery of Art, Hanover [N.H.]: Distributed by the University Press of New England, 1989.

Saint-Georges, Benedicte Bonnet. "Les exceptionelles collections du Palais Fesch." *L'Objet d'Art* 461 (2010): 30-9.

San Juan, Rose Marie. "The Court Lady's Dilemma: Isabella d'Este and Art Collecting in the Renaissance." *Oxford Art Journal* 14(1991), 67-78.

Schama, Simon. *The Embarrassment of Riches: An Interpretation of Dutch Culture in the Golden Age*, New York: Alfred A. Knopf 1987.

Schofield, Bertram, ed. *The Knyvett Letters, 1620-1644*, London: Constable, 1949 [volume 20 of Norfolk Record Society Publications].

Segal, Sam. *A Flowery Past—A Survey of Dutch and Flemish Flower Painting from 1600 until the Present*, exhibition catalogue. Hertogenbosch, Amsterdam: Gallery P. de Boer's-Noordbrabants Museum, 1982.

Seling, Helmut. *Die Kunst der Augsburger Goldschmiede 1529–1868*, vols. I–III. München: C. H. Beck, 1980.

Sikkens-de Zwaan, Marisca. "Magdalena Poulle (1632-99): a Dutch Lady in a Circle of Botanical Collectors." *Garden History* 30.2: Dutch Influences (winter 2002): 206-20.

Slive, Seymour. *Dutch Painting, 1600–1800*. New Haven, Yale University Press, 1995.

Sloan, Kim. "'Aimed at Universality and Belonging to the Nation:' the Enlightenment and the British Museum". In *Enlightenment: Discovering the World in the Eighteenth Century*, edited by Kim Sloan and Andrew Burnett, 12-25. London: British Museum Press, 2003.

Sloan, Kim and Andrew Burnett, eds. *Enlightenment: Discovering the*

World in the Eighteenth Century. London: British Museum Press, 2003.

Sloboda, Stacey. "Displaying Materials: Porcelain and Natural History in the Duchess of Portland's Museum." *Eighteenth-Century Studies*, 43, 4 (2010): 455-72.

Smart, Alastair. *Allan Ramsey. A Complete Catalogue of his Paintings.* New Haven and London: Yale University Press, 1999.

Smart, Carol, ed. *Regulating Womanhood: Historical Essays on Marriage, Motherhood, and Sexuality.* London: Routledge, 1992.

Smith, John P. *James Tassie, 1735-1799. Modeller in Glass. A Classical Approach.* London: Mallett, 1995.

Snodin, Michael and Nigel Llewellyn, eds. *Baroque 1620-1800: Style in the Age of Magnificence*, exhibition catalogue V&A. London: Victoria and Albert Museum: 2009.

Southron, Janet. *Power and Display in the Seventeenth Century: The Arts and their Patrons in Modena and Ferrara.* Cambridge: Cambridge University Press, 1988.

Spear, Richard and Philip Sohm, eds. *Painting for Profit: The Economic Lives of Seventeenth-Century Italian Painters.* New Haven and London: Yale University Press, 2010.

Stangl, Anja, Verena Helfert, Frank T. Lang, eds. *Sybilla Augusta. Ein barockes Schicksal. Die badische Markgräfin zwischen Familie, Kunst und Politik.* Exhibition catalogue. Rastatt. Stuttgart: Staatsanzeiger-Verlag, 2008.

Stangler, Gottfried and Dagmar Leindl, eds. *Zeugen der Intimität. Privaträume der kaiserlichen Familie und des böhmischen Adels. Aquarelle und Interieurs des 19. Jahrhunderts.* Exhibition catalogue Schallaburg, Horn: Niederösterreichisches Landesmuseum, 1997.

Starkey, David, ed. *The Inventory of King Henry VIII. Society of Antiquaries MS 129 and British Library MS Harley 1419.* London: Harvey Miller Publishers for the Society of Antiquaries of London, 1998.

Stott, Rebecca. *Duchess of Curiosities: The Life of Margaret, Duchess of Portland.* Worksop: Pineapple Press for the Harley Gallery, 2006.

Stourton, James. *Great Smaller Museums in Europe.* London: Scala Publishers, 2008.

Straussman-Pflanzer, Eve. *Court Culture in 17th-Century Florence: The Art Patronage of Medici Grand Duchess Vittoria della Rovere, 1622-1694.* Ph.D. diss. New York University, 2010.

Strunck, Christina, ed. *Medici Women as Cultural Mediators (1533-1743).* Cinisello Balsamo: Silvana Editoriale, 2012.

Sutton, Denys. "Aspects of British collecting, I-XVII". *Apollo*, 237 n.s. (November 1981), 282-339 (I-IV); 250 n.s. (December 1982), 358-420 (V-VIII); 267 n.s. (May 1984), 312-372 (IX-XIII); 282 n.s. (August 1985), 84-129 (XIV-XVII).

Szerémi [Odescalchi, Artúr]. "Rákóczy Erzsébet ingóságai a hrussói és kis-tapolcsányi várkastélyokban", *Archaeologiai Közlemények*, 12, ú.f. 9. (1878): 126-30.

Tebbe, Karin, Thomas Eser, Ursula Timann [et al.], eds. *Nürnberger Goldschmiedekunst, I. Meister, Werke, Marken*. Nürnberg: Verlag des GNM, 2007.

Teolato, Chiara. *Tra Serialità e Originalità: la Produzione di Bronzi Decorativi a Roma (1760-1820)*. Ph.D. dissertation, Università di Roma Tre, 2010.

Thackray, John. "Mineral and Fossil Collection." In *Sir Hans Sloane: Collector, Scientist, Antiquary, Founding Father of the British Museum*, edited by Arthur MacGregor, 123-35. London: Published for the Trustees of the British Museum by British Museum Press in association with Alistair McAlpine, 1994.

Thaly, Kálmán. "Gr. Rákóczi Erzsébet, mint költő", *Századok*, 34 (1900): 481-94.

Thornton, Dora. *The Scholar in his Study: Ownership and Experience in Renaissance Italy*, New Haven and London: Yale University Press. 1997.

Thornton, Peter. "Furniture from the Netherlands at Ham House." *Nederlands Kunsthistorisch Jaarboek* (1980): 239-43.

—. *The Italian Renaissance Interior: 1400-1600*. London: Weidenfeld & Nicolson, 1991.

Thornton, Peter and Maurice Tomlin. "The Furnishing and Decoration of Ham House." *Furniture History*, XVI (1980).

Tinagli, Paola. *Women in Italian Renaissance Art: Gender, Representation, Identity*. Manchester: Manchester University Press, 1997.

Todd, Kim. *Chrysalis:Maria Sibylla Merian and the Secrets of Metamorphosis*. New York: Harcourt publishers, 2007.

Tollemache, E. D. H (Edward). *The Tollemaches of Helmingham and Ham*, London: W.S Cowell Ltd, 1949.

Történelmi Főcsoport Igazgatósága ed. *1896-iki Ezredéves Országos Kiállítás. A Történelmi főcsoport hivatalos katalógusa*. Budapest: Történelmi Főcsoport Igazgatósága, 1896.

Trachtenberg, Marvin. "Archaeology, merriment, and murder: the first cortile of the Palazzo Vecchio and its transformations in the late Florentine Republic." *The Art Bulletin*, 71 (1989): 565-609.

Treydel, Renate. "Faesch (Fasch; Fäsch; Fesch), Johann Ludwig Wernhard (Jean-Louis-Wernhard)". In *Saur's allgemeines Künstlerlexikon: die bildenden Künstler aller Zeiten und Völker*, XXXVI, 192. München-Leipzig: K.G. Saur, 2003.

Trusted, Marjorie. *The Arts of Spain: Iberia and Latin America 1450-1700*. University Park, PA: Pennsylvania State University Press, 2007.

Turbide, Chantal. "Catherine de Médicis, mécène d'art contemporain: l'hôtel de la Reine et ses collections". In *Patronnes et Mécènes en France à la Renaissance*, edited by Kathleen Wilson-Chevalier, 511-26. Paris: Université de Saint-Etienne, 2007.

Uhl, Gabriella. "Esterházy Pál és Rákóczi Erzsébet", *Irodalomismeret*, 2, 1-2 (1995): 82-8.

van den Ploeg, Peter and Carola Veemeren, eds. *Princely Patrons: The Collection of Frederick Henry of Orange and Amalia of Solms in The Hague*, exhibition catalogue. Zwolle: Mauritshuis, The Hague, 1998.

van der Graft, C. "Agnes Block en haar liefde voor tropische gewassen." *Jaarboekje van Oud-Utrecht* (1962) 117-24.

van Eeghen, I.H., "Het poppenhuis van Petronella de la Court huisvrouw van Adam Oortmans." *Maandblad Amstelodamum* 47 (1960): 159-67.

van Gelder, J.G. "'Beelden en rariteiten" in de verzameling Valerius Röver.'" *Nederlands Kunsthistorisch Jaarboek* 31 (1980): 341-54, 349-50.

Vasari, Giorgio. *Le vite de' più eccellenti pittori scultori e architettori: nelle redazioni del 1550 e 1568*. Edited by Rosanna Bettarini and Paola Barocchi. 6 vols. Florence: SPES, 1966-87.

—. *Lives of the Painters, Sculptors and Architects*. Translated by Gaston du C. de Vere. 2 vols. New York and Toronto: Alfred A. Knopf, 1996.

Veenendaal, Jan. "Furniture in Batavia." In *Domestic Interiors in the Cape and in Batavia 1602-1795*, edited by Titus M. Eliëns and Monique van der Geijn, 23-39. Verhoeven, Vlaeberg: Fernwood Press, 2002.

Venditti, Mauro. "Una presenza vicereale a Pozzuoli: la dimora fortificata di Don Pedro de Toledo." *Archivio storico per le province napoletane* 124 (2006-2007): 251-87.

Vergara, Alejandro and Ana Cabrera, eds. *El arte en la corte de los archiduques Alberto de Austria e Isabel Clara Eugenia, 1598-1633: un reino imaginado*. Madrid: Sociedad Estatal para la Conmemoración de los Centenarios de Felipe II y Carlos V. Patrimonio Nacional, 1999.

Vetter, Gerlinde. *Zwischen Glanz und Frömmigkeit. Der Hof der badischen Markgräfin Sibylla Augusta*, Gernsbach: Katz 2007.

Waddy, Patricia. *Seventeenth-century Roman Palaces: Use and the Art of the Plan*. The Architectural History Foundation, MIT Press: New York, N.Y., Cambridge/Mass., 1990.

Walpole, Horace. *A Description of the Villa of Horace Walpole* [...] *at Strawberry-Hill, near Twickenham. With an Inventory of the Furniture, Pictures, Curiosities, &c.* London, Strawberry-hill: Printed by Thomas Kirgate, 1774.

Weatherill, Lorna. "A Possession of One's Own: Women and Consumer Behaviour in England, 1660-1740". *The Journal of British Studies*, 25(1986), 131-56.

Weber, Gordian A. *Die Antikensammlung der Wilhelmine von Bayreuth.* Munich: tuduv-Verlagsgesellschaft mbH, 1996.

Welch, Evelyn. "The Art of Expenditure: the Court of Paola Malatesta Gonzaga in Fifteenth-Century Mantua," *Renaissance Studies* 16 (2002), 306-17.

—. *Shopping in the Renaissance.* New Haven and London: Yale University Press, 2005.

Westermann Bugarella, Mary. "The Burial Attire of Eleonora di Toledo." In *The Cultural World of Eleonora di Toledo: Duchess of Florence and Siena*, edited and with an introduction by Konrad Eisenbichler, 207-24. Aldershot: Ashgate, 2004.

Wilson-Chevalier, Kathleen, ed. *Patronnes et Mécènes en France à la Renaissance.* Paris: Université de Saint-Etienne, 2007.

Wright, David R. *The Medici Villa at Olmo a Castello: its History and Iconography.* Ph.D. thesis, Princeton University, 1976.

Yorke, James. "French Furniture Makers at Ham House." *Furniture History*, XXVI (1990): 235-8.

Zedler, Johann Heinrich. *Großes vollständiges Universal-Lexicon aller Wissenschaften und Künste.* Halle-Leipzig: Johann Heinrich Zedler and Johann Heinrich Wolff, 1732-1750.

Zeri, Federico. *La Galleria Pallavicini in Roma; catalogo dei dipinti.* Florence: Sansoni, 1959.

Zinnkann, Heidrun. *Furniture Woods.* Munich, Berlin, London and New York: Prestel, second edition 2003.

Zvereva, Alexandra. *Les Clouet de Catherine de Médicis: chefs-d'œuvre graphiques du Musée Condé.* Paris: Somogy, Chantilly: Musée Condé, 2002.

—. "Catherine de Médicis et les Portraitistes Français." In *Patronnes et Mécènes en France à la Renaissance*, edited by Kathleen Wilson-Chevalier, 527-43. Paris: Université de Saint-Etienne, 2007.

—. *Portraits dessinés de la cour des Valois: les Clouet de Catherine de Médicis*. Paris: Arthena Editions, 2011.

Sales Catalogues

Catalogue de la Riche Bibliotheque de Rosny. Rosny, 1837.

Mussell, Ebenezer. *A Catalogue of the Genuine and Curious Collection of Roman and Egyptian Antiquities, Mummies, Urns, Lamps, Figures, Etruscan Vases and other Effects, of Ebenezer Mussell, Esq.*[...] *which* [...] *will be sold by auction, by Mr. Langford and Son, at their house in the Great Piazza, Covent Garden* [...] 5-6 June 1765.

Sotheby's, 11 April 1951. *Catalogue of Fine Engravings and Etchings. Comprising* [...] *the Print Library from Syon House* [...] *the Property of His Grace the Duke of Northumberland*.

—. 26 March 1952. *Catalogue of Important Old Master Paintings* [...] *also a Collection of Dutch 17th-Century Paintings, the Property of His Grace the Duke of Northumberland, Removed from Syon House.*

—. 3 December 1980. *European Historical Medals from the Collection of His Grace the Duke of Northumberland* [...] *Removed from Alnwick Castle.*

—. 17 June 1981. *European Historical Medals of the Holy Roman Empire, Germany, France, Italy and the Vatican, Spain, Switzerland and Great Britain.*

—. 4 November 1982. *Roman Coins from the Collection of His Grace the Duke of Northumberland* [...] *Removed from Alnwick Castle.*

—. 14 April 2011. *Noblesse Oblige.*

Online Resources

Bucholz, Robert. "Algernon Seymour, 7th Duke of Somerset (1684–1750)" in "Seymour, Charles, 6th Duke of Somerset (1662–1748)". In *Oxford Dictionary of National Biography*. Oxford: Oxford University Press, 2004; online edn, May 2008 [http://www.oxforddnb.com/view/article/25158, accessed 7 Dec 2010].

Coppens, Thera. "Ananas: een zoete historie." *Nouveau*, July 2005: http://www.historisch-toerisme-bureau.nl/artikelen/ananas.htm.

Craske, Matthew and Lesley Craske. "Gosset, Isaac (1713–1799)". In *Oxford Dictionary of National Biography*. Oxford: Oxford University Press, 2004 [http://www.oxforddnb.com/view/article/11116, accessed 24 Nov 2010].

Fallon, Melinda van der Ploeg "Petronella de la Court and Agneta Block:

Experiencing Collections in late Seventeenth Century Amsterdam."
    Aurora Journal of the History of Art IV (2003):
    http://www.aurorajournal.org/contents%20volume%204.htm.
Getty Provenance: Provenance Index Database of the Getty Institute:
    http://piprod.getty.edu/starweb/pi/servlet.starweb
Hutton, R. "Maitland, John, duke of Lauderdale (1616-82), Politician."
    Oxford Dictionary of National Biography, Oxford: Oxford University
    Press, 2004 online edition, May 2006.
Laurie, Kedrun. "Zähringen, House of." *Grove Art Online*. *Oxford Art
    Online*. 1 June 2011,
    [http://www.oxfordartonline.com/subscriber/article/grove/art/T093155
    pg3].
Luard, Henry Richards. "Dutens, Louis (1730–1812)", rev. Elizabeth
    Baigent. In *Oxford Dictionary of National Biography*. Oxford: Oxford
    University Press, 2004 [http://www.oxforddnb.com/view/article/8331,
    accessed 25 Nov 2010].
Manno Tolù, Rosalia. *Firenze-Praga, 40 anni di studi storico-archivistici.*
    Archivio di Stato di Firenze: Florence, 2007. (available at
    http://www.archiviodistato.firenze.it)
    http://www.archiviodistato.firenze.it/nuovosito/fileadmin/template/alle
    gati_media/materiali_studio/progetti/firenze_praga.pdf
Marshall, Rosalind "Murray, Elizabeth, Duchess of Lauderdale and *suo
    jure*, Countess of Dysart, *bap.* 1626, *d.* 1698', *Oxford Dictionary of
    National Biography*, Oxford 2004, and online ed.
Oresko, Robert. "Verrue, Jeanne-Baptiste d'Albert de Luynes. " *Grove Art
    Online*. *Oxford Art Online*. 1 Jun. 2011,
    [http://www.oxfordartonline.com/subscriber/article/grove/art/T089057]
Rogers, Pat. "Bentinck, Margaret Cavendish [Lady Margaret Cavendish
    Harley], Duchess of Portland (1715–1785)." In *Oxford Dictionary of
    National Biography*. Oxford: Oxford University Press, 2004; online
    edn, Oct 2006 [http://www.oxforddnb.com/view/article/40752,
    accessed 25 July 2011].
Rossi, Lorenza. "Doria." *Grove Art Online*. *Oxford Art Online*. 1 Jun.
    2011,
    [http://www.oxfordartonline.com/subscriber/article/grove/art/T023381]
Sambrook, James. "Seymour [Née Thynne], Frances, 7th Duchess of
    Somerset (1699-1754)." In *Oxford Dictionary of National Biography*.
    Oxford: Oxford University Press, 2004; online edn, Jan 2008
    [http://www.oxforddnb.com/view/article/53787, accessed 7 Dec 2010].
The Medici Archive Project, http://documents.medici.org.

Thomson, Duncan. "Tassie, James (1735–1799)". *Oxford Dictionary of National Biography*. Oxford: Oxford University Press, 2004 [http://www.oxforddnb.com/view/article/26977, accessed 25 Nov 2010].

AUTHORS' BIOGRAPHIES

Sheila ffolliott

Sheila ffolliott is Professor Emerita in the Department of History and Art History at George Mason University, Fairfax, Virginia, USA. She serves currently as Vice President of the Sixteenth-Century Studies Association and as a Director of the American Friends of Attingham, the US support group for the Attingham Trust. From 2006-09, she participated in the *Medici-Frauen Interdisziplinär: Soziale Rollen, kultureller Transfer, mäzenatisches Oeuvre*, funded by the Deutsche Forschungsgemeinschaft (DFG), resulting in several publications, including: "'La Florentine' or 'La bonne Françoise?'" Some Sixteenth-Century Commentators on Catherine de' Medici and her Patronage." In: *Medici Women as Cultural Mediators (1533-1743)*, edited by Christina Strunck. Milan: Silvana Editoriale, 2012.

Other publications include: "Wife, Widow, Nun, and Court Lady: Women Patrons of the Renaissance and Baroque." In: *Italian Women Artists, Renaissance to Baroque*, edited by J. Pomeroy and C. Strinati, 31-40. Milan: Skira, 2007; "Catherine de' Médicis: La Reine-Patronne Ideale de la Rénaissance?" In: *Les Femmes et les arts à la Renaissance: Patronnes et mécènes, d'Anne de France à Catherine de Médicis*, edited by K. Wilson-Chevalier (Paris: Université de Saint-Étienne, 2007) and the forthcoming "Tapestry" for *The Cambridge Shakespeare Encyclopedia, Volume I: Shakespeare's World*, edited Bruce R. Smith, and "Women Artists" for the *Ashgate Research Companion to Women and Gender in Early Modern Europe*, edited by Jane Couchman, Katherine McIver, and Allyson Poska.

Andrea Gáldy

Andrea Gáldy received her Ph.D. from the School of Art History and Archaeology at the University of Manchester in 2002. She has held fellowships from the Henry Moore Foundation and from the Harvard University Center for Italian Renaissance Studies at Villa I Tatti. In 2004 she founded the working group Collecting & Display (100BC to AD1700) with Adriana Turpin and Susan Bracken as an international forum of discussion for the history of collecting. The author of numerous articles and reviews, Andrea Gáldy published *Cosimo I de' Medici as Collector: Antiquities and Archaeology in Sixteenth-century Florence* with CSP in 2009.

Robert G. La France

Robert G. La France (www.robertglafrance.com) is curator of pre-modern art at Krannert Art Museum at the University of Illinois at Urbana-Champaign. His monograph on the Medici court artist Bachiacca (2008) restores the career of Pontormo and Bronzino's friend and peer. While his main interests traditionally lie in the painters of the Renaissance in Florence and Rome, his new research focuses on the artistic centres of Urbino and Bologna, particularly the circles of Raphael and Francesco Francia.

He is presently writing a monograph on the artist Timoteo Viti, while mounting exhibitions and gallery installations ranging from the art of Ancient Greece to Beaux-Arts sculpture in France and America.

Christopher Rowell

Educated at Winchester, Magdalen College, Oxford, and the Courtauld Institute of Art (MA), Christopher Rowell joined the curatorial staff of the National Trust in 1977. His major team projects included the restoration of Uppark after the 1989 fire, which won the joint *Museum of the Year Award* (1995); the re-display of Ham House (1990-), and the restoration of the state rooms at Petworth (1991-2002), culminating in his curatorship—with Tate Britain—of the exhibition *Turner at Petworth* (2002). In 2002, he was appointed the National Trust's first full-time national specialist Furniture Curator. His publications include numerous National Trust guidebooks and articles in learned journals, as well as the joint-authorship of *Treasures from India: The Clive Collection at Powis Castle* (1987), *Uppark Restored* (1995), and the exhibition catalogue, *Turner at Petworth* (2002). He contributed the articles "Display of Art" and "Exhibition" to *The Dictionary of Art* (1996; now *Oxford Art Online*). He is currently editing and contributing to *Ham House: 400 Years of Collecting and Patronage*, to be published in 2012 by Yale University Press in association with the National Trust and the Paul Mellon Centre for Studies in British Art.

Joy Kearney

Joy Kearney studied Philosophy and Art History at University College, Dublin. She spent seven years working at the education department of the National Gallery of Ireland before winning a fellowship to study at Utrecht University, having written her Master's thesis on the painting of birds and fowl in the Low Countries in the seventeenth century. She is presently completing the *catalogue raisonné* of Melchior de Hondecoeter for a PhD at Radboud University Nijmegen. She contributed to the publication

Vorstelijk Vee (Royal Livestock) accompanying the exhibition of the same name at the Palace of Het Loo in Apeldoorn. She now works at Erasmus University in Rotterdam.

Orsolya Bubryak
Orsolya Bubryák obtained her MA at the Péter Pázmány Catholic University where she studied Art History, German and Hungarian Literature. She received her Ph.D. in 2010 from the ELTE University of Budapest. She wrote her dissertation on the history of the collections of the Erdődy family concentrating mainly on the reconstruction of the family entail treasury created by György Erdődy in the eighteenth century at Galgóc (Hlohovec, Slovakia).

Orsolya Bubryák has been research fellow at the Research Institute for Art History of the Hungarian Academy of Sciences (www.arthist.mta.hu) from 2002 onwards. In 2011 she was appointed chief curator of the Art Collection of the Hungarian Academy of Sciences.

Orsolya is currently embarking on a large-scale provenance research project on the treasuries of Hungarian noble families of the seventeenth and eighteenth century.

Adriano Aymonino
Adriano Aymonino obtained his MA at the Warburg Institute and completed his PhD at the University of Venice with a doctoral dissertation on the collections, patronage and cultural interests of the 1st Duke and Duchess of Northumberland. He has recently expanded his dissertation as a postdoctoral fellow at the Paul Mellon Centre for Studies in British Art and at the Getty Research Institute in Los Angeles, where he also started research for a future project on the impact of antiquarian publications in seventeenth- and eighteenth-century European art and decoration. His parallel field of interest is provenance research, having worked as senior researcher for the Commission for Looted Art in Europe during the last two years. He currently works as Coordinator of Undergraduate Programmes at the department of Art History and Heritage Studies of the University of Buckingham.

Heike Zech
Heike Zech studied art and architectural history and historical building archaeology in Germany and Italy and received her Ph.D. from the University of Bamberg. In 2001 she held a scholarship at the Centro Tedesco di Studi Veneziani in Venice. Her interest in the decorative arts and related aspects of collecting was first sparked when she collaborated

on a research project on Nuremberg silver at the Germanisches Nationalmuseum, and further nurtured during her time with Sotheby's Munich where she worked from 2003. In 2008 she moved to London to join the Metalwork Department of the Victoria & Albert Museum, where she works as curator of the Gilbert Collection at the Victoria & Albert Museum.

Philip Mansel

Philip Mansel (www.philipmansel.com) is a historian of France and the Ottoman Empire. His books include the lives of Louis XVIII (1981) and of the Prince de Ligne (2003); a study of the court of France after 1789 (1989); a history of Paris in the nineteenth century (2001); and *Dressed to Rule*, a history of royal dress (2005). He is editor of *The Court Historian*, journal of the Society for Court Studies (www.courtstudies.org), a Fellow of the Institute of Historical Research, and a member of the committee of the Research Centre of the Château de Versailles. Philip is currently working on a biography of Louis XIV.

INDEX